PRAYING WITH ST MARK

*In memory of Hugh and Jean, parents who taught us to read
and be thoughtful; and to the many like them
who have had little access to bible study,
but who possess
'the implanted word that has the power to save your souls'
(James 1:21).*

Albert McNally

Praying with St Mark

Sr. Mary,

Albert McNally
Christmas 2011

the columba press

First published in 2011 by
the columba press
55A Spruce Avenue, Stillorgan Industrial Park,
Blackrock, Co Dublin

Cover by Bill Bolger
Origination by The Columba Press
Printed in Ireland by Gemini International

ISBN 978-1-85607-750-7

The Scripture quotations contained herein are (except where otherwise stated) from the New Revised Standard Version Bible, copyright © 1989 by the Division of Christian Education of the National Council of the Churches of Christ of the USA., and are used by permission. Psalms are numbered in accordance with NRSV. Used by permission.

Nihil Obstat:
Paul Fleming
Censor Deputatus

Imprimatur:
Noel Treanor
29 September 2011

Contents

Preface

In these times we need a strong diet to nourish our faith, and the good news is that it is freely available to everyone in the word of God. I have received so much food for the soul by returning to St Mark after many years and living with it for the last nine months, that I am delighted to offer a share in what I have found there to all who are open to it. The Gospels are not only for trained experts, but for everyone. We are people of the New Covenant, and believe in God's promise to Jeremiah, 'I will write it on their hearts, and I will be their God, and they shall be my people' (Jeremiah 31:33). James has the lovely idea that the word of God is implanted in our hearts: 'Welcome...the implanted word that has the power to save your souls' (James 1:21). The Holy Spirit is also present in our hearts, waiting to help us when we pay attention to that word within us.

So would you like to be able to pray better with the word of God in St Mark's Gospel? Do you wish that you could use the liturgical year to really get to know the Gospel of Mark? This book is offered to those who would say yes to one or other, or even both, of those questions. When we try to do two things together, we run the risk of doing neither well. But I believe that the two are as close as twins, the getting to know and the praying. The first aim is, then, to help the growing number of people who wish to pray with the scriptures to try their hand with St Mark's Gospel, and secondly, to help those who hear Mark's Gospel, or prepare homilies on it, during year B of the lectionary, to use the opportunity to explore it. This is a continuation of my *Blessed be the Lord: Praying with St Luke*, (Columba Press, 2009), using the same methodology, which many were kind enough to tell me they found helpful.

I wish to thank all who have helped and encouraged me, the writers of Commentaries on whom I have so obviously relied, The Columba Press for their patience and support, and MB for help with proof reading.

Albert McNally
a.mcnally191@btinternet.com
August 2011

Introduction

Do you wish that the gospels had been written for today, instead of being nearly two thousand years old? Today our faith is under attack, membership of the church is declining, increasing numbers have only a shallow understanding of the Christian message, ministers of the gospel have been guilty of betraying their trust, leaders of the church are under pressure, militant atheism is undermining our certainties, we are unsure of the way forward. Enter St Mark! Exactly like my own day, he says, except that we also faced martyrdom. The word is alive; we will see how well Mark addresses the present concerns of the church. A close and prayerful reading of St Mark can be as fruitful today as in the time of Mark himself. The method of *lectio divina* is a wonderful way to discover how the gospel speaks to our own life and times.

Lectio divina (divine reading) is something most of us have heard of, but perhaps never tried seriously. It was recommended to all Catholics at the Synod of Bishops held in Rome in 2008, and again in *Verbum Domini*, (86-87, CTS, 2010, pp 104-108), the recent work of Pope Benedict XVI giving the recommendations of the synod. *Lectio divina* is also being recommended by the team preparing for the International Eucharistic Congress in Dublin in 2012. There are some variations in approach to the method, and for those who wish to investigate further, see the titles in the select bibliography at the end of this introduction. The basic stages are *lectio*, reading; *meditatio*, reflection, with the help of the Spirit, that enables the text to speak to us; *oratio*, our personal prayer in response to the text; *contemplatio*, contemplation or allowing the words of the text to resonate in our minds and hearts so that with the help of the Spirit they may be a constant source of nourishment for our spirits. *Verbum Domini* adds: 'We do well also to remember that the process of *lectio divina* is not concluded until it arrives at action (*actio*), which moves the believer to make his or her life a gift for others in charity' (87). We will replace the Latin terms, as before, with Familiarisation (*lectio*), Reflection (*meditatio*), Response (*oratio*), and Contemplation (*contemplatio*). Each session is intended to give food for thought for many days, at least a week.

The method may be described briefly as follows:

- Reading the text slowly and attentively, believing that it is God's word to us (*lectio*/familiarisation); thinking carefully about what the text is saying about Jesus or about his mission.

- Thinking about what the words are saying to us now, and turning the message over in our minds (*meditatio*/reflection).

- Responding to the word of God with our own prayers of praise, thanksgiving, repentance, petition; making decisions about what we see ourselves called to be or to do (*oratio*/response).

- Keeping the text alive in our minds and hearts, allowing it to speak to us through the power of the Spirit (*contemplatio*/contemplation).

This method engages our eyes and ears (reading or listening to the text); our minds (thinking about its meaning, in the time of Jesus and now in our lives); our hearts (welcoming the message with love, responding to it in prayer); our wills (deciding what we are called to do or to be as a result).

Most of us need help to understand the text and see how it applies to us and to our times. Benedict XVI says: 'The reading (*lectio*) of a text ... leads to a desire to understand its true content: what does the biblical text say in itself? Without this, there is always a risk that the text will become a pretext for never moving beyond our own ideas' (*Verbum Domini*, 87). Lack of knowledge may lead to our imposing personal, and perhaps eccentric, interpretations on the text.

The approach to lectio in this book gives 'reading' a wide interpretation, beginning from an attempt to discover what the writer meant to say at the time of writing, and allowing that to guide us as to what it says to us now. It is possible to pray using short quotations; but trying to pray with longer passages, as we will do, helps us to appreciate the context of a particular verse. This is a surer guide that we are listening to God's word and not our own, though I would not wish to limit the power of the Holy Spirit, who may inspire those leaps of intuition that sometimes illuminate a text for us. Intuitions benefit by being checked out in line with the findings of biblical scholars and the teaching of the church. Therefore 'reading' (familiarisation) will include some study of the context and the language of the text, its allusions to Old Testament texts, and some guide to understanding the difficulties that often face us in reading St Mark. This will take a little time, but it will be well spent. Then 'reading' becomes 're-reading' with a broader understanding of what the text means. Reflection (*meditatio*) begins only then. However, the reader is encouraged to use this book in a flexible way. Where the 'background' notes get in the way of prayer, select from them or leave them out and go to the next stage. But remember that the purpose of this book is defeated if you just 'read' it, without personal reflection and prayer at each stage.

To pray meaningfully with any of the gospels it is good firstly to have an overview of the whole gospel. It is highly recommended that you sit down and read the gospel of Mark at one sitting (and repeat the exercise occasionally). Mark is the shortest gospel and can be read in about an hour and a half. Below I give only a short introduction to St Mark, with a simplified structure which the reader may use to fit individual texts into the narrative context. In each session I will offer a fairly structured text in 'sense lines', using the NRSV, with some headings (mine, not the NRSV's, and mostly not Mark's) to focus our attention. Reflection on the text can be the most difficult part of the process for those who are not trained to it, so I will give help for reflection by proposing four keywords (really aspects of Mark's thought), which will give us four differing but complementary approaches to the text (see below).

The Year of Mark: The second important aim of the book is to help readers to get to know Mark's Gospel much better. There are, of course, good commentaries available to help (see the Bibliography at the end of this introduction). But we need to go beyond the commentaries, to allow the text to nourish our spiritual lives and guide our living, by reflection and prayer. Though the book is meant to help in the year of Mark, Year B in the Lectionary cycle, I do not intend to follow the layout of the Sunday readings for Year B. This is not another book of homilies on the Sunday gospels, of which there is a rich variety already in print. If you wish to preach Mark, nothing beats the attempt to pray with the text, so that you bring to it your personal insights.

Reflecting on the Sunday readings is important, but of course in Year B they are not always taken from Mark. Because Mark has no infancy narrative and no resurrection appearances, the other gospels supply much of the seasons of Advent, Christmas, and Easter. Mark, being shorter than Matthew or Luke, is interrupted also in the lectionary by the use of John chapter 6 from the 17th to the 21st Sunday. On Palm/Passion Sunday we meet the whole of Mark's passion narrative, too much to digest on one day, with no time to explore its depths or emphases, so we will take it scene by scene. The choice of texts offered from St Mark is therefore to help us to get a better feel for the whole gospel, to let it become a familiar friend in our reflecting and praying, so that we will become more capable of appreciating any text from Mark that occurs on a Sunday of Year B. I like the approach of the famous preacher who outlined his method thus: 'I read myself full, I think myself clear, I pray myself hot, and I let myself go!' Isn't he almost proposing the stages of lectio?

A Gospel for a time of persecution

Mark's Gospel has no information about Jesus' human origins or background, except that he came from Nazareth in Galilee (1:9). When he visits Nazareth, and preaches in its synagogue, he is said to be 'the carpenter, the Son of Mary' (6:3); there is no mention of Joseph, but there is an extended family of 'brothers and sisters' (3:31, 6:3), who mostly do not seem to comprehend what Jesus is doing. Mark has no resurrection narrative either, apart from the finding of the empty tomb (16:1-8), which ends mysteriously with a command to the women at the tomb to go and tell the disciples that Jesus would meet them in Galilee, but they are afraid and tell no one. The current ending of the Gospel (16:9-20) is unanimously agreed to be a later addition, not part of the original Mark. It appears to be mostly a summary of the events developed by the other evangelists.

It is the common, though not unanimous, consensus that Mark is the first Gospel to be written, between 65 and 75 AD. For what its worth, I think it probably should be placed in 69 AD, shortly before the destruction of the temple and the city of Jerusalem in 70 AD. Each Gospel was written for a particular church community, not originally for the universal church.

Most commentators place the Markan community either in Rome or in the Near East, close to the Holy Land, perhaps Syria. In either place at that time the Christian community faced great turmoil and the possibility of martyrdom. In Rome the emperor Nero (54-68 AD) had picked on the Christians as scapegoats after the burning of Rome. In the Near East the rebellion of the Jews against Rome (65-70 AD) caused great upheaval, the destruction of Jerusalem and the temple, with a scattering of the Jewish community. In the endeavour of the Jews under the leadership of the Pharisees to preserve their identity they separated themselves from the Christian Jews who up to then had seen themselves as the true flowering of Judaism, and relations between Christians and Jews rapidly deteriorated. Reading between the lines in Mark it is clear that there was much fear in the Christian community, persecution and probably apostasy and betrayal on the part of weaker Christians. 'Brother will betray brother to death, and you will be hated by all because of my name. But the one who endures to the end will be saved' (13:12-13).

This background coloured Mark's approach to the Gospel. Many in the community had been glad to accept Christianity as good news in times of relative peace, focusing on the great hopes derived from the resurrection and the expectation of Jesus returning in glory to claim his people. Now faced with persecution and the real possibility of death, the community needed a deepening of faith, an understanding that they followed a Jesus who was persecuted and crucified, and who asked his disciples to take up the cross and follow him. Their survival depended on people who would be able to face hard times with courage and faith in Jesus. So Mark is a Gospel which can speak to us in hard times.

The structure of the gospel
A literary structure is imposed by Mark on the life of Jesus, a simplification of what happened historically. Basically Mark first tells us all that Jesus did in and around Galilee, then there is a journey to Jerusalem, Jesus' only recorded visit (he probably went there more often, as John's Gospel shows). Then we have a period of mission in Jerusalem, followed by the account of Jesus' arrest, condemnation, suffering and death on the cross, climax-

ing in the finding of the empty tomb and the announcement that Jesus has been raised up. Mark's account breaks off mysteriously there, with no resurrection appearances such as we find in the other Gospels. Later an ending was supplied, though clearly not written by Mark. I have not felt it necessary to give detailed attention to the structure, except to indicate from time to time how expertly Mark links his material together. The respect now paid to Mark as a skillful editor of his material is remarkable, since in the first half of the twentieth century people could still say that Mark 'is not a stylist, not even a clever storyteller; he is a faithful, artless reporter,' whose units of material are strung together as if a string of pearls had broken and their original order could not be restored. One of the people who put that to rest was the actor, Alec McCowen, who demonstrated what a dramatic and coherent story Mark tells by his very successful one-man show, simply reciting Mark on stage – to packed houses. Below I give a brief outline; for more details see the commentaries listed in the bibliography. The square brackets refer to the sections treated in this book.

AN OUTLINE STRUCTURE

Prologue: Mark 1: 1-13 [Sessions 1 and 2]
Section A: Ministry of Jesus in Galilee 1:14-8:26
      A1 Authority of Jesus in word and deed 1:14-3:6
      [Sessions 3-6]
      A2 Jesus and disciples and family 3:7-6:6
      [Sessions 7-9]
      A3 The 'bread section' 6:7 – 8:26 [Sessions 10- 13]
Section B: Learning about Jesus on the way to Jerusalem, 8:27-
      10:52 [Sessions 14-16]
Section C: Last Days in Jerusalem 11:1-16:8
      C1 Ministry in and around the temple 11:1-13:37
      [Sessions 17-19]
      C2 Passion and death 14:1-15:47 [Sessions 20-24]
      C3 The empty tomb 16:1-8 [Session 25]

Difficulties of interpretation
Permission is hereby granted to 'skip' where difficulties of interpretation prevent you from praying with the word. Mark is

often enigmatic, mysterious, for of course we are dealing with divine things beyond our understanding. There are notorious places where the interpretation is not only much disputed, but is also critical for our understanding of the gospel. I have tried to grapple with these and come to a conclusion, and the reader is warned that the going may be heavy in those places. They are (1) 3:20-21 and 31-35, the attitude of his family to Jesus [Session 8, Jesus' New family]; (2) 4:10-12, the meaning of 'the mystery [secret] of the kingdom of God'; [Session 9, The Sower]; (3) 6:45-52, Walking on the Water [Session 11]; (4) The fig tree, 11:12-14, 20-25, which I have only referred to in passing in Session 18, Cleansing the Temple; (5) Chapter 13, the 'Little Apocalypse' [Session 19, The Son of Man in Glory]; (6) The abrupt ending at 16:8 [Session 25, The Empty Tomb].

Keywords

As I did for Luke, I will suggest four keywords that will help to focus our reflection stage in Mark. They are to be seen as starters to get us going. To be helpful, the keywords need to facilitate reflection on (almost) every passage of the Gospel, and must be able to be deepened as we move further and further into the Gospel, as God's plan for our salvation becomes gradually clearer. My suggestions are culled from Mark 1:14-20 (Session 3), the proclamation of the kingdom of God and the call of the first disciples.

1. Mystery: Jesus comes into Galilee to begin his ministry, proclaims 'the good news of God' and says: 'The kingdom of God has come near [is at hand]; repent, and believe in the good news.' Immediately afterwards he calls the fishermen, Simon, Andrew, James and John to follow him and become 'fishers for people'. Getting to know what Jesus means by 'the kingdom of God' will not only test, but enrich our understanding right through the Gospel, and to encapsulate it I will take the word 'mystery' from the difficult passage in Mark 4:10-12, where Jesus said to 'those who were around him along with the twelve': 'To you has been given the mystery [secret, NRSV] of the kingdom of God, but to those outside, everything comes in parables.' Much ink has been spilled in trying to find what precisely Mark thought Jesus intended by the word mystery (or secret). In Session 9, The Sower, we will treat that question in more detail, but I propose the word mystery as our first key-word, to embrace the whole complex of ideas that surround the kingdom of God and its mysterious, ie. divine, nature. It is not a 'secret', something that once revealed is known and can be shared with others, but a mystery, into which disciples are drawn by Jesus, and by the Holy Spirit. Though it is beyond human understanding, it is something living, growing, freeing and transforming us if we have the new 'mindset' and the faith that Jesus asks us to have.

2. *Christology:* Since it is Jesus who announces and in some way embodies the kingdom, our second keyword must focus on him, seeking our answer to the continuing question in this Gospel, 'Who can this be?' Mark tells the readers in the first verse that Jesus is Messiah (Christ), the Son of God, and at least from the baptism story, 1:9-11, Jesus is aware of that, and soon too the demons, but nobody else in the developing story knows this. There has to be a slow and difficult learning experience even for those closest to Jesus. So for us who know in theory who Jesus is, it is good to follow the learning experience of the disciples and others in the Gospel as they struggle to understand who is this wonderful, strange, bewildering person who does not fit with their mindset or expectations. Jesus is still saying to us: 'Who do you say I am?' (8:29). The word 'christology' has been used for our understanding of who Jesus is and the meaning of his mission, our '-ology' about 'the Christ'. So christology will be our second keyword.

3. *Discipleship:* We identify with the disciples who respond to his call, struggle to know Jesus and understand the implications of following him, so our third keyword is discipleship. This call was a heady experience for the disciples, and a tough one, and they felt the frustration and apparent disappointment of Jesus at their slowness to comprehend. It may be a heady and a tough experience for us too, as we try to follow the same learning curve, but it will be interesting and challenging!

4. *Conversion:* The fourth one is conversion (repentance), representing the Greek word *metanoia*, which literally means 'change of mind' or 'change of mindset'. It seems dangerous to suggest a noun that occurs only once in the gospel, and that on the lips of

John the Baptist, who preaches a 'baptism of repentance (*metanoia*) for the forgiveness of sins' (1:4). The equivalent verb, *metanoein*, (*noein*, to perceive, *meta*, afterwards, or too late; to change one's mind, to repent) is used only twice, once to describe Jesus' preaching: 'Repent and believe in the good news' (1:15), and once to describe the preaching mission of the twelve: 'So they went out and proclaimed that all should repent' (6:12). But it represents the new set of values, the new mind-set that the kingdom of God calls for, and acquiring that new mind-set will severely test the disciples throughout the Gospel, and can take a lifetime for any of us. The idea deepens in the section on discipleship following the first prophecy of the passion, after Jesus rebukes Peter for doing the work of Satan, by trying to steer him away from the path of suffering, saying: 'Get behind me, Satan! For you are setting your mind not on divine things but on human things.' (8:33) The Greek may be translated literally: 'For you do not think (understand, pay heed to) the things of God but the things of men', and I much prefer the Jerusalem Bible translation here: 'For the way you think is not God's way but man's way.' To follow the NRSV in the attempt to use inclusive language, it would become 'not God's way but the human way'. *Metanoia* is the gradual process by which we come to think more in God's way, not in our own human way. I feel conversion, which means 'turning towards [God]', better represents the whole complex of ideas than 'repentance'.

These four keywords, Mystery, Christology, Discipleship, Conversion, need not all be used at any one time, and the two most prominent in Mark are Christology and Discipleship. But the others should not be ignored.

Recommendations for group leaders
Group leaders should plan the meetings and begin with initial calming and focusing of minds. Communal prayer and singing of hymns unites the group.

Focus
Use what skills you have, and the talents of other members of the group. Determine to take seriously the need to create a calm, prayerful atmosphere. Guidance will be given in the text only in Session 1. Prayers given there for beginning and end are usable

in any session, but leaders are recommended to vary the prayers used and to use hymns – you need some hymnbooks and someone with the confidence to start them off.

1. Familiarisation

1.1 Text: Have the text read aloud, slowly and clearly; encourage members to read it again quietly. The leader's task is to ensure that the 'reading' helps members to see the text freshly, note its shape, the narrative sequence, the people involved, the reaction of observers. Ask members to imagine they are there, and re-tell to themselves what is happening.

1.2 Background: At the first meeting the leader needs to be more active, say a few words about the key points, clarify difficulties for the members, highlight central issues. Do not spend too long at this stage; not all difficulties need to be addressed; the notes are there to help leaders deal with questions, but remember that we are here to pray, not to listen to a talk from the leader. For subsequent sessions, try to encourage the members to have looked at the background notes in advance. So sessions will end with the announcement of the text for the next session, and some gentle persuasion to continue the prayer during the week, and to prepare for the next time by reading the background notes.

2. Reflection

Allow a pause to recall the text itself; re-read it in the light of the new information. The leader has to decide on the time available, and restrict reflection to suit, eg on a portion of the text (the rest gives it context), and chose perhaps two, perhaps only one of the keywords to use. Most important for Mark are always Christology and Discipleship. The others can be looked at later by individual members continuing the prayer during the week. Make sure time is always allowed for response in each session. The leader needs to have a range of prompt questions to help participants to ponder the text (though they do not need to voice their answers).

Prompt questions: Is there one outstanding idea for you in this passage? Is Jesus guiding us, by word, by example? What do we learn about God from this passage? About Jesus? About the disciples? About ourselves? What about opponents of Jesus?

Do you have some sympathy with them? Are they malicious, sincere, unable to face change? Are there some like that today? Are there people in the passage who remain uncommitted, postponing decision? Am I like that? Can you identify with the disciples, or with his opponents? What are their feelings, attitudes, misunderstandings? Do you experience these same feelings/ attitudes? What do you find nourishing and affirming in this passage? What do you wish to give thanks for? What do you find difficult, challenging? Does it make you see more clearly who you are? Does it ask you to make some decisions?

3. Response
This is quiet time, though the leader may allow members to say briefly what part of the text strikes them most, without comment from others. A period of silence must be given for each one to make a personal response. Ask the members to read the text quietly and stop at a phrase or sentence which speaks to them and use it for their prayer. Some of the suggestions given in the response section may be used afterwards, but it is not always necessary.

4. Contemplation
The important task of the leader is to help the participants to take the mood of the prayer with them and be able to continue it in their quiet times and daily activities. So ask them to keep a phrase or sentence, even a word, in their minds and turn it over in their thinking. In this way God's word continues to nourish us.

Conclusion
End with a prayer; it may be led by an individual or said together. Thank everyone for being there, encourage them to come to the next meeting, announce the text to be used, and suggest they read the background notes beforehand.

Recommendations for beginners
If you have not tried to pray like this before, be patient with yourself and with the method. This method is about listening to God, and not talking all the time, letting God have the first word. Listening attentively requires us to calm ourselves, free our minds from stress and distractions (as far as possible!).

When you get interested in listening to the word of God, distractions begin to fade away. You have to believe that God is able to speak to you through the Gospel, which was always intended for God's people gathered together in prayer. So it continues to be alive when we gather together in faith, or even when we sit down alone but remain tuned in to the people of the church. Individuals can use the prompt questions outlined above for leaders (Recommendations for Leaders, under Reflection). For prayer to work, we must not restrict ourselves to requests. You will soon find yourself praying more in thanksgiving and praise. Use the time-honoured four headings to start you off: adoration, contrition, thanksgiving, supplication (asking): A-C-T-S. Later you may become a free spirit. Do not be too worried about parts of the text you do not understand: use the parts that speak to you. We can enjoy a drink without emptying the well. Do not give up; if you do, begin again. 'Man or woman does not live on bread alone, but on every word that comes from the mouth of God.'

Bibles

The bible used in this book is *The New Revised Standard Version* (NRSV), except where otherwise noted. It is close to the Greek and uses inclusive language. You may of course continue to use your own bible: recommended also are the Revised Standard Version, The Jerusalem Bible, The New American Bible, The New English Bible, even the Good News Bible.

Select bibliography

Commentaries

Achtemeier, Paul J, *Invitation to Mark*, Image Books, Doubleday 1978

Anderson, Hugh, *The Gospel of Mark*, (New Century Bible), Eerdmans/Marshall, Morgan & Scott, 1976

Donahue, John , Harrington, Daniel, *The Gospel of Mark*, (Sacra Pagina), Liturgical Press, 2002

France, R. T., *The Gospel of Mark, A Commentary on the Greek Text*, (New International Greek Testament Commentary) Eerdmans/ Paternoster Press 2002

Harrington, Wilfred, *Mark*, (Revised) Glazier 1985

La Verdiere, Eugene, *The Beginning of the Gospel, Introducing the Gospel According to Mark*, 2 Vols, Liturgical Press, 1999

Moloney, Francis J, *The Gospel of Mark*, Hendrickson, 2002

Montague, George T, *Mark, Good News for Hard Times*, Servant Books, Ann Arbor, Michigan, 1981

Mullins, Michael, *The Gospel of Mark, A Commentary*, The Columba Press, 2005

Nineham, D. E., *Saint Mark*, (Pelican) Penguin Books, 1963

Schweizer, Eduard, *The Good News According to Mark*, SPCK, London, 1971

Taylor, Vincent, *The Gospel According to St Mark* (Commentary on the Greek text), 1952, 2nd Ed, Macmillan, 1966.

Other works

Benedict XVI, *Verbum Domini*, Post-Synodal Exhortation on the Word of God, CTS 2010

Byrne, Brendan, *A Costly Freedom, A Theological Reading of Mark's Gospel*, Liturgical Press, 2008

De Verteuil, Michel, *Lectio Divina with the Sunday Gospels, The Year of Mark*, Year A, Columba Press

Harrington, Wilfred, *Mark: Realistic Theologian, The Jesus of Mark*, Columba Press 1996

Hengel, Martin, *Studies in the Gospel of Mark*, SCM, 1985

Lightfoot, R. H., *The Gospel Message of St Mark*, OUP, 1950

Reilly, John, *Praying Mark*, St Paul Publications, 1992

Senior, Donald, *The Passion of Jesus in the Gospel of Mark*, Glazier, 1984

Stock, Augustine, *Call to Discipleship, A Literary Study of Mark's Gospel*, Glazier/Veritas 1982

Van Iersel, Bas, *Reading Mark*, Clark, Edinburgh, 1989

Praying with scripture

Foster, David, *Reading with God, Lectio Divina*, Continuum, London/NY 2005

Hall, Thelma, *Too Deep for Words. Rediscovering Lectio Divina*, Paulist Press, NY/Mahwah, 1988

Hough, Stephen, *The Bible as Prayer. A Handbook for Lectio Divina*, Continuum, London/NY 2007

Khoury, Jean, *Lectio Divina, Spiritual Reading of the Bible*, CTS 2006

Pennington, Basil M, *Lectio Divina*, Crossroads Publishing Co, NY, 1998

Schultz, Karl A, *How to Pray with the Bible, The Ancient Prayer Form of Lectio Divina Made Simple*, Our Sunday Visitor, Indiana, 2007

GROUP MEETINGS

Welcome and brief outline of the format of the meeting.

FOCUS

Each session should begin with calming the mind and praying for guidance from the Holy Spirit.

1. FAMILIARISATION

(a) Getting to know the text.

(b) Background – notes on the text to guide reading.

2. REFLECTION

Use one or more of the Keywords to help reflection; use the others later.

(a) Mystery

(b) Christology

(c) Discipleship

(d) Conversion

3. RESPONSE

4. CONTEMPLATION

Closing Prayer

Thanks and instructions for the next meeting.

John the Baptist (Mark 1:1-8)

More 'stage directions' will be given in this session than hereafter. Experienced users will not need them; they are intended for newcomers to this method of praying, that they may become familiar with the methodology proposed. 'Focus' and 'Prayers' will be given here, but not subsequently.

Focus

Two things are necessary: that we still our minds, and implore the Holy Spirit to inspire us. Firstly, sit comfortably but upright in your chairs, relax shoulders and neck muscles, breathe deeply, slowly. Pay attention to inhaling and exhaling: find a comfortable rhythm. The Holy Spirit is the living breath of God. As we exhale, breathe out the tensions that fill our minds, as we inhale, quietly ask the Holy Spirit to come into our souls and live in us. The Spirit has inspired (literally, breathed into) the author of St Mark's Gospel. We ask the Spirit to breathe into us also, to inspire us, as we read and pray with Mark's Gospel. We pray 'Come, Holy Spirit' (*Veni Sancte Spiritus*) in rhythm with our breathing, or sing with the Taize chant, *Veni Sancte Spiritus*.

Prayer

After a few minutes, the leader or the whole group prays aloud the following prayer (or another of your choice):

God our Father, send us your Holy Spirit to prepare our minds and hearts to hear the words of the Gospel and allow them to nourish our spirits. Let the breath of your Spirit quieten our over-crowded minds that we may allow your word to take firm root within us. We ask this through Jesus Christ, your Word made flesh, who lives and reigns for ever and ever. Amen.

1. FAMILIARISATION

This stage involves reading the text carefully until we become familiar with it, noting the things that puzzle us, then reading the background notes, with an eye always on the text.

Group leaders will decide how long to spend on each section (not more than an hour in total!). Individuals should try to set aside at least a half hour, and please do not worry if you only get the Familiarisation section done in that time. Make a few minutes personal response, and come back to it tomorrow. Be happy if you take a week to get through a session: there are no points for hurrying!

1.1 Getting to know the text (Mark 1:1-8)
Read the text a few times, aloud if possible, and note the sequence of events; the suggested paragraph headings will help you to focus on the important ideas in the passage. You are ready to move on when you can close your eyes and retell the passage to yourself fairly accurately. That may take a few tries!

The Headline
1   The beginning of the good news of Jesus Christ, the Son of God.

Prophetic hopes are coming true
2   As it is written in the prophet Isaiah,
     "See, I am sending my messenger ahead of you,
     who will prepare your way;
3   the voice of one crying out in the wilderness:
     'Prepare the way of the Lord,
     make his paths straight,'"
4   John the baptizer appeared in the wilderness,
     proclaiming a baptism of repentance
     for the forgiveness of sins.

The People of God cleansed and prepared
5.   And people from the whole Judean countryside
     and all the people of Jerusalem were going out to him,
     and were baptized by him in the river Jordan,
     confessing their sins.

The Forerunner and the Stronger One
6   Now John was clothed with camel's hair,
     with a leather belt around his waist,
     and he ate locusts and wild honey.

7 He proclaimed, 'The one who is more powerful than I am
   is coming after me;
   I am not worthy to stoop down
   and untie the thong of his sandals.
8 I have baptized you with water,
   but he will baptise you with the Holy Spirit.'

1.2 Background

These notes are meant to help you re-read the text with more insight. They attempt to put you in line with what Mark intends by his choice of words, the sequence of ideas, and the context in which he places them. I feel we often rush to pray with the text too quickly, and are disappointed with results. Ground needs to be cultivated before the seeds can grow. Group leaders may have to summarise the material for a first session. For subsequent sessions group members should be asked to read the text and the background notes for the next session before they attend.

1.2.1 *The Prologue:* Commentators are agreed that Mark intends the first section of chapter one to be a prologue to the dramatic action of the public ministry of Jesus. But they do not agree where it ends. They used to be fairly unanimous that it ends at v 13, with Jesus' testing in the desert, but now about half the commentators believe that Mark intended vv 14-15, Jesus' proclamation of the kingdom, as the conclusion of the prologue rather than the beginning of the ministry. There are good arguments on both sides, but the decision does not deeply affect our purposes. I still favour ending the prologue at v 13, and beginning the ministry with v 14. I have divided the prologue into two sections for convenience, 1-8 and 9-13, to avoid overload in our first session. The outstanding characteristics of the prologue are: (1) Mark there gives the reader privileged information about the identity of Jesus (1:1; 1:11), information not available to the participants in the story, who have to learn the hard way. (2) The action takes place in the 'desert', remote and uninhabited places, whereas the ministry beginning at 1:14 is normally in crowded villages and towns. (3) Through quotations from scripture Mark announces the story of Jesus as the fulfilment of all the prophetic hopes for Israel.

23

1.2.2 The 'headline' (1:1): 'The beginning of the good news of Jesus Christ, the Son of God.' Mark is writing for Christians who know who Jesus is, and to whom at least some of the writings of Paul would be known. So he states at the beginning the full Christian message: it is a kind of title, telling what Mark believes about Jesus, and what the original disciples will only find out very gradually. Jesus is the 'Messiah' (the 'Christ' in Greek), the chosen one sent by God to bring good news, or to be the good news. In Christian usage the word Christ, which originally described a role, has become almost a name, Jesus Christ. He is also 'Son of God', a title which can be used as simply another description of the Messiah, but seems intended by Mark to mean the divine Son of God. Both the titles will be picked up again at strategic points in the gospel, Messiah at the turning point in 8:29, when in answer to Jesus' question: 'Who do you say I am?' Peter answers: 'You are the Messiah.' It is soon apparent that Peter's understanding of Messiah and that of Jesus are far apart, and the disciples thenceforth struggle to comprehend how Jesus can be Messiah and still suffer and be rejected as he foretells. It is only when Jesus stands on trial before the High Priest that he admits openly that indeed he is the Messiah and more, the Son of Man, who will come in glory (14:62). The title 'Son of God' is confirmed by the heavenly voice at Jesus' baptism (1:11) and transfiguration (9:7), but only to privileged hearers, Jesus alone at his baptism and the three chosen disciples at the transfiguration. The full Christian faith is put on the lips of the centurion when Jesus dies: 'Truly, this man was God's Son' (15:39). Readers need to identify with the disciples' struggle to understand, because it helps us to comprehend the struggle for faith in our own circumstances. As Jesus says in Matthew 7:21, it is easier to give Jesus titles like 'Lord', than to understand the implications for our lives.

1.2.3 'As it is written' (1:2-3): The scripture quotation is said to be from Isaiah, but is in fact a combination of Malachi 3:1 (with some modification from Exodus 23:20), and Isaiah 40:3, again with modifications. It is principally the Isaiah quotation in which Mark is interested (the whole complex may have been part of a collection of prophetic texts used by the early church). A number of Greek translations existed as well as the best known, the Septuagint (LXX), and Mark may have used one of them. Malachi 3:1 reads: 'See, I am sending my messenger to prepare the way before me', 'me' of course referring to God himself, who was expected to come on the 'great and terrible day of the Lord' (Malachi 4:5). Mark has modified Malachi 3:1 by part of Exodus 23:20, 'I am going to send an angel (=messenger) in front of you', so that Mark's 'I am sending my messenger ahead of you who will prepare your way' can only refer to the 'more powerful one' (v 7) who will baptise with Holy Spirit (v 8), that is, Jesus rather than God himself. Interestingly then, Mark feels able to retain from Isaiah 40:3 'prepare the way of the Lord', for preparing the way of Jesus. 'Lord' is a title reserved for God himself in the Old Testament, which means that Mark is accepting the early Christian faith that gave the title Lord to Jesus, considering him the divine Son of God.

1.2.4 *'A baptism of repentance for the forgiveness of sins'*: John's baptism was probably unique, administered by him and not repeatable, unlike other Jewish ritual washings of the time, which were self-administered and repeated often. It was a sign of a person's repentance and readiness for the events to come. V 5 tells us the people were baptised by him, 'confessing their sins'. It takes place 'in the wilderness', which for Jews would conjure up thoughts of the Israelites delivered from Egypt and finding God in the desert. It was also the place were the Israelites were tested, sinned and found forgiveness. The flocks of people from Judea and Jerusalem receiving baptism represent a renewed people of God cleansed and seeking forgiveness.

1.2.5 *The Baptist's task is to proclaim the coming one (vv 6-8)*: Mark presents the Baptist, unlike Matthew and Luke, not as a preacher of morality condemning specific sins, but simply as the one who prepares the people for the great coming of the 'more powerful one', whose slave he is not worthy to be, and who will bring a much superior baptism in the Holy Spirit. V 6 deliberately describes John's mode of dressing as similar to that of Elijah (2 Kings 1:8). As he proclaims the coming of the 'more powerful one', Mark seems to have in mind Malachi 4:5, 'Lo, I will send you the prophet Elijah before the great and terrible day of the Lord comes.' Again, prophetic expectation was that God himself would pour out the Spirit when the day of the Lord came (Peter in Acts 2:16ff explains Pentecost in terms of the fulfilment of Joel 2:28-32 NRSV). The 'more powerful one', whom John does not name, will be the fulfiller of the promises of God.

2. REFLECTION

We refresh our memories of the text if necessary at this point and prepare to reflect upon it. Leaders may wish to allow participants (briefly, and without comment, except 'thank you') to voice what strikes them most vividly about the text before taking the keywords (one or more depending on time available) as helps to reflection. Prompt questions are found in *Recommendations for Group Leaders, Reflection* (Introduction, p 17). Unused keywords may be continued privately. Time must be left for response.

2.1 Mystery

The mysterious ways of God are everywhere in the air. There is a tremendous sense of anticipation, the beginning of mysterious good news, centred on Jesus, as the reader knows, though not the people of the time. God's promises to the people of Israel are on the point of fulfilment. Feel with them the excitement at the coming of the wonderful and terrible 'day of the Lord'. There has not been a prophet in Israel for such a long time, but now a wild man, dressed like Elijah, appears in the desert of Judea, the voice in the wilderness that Isaiah spoke about, opening up vistas of a new great act of God. The last prophet Malachi said: 'Lo, I will send you the prophet Elijah before the great and terrible day of the Lord comes' (4:5). And John is dressed like Elijah. His preaching in the desert, the place of hope, where God in the past prepared a people for himself, is enough to draw great crowds from Jerusalem and all Judea. He wants them to prepare for something great. But this Elijah figure is focused on the coming of a 'more powerful one', whose sandals he isn't worthy to unloose. Who that mysterious person may be, John does not – perhaps cannot – say, but he knows that his water baptism will pale into insignificance before the Spirit baptism of the more powerful one. God himself had promised to pour out the Spirit when the time would come. Joel pictures the Lord pouring out his Spirit on a repentant people: 'I will pour out my spirit on all flesh; your sons and your daughters shall prophesy, your old

men shall dream dreams, and your young men shall see visions.'
(Joel 2:28-29, quoted by Peter on Pentecost Sunday, Acts 2:16-
18.) Read all of Joel chapter 2 to feel the power of the Lord's
coming.

2.2 Christology

Pick out for yourself from the text what Mark says about Jesus.
He both gives privileged information to the reader, and asks us
to learn with John the Baptist and the people who witnessed the
events. Though John and those whom he baptises do not know
who the 'more powerful one' is, the readers are told in v 1 that
he is [the] Christ, and the Son of God. It is possible that Son of
God could simply be another term for Messiah, but the context
shows it must be more. Nobody at the time expected the
Messiah to be the divine Son of God, yet Mark had not been
afraid to adapt the composite scripture quotation (vv 2-3),
which spoke of the coming of God, so that it now gives God's
prerogatives to Jesus. The Baptiser goes 'ahead of you', prepares
'your way' (v 2), and that is paralleled with 'prepare the way of
the Lord' (v 3). The Baptist (vv 7-8) makes it clear that he is
preparing for the coming of this mysterious 'more powerful
one'. John is not fit to be his slave, and he will baptise with Holy
Spirit, so he must be a very powerful one. The surprise is that
Mark can give him the title 'Lord', which in the Greek Old testament (LXX) is the translation of the divine name of God, and
was only given to Jesus by the early Christians after the resurrection. So this more powerful one is given the divine name. We
can still feel the excitement of a people who have been waiting
patiently for the 'day of the Lord', who now feel that perhaps
something wonderful is coming with this new promised one.

2.3 Discipleship

Mark likes prophetic exaggeration: John the Baptiser drew out
to the desert 'people from the whole Judean countryside and all
the people of Jerusalem', and they accepted his baptism and
confessed their sins (v 5). We may call them disciples of John,
but John's whole focus is to prepare for the coming of the 'more
powerful one', to cleanse and renew the people of God for his
coming. John himself is very humble before the coming one, so
his followers are called to be humbly repentant and to wait with

great anticipation for God's initiative. As we begin our prayerful journey through Mark's Gospel, we unite ourselves to them. We are preparing for what God may do for us through praying the Gospel, humbly repentant, open to God's gifts, hoping that the coming one will accept us as his disciples.

2.4 Conversion

John proclaims a 'baptism of repentance' (*baptisma metanoias*) for the forgiveness of sins (v 4), that is, a baptism that is a visible sign of inner repentance, accompanied by confession of sins. Mark uses the noun *metanoia* only here, and the equivalent verb only twice (1:15, 6:12). Nevertheless the underlying idea is a useful key to facing the challenge of each passage. Literally the Greek word *metanoia* means 'change of mind', the acquiring of a new mindset, and behind it is a Hebrew concept of repentance as 'returning' to God and to a better relationship with God. We will see that this is a frequent idea in Mark, even when he does not use the exact words. As we begin our journey through the gospel we humbly pray for the grace to be open to the changes in thinking and acting that the gospel may ask of us. We too are challenged to repent and confess our sins.

3. RESPONSE

It is vital for all users to take time to make a personal response to the text before looking at my suggestions. Individuals within groups should be reassured that they will not be asked to share aloud anything they feel uncomfortable about sharing. Reread the text slowly, pausing at any word, phrase or verse that strikes. A short response is enough, sometimes just 'thank you'.

The beginning of the good news of Jesus Christ, the Son of God. God is taking action. Thanks be to God, we depend always on God and his powerful action among us. This is the beginning of the good news of God's fulfilment of his plans for our salvation. Lord, your desire for our salvation never changes. We are blessed by being able to relive the saving events at all times through the gospel. Thank you, Lord, for we are truly concerned about our faith and the state of the world and the church: only you, Lord, can fix it. Lord, we are truly glad that we are always in your hands; help us to renew our faith in your promises and your goodness to us in Jesus, your beloved Son. Help us to have faith that your plans will be fulfilled, in spite of all setbacks and failures. Take a little time on 'the good news of Jesus Christ' and respond in your own way.

Prepare the way of the Lord, make his paths straight. Lord, you are a liberator who wish to set people free. Centuries ago you freed your people from Egypt and Babylon. We are now hoping for a new deliverance, a third 'exodus', a new experience of salvation through this promised one that John the Baptist is expecting. We know he is your Beloved Son, and will deliver us from sin and the power of the devil. Deliver us, Lord from all evil through this 'more powerful one'. We need to prepare the way to our hearts, our inner being, so as to be healed and made new. Help us to prepare ourselves to come closer to your Son.

Proclaiming a baptism of repentance for the forgiveness of sins. Lord, we know that John's baptism was only a sign that people wanted to turn towards you, to beg for your forgiveness. You have left us the real thing, baptism which cleanses us from within, and the sacrament of reconciliation, where we can be reconciled to you and to your people. Even so, it doesn't always change our hearts. So we unite ourselves to those who came to John, humanity seeking God, feeling the need of healing. We pray that your people may turn to you in earnest. Forgive our shallowness, give us the desire for inner healing. 'More powerful one', immerse us in Holy Spirit.

People from the whole Judean countryside and all the people of Jerusalem ... were baptised, confessing their sins. Mark suggests a whole people were trying to be ready for God's plans to be fulfilled. Some of those hopes were realised, others came to nothing. Help us not to miss opportunities for growing in your grace. Lord, help us to pray with and for the whole people in the church today, that there may be a great turning towards your Messiah. Forgive our faith-fatigue that first strips the marvels you perform for us of their wonder, soon makes us think of them as commonplace, then as 'old-fashioned', beyond the belief of moderns like ourselves. Lord, through your Spirit, rekindle in us wonder and awe in your presence.

He will baptise you with the Holy Spirit. Jesus, we thank you for bringing us the gift of the Spirit. Holy Spirit, renew the gifts of baptism and confirmation within us. You inspired Mark to write his Gospel; inspire us also by his words, and help us to understand them better, and to put them into practice in our lives.

4. CONTEMPLATION

Contemplation is a scary word for beginners, which means most of us. There are no limits to its power in the hands of saints. For us it means simply (or amazingly) keeping alive in our minds and hearts the thoughts and feelings that we experienced in praying with this passage of Mark. We can do this while going about our daily activities. To help us to love and reverence the text, it is good to choose a phrase or sentence that we found helpful and repeat it to ourselves often. Suggestions might be 'prepare the way of the Lord', 'the one who is more powerful ... is coming', 'he will baptise you with the Holy Spirit'. Our task here is to allow God to work on us by being mindful.

Prayer

Holy Spirit of God, we thank you for the Word which you have inspired and which nourishes our spirits. Help us to be faithful in our resolve to continue praying with St Mark, and inspire us too with your presence. Help us to come to know better the Son of God who is always coming into our lives, and help us to be open to his teaching and his healing love. Come, Lord Jesus, and pour out your Spirit upon us. Amen.

Note: Leaders of groups should encourage participants to continue their prayer on their own, by looking at the key words not used, to read the text for the next meeting and its background notes before they come to the meeting.

Baptism and Testing of Jesus (Mark 1:9-13)

1. FAMILIARISATION

1.1   Getting to know the text (Mark 1:9-13)

The baptism of Jesus

1:9   In those days Jesus came from Nazareth of Galilee
        and was baptised by John in the Jordan.

10   And just as he was coming up out of the water,
        he saw the heavens torn apart
        and the Spirit descending like a dove on him.

11   And a voice came from heaven,
        'You are my Son, the Beloved,
        with you I am well pleased.'

The testing of Jesus

12   And the Spirit immediately drove him out
        into the wilderness.

13   He was in the wilderness forty days,
        tempted [tested] by Satan;
        and he was with the wild beasts;
        and the angels waited on him.

1.2 Background

1.2.1 *Jesus from Nazareth of Galilee:* Solemnly Jesus is introduced and it is clear that he is the 'more powerful one' (1:7). Unlike Matthew and Luke, Mark lacks information about Jesus' family and background. All we are told is that he comes from Nazareth in Galilee. Later we will meet his family in 3:21, 31-35, and be puzzled to find that they think his behaviour is very strange, to say the least! In 6:1-6, Jesus visits Nazareth and gets a bad reception. He is called 'the carpenter, the son of Mary' (no mention of Joseph), four 'brothers' are named, and 'sisters' without names (they may be cousins). No family stories get in the way of Mark's focus on Jesus' mission from God. Jesus is the only Galilean mentioned among the crowds from Judea who came to be baptised by John, though John 1:35-42 tells us that Jesus' first disciples, Galileans all, were already disciples of John the Baptist. It is best to try to stay with the information Mark gives us, which is all the information the other actors in the drama are deemed to have.

1.2.2 The 'more powerful one' is baptised by the lesser one. The one who is to baptise with the Spirit submits to John's 'baptism of repentance for the forgiveness of sins (1:4)'. Each evangelist has trouble with this, for we know the Baptist still had many followers in the early years of Christianity, who claimed that John was the more important one. Only Mark states bluntly that John baptised Jesus, Matthew and Luke put it in a subordinate clause without John's name, and the fourth gospel doesn't mention that he was baptised at all. Mark therefore makes sure that he has John's declaration beforehand that the coming one is more powerful than he, with a superior baptism (1:7-8). Unlike Matthew 3:14-15, Mark has no problem with Jesus accepting a baptism of repentance for the forgiveness of sins. He surely intends to convey that Jesus consciously identified with the People of God (represented by the crowds from Jerusalem and all Judea, 1:5), cleansed and repentant, seeking God's mercy. This he will do again on the cross, which he refers to as a 'baptism' (10:38). Both at John's baptism and after his 'baptism' on the cross, he is acclaimed as 'the Son of God' (by the centurion 15:39).

1.2.3 Privileged insights: Mark is much more interested in the events accompanying the baptism, privileged revelation for Jesus that is also given to the reader. Three wonderful things happen: the heavens are torn open, the Spirit descends (visibly, dove-like) on Jesus, and a voice from heaven addresses him in words that at once affirm his identity, show God's delight in him, and point strongly towards his mission. We call this an 'epiphany', a divine revelation, and in Mark it is only for Jesus ('he saw', 'you are my Son'). In Matthew 3:17 it becomes a public announcement: 'This is my Son'. These same three things happen, implicitly or explicitly, in the call of prophets: see the call of Ezekiel (1:1 the heavens were opened; 1:28 he hears a voice; 2:2 a spirit enters into him). The heavenly voice of God tells Jesus: 'You are my Son, the Beloved', reaffirming what Mark told us in 1:1, and what the heavenly voice at the transfiguration (9:7) will say to the three disciples: 'This is my Son, the Beloved'. These are important moments in Mark's gospel, and the acclamation is echoed on Calvary after Jesus' death, this time surprisingly on the lips of the gentile centurion who has just overseen his execution: 'Truly this man was God's Son' (15:39). 'With you I am well pleased' could refer to God's pleasure in all that Jesus is and does, but the Greek verb, *eudokésa*, is an aorist tense (past action), and it seems proper to suggest that God was also well pleased with what Jesus has just done, identifying himself with the people turning to God in repentance in preparation for God's great initiative.

'He saw the heavens torn apart' (v 10): the verb used here, *schizein*, to tear, is used again when Jesus dies on the cross: 'And the curtain of the temple was torn (*eschisthē*) in two, from top to bottom' (15:38). The curtain intended is probably the curtain before the 'holy of holies', which was seen as the place where God dwelt with his people, and was accessible only to the High Priest on the Day of Atonement. The tearing of the curtain symbolises the opening up of the presence of God to all those who come 'through, with and in' Jesus. These links between the baptism scene and the death of Jesus help our reflection.

1.2.4 Jesus' vocation: As well as being an affirmation of Jesus' identity, the words of the heavenly voice point strongly to his vocation and call him to begin his mission. 'You are my Son' comes from Psalm 2:7, a psalm which describes the enthronement of the kings of the line of David and acclaims them as God's son from that day (the king embodied the People of God, collectively called God's son). With the Babylonian Exile the line of kings from David was broken, and the psalm took on a new life as a prayer that one day an anointed one (Messiah) of the line of David would be restored. Jesus, who prayed the psalms, has to know that the words imply the fulfilment of that hope, and that therefore he is being called to the role of Davidic Messiah (something that all Jews awaited with longing). But the role is tempered by the unexpected combination of the Davidic hope with the words 'with you I am well pleased', which echo another famous biblical theme, the Servant of God who will suffer for others and be put to death with sinners. Isaiah 42:1 reads: 'Here is my servant, whom I uphold, my chosen, in whom my soul delights; I have put my spirit upon him.' The words 'in

33

whom my soul delights' are thought to be reflected in 'with you I am well pleased', in the context of the outpouring of the Holy Spirit upon Jesus. The Spirit will take charge of Jesus' mission and first 'drive' him out into the desert to be tested (better than 'tempted'), to realise the implications of the dual roles as king and servant, and the opposition that awaits him, embodied in Satan. The Servant Songs from 'Isaiah of the Exile' (Second Isaiah, 40-55) have never been associated with the expected Davidic Messiah in Jewish thinking, and the combination of the two is a new and strange thing, extremely difficult for the Jewish people, then or now, to accept. This is part of 'the mystery of the kingdom of God', which even Jesus' closest disciples found very difficult to digest. The implications for disciples certainly challenged the community for which Mark was writing, and continue to challenge us today.

1.2.5 The testing: John's baptisms took place 'in the desert' beside the Jordan, but there were crowds about, and the Spirit immediately 'flings out' Jesus (the verb used, *ekballein*, is one you would use for throwing a javelin, or for what an ejector seat does to a pilot) into uninhabited places. He spent 40 days there, reminiscent of the 40 days Moses fasted on Mt Sinai (Deut 9:9, a fast repeated in intercession when he discovered Israel's sinful behaviour, Deut 9:18), or the 40 days that Elijah spent travelling without food to Sinai (1 Kings 19:8) – Moses and Elijah will appear at the Transfiguration – or just perhaps of the 40 years during which Israel was tested in the desert (read Deut 8:2-5). There is a confrontation with Satan, with no result given, a contest to be renewed often during the ministry. Detailed 'temptations' as in Matthew and Luke are not found in Mark. We find just the cryptic remark: 'He was with the wild beasts', which I think means that he was in a lonely and dangerous place (other explanations are given by commentators). Finally, God's angels looked after him, as an angel did for Elijah on his way to Sinai. We are to assume that no matter what happens to Jesus on his wonderful and perilous mission, God will be with him.

2. REFLECTION

2.1 Mystery
Reflect on the plan of God. Though God's plan is taking shape,

and we know that it is centred on Jesus, there is an up-down, high-low feel about this passage. Jesus comes as a humble pilgrim to be baptised by John; and there is no sign of any expectation in Nazareth when Jesus visits it later that 'the carpenter, the son of Mary' was ever going to be anything else (6:1-6). Then he is acclaimed by the divine voice as God's beloved Son, filled with the Spirit, assured of God's love and good pleasure. He is given a mission which combines the glory of kingship with the lowliness of a servant, then flung into solitude by the Spirit, confronted by Satan the Adversary, testing his metal, and finally ministered to by angels. Mark does not minimise the strangeness of it all. Jesus is sent on a mission by God, but God will not give the Son power to wipe out all opposition from Satan, who embodies all that is opposed to God's plan. Jesus is tested, but does not fail the test, and disciples may be reassured that one so loved by God and filled with God's Spirit will, in the end, carry out God's plan.

2.2 Christology

Reflect on the one who is to carry out the plan of God. Mark plunges Jesus into the scene. He comes to be baptised by John, and is suddenly startled by the enormity of what happens. Mark cannot tell us if he had any prior knowledge of what was to come, and we can only imagine that the tremendous feeling of being loved and enlivened by the affirmation of the One he will come to call Abba, Father, and being filled by the power of the Spirit will far override the strangeness of his call to mission. The long awaited 'day of the Lord' must be at hand. So Jesus is Son of God, the Beloved, the source of the Father's joy, the royal Messiah ('You are my Son', Psalm 2:7), but a servant (reference to Isaiah 42:1f). John said he was not worthy to be Jesus' servant, but Jesus is to be the servant of everyone. The Spirit, who we would humanly expect to lead him to a public proclamation of the good news, propels him instead into a 40 day retreat to be tested, pondering what a servant-messiah may mean, and learning the hard way that his mission will be obstructed by all the wiles of Satan and his power over people. We know what it will cost him to give us his baptism in the Spirit; we know he has another baptism to receive first (10:38). But he is the beloved Son of

God, and when he undergoes that baptism on the cross, he will be acknowledged as God's Son by the one who presides over his death (15:39). For us, it is important that he is the Son of God who identifies with us in our sinfulness and our needs.

2.3 Discipleship

There is nothing explicit yet about discipleship, but if Jesus is the one who identifies with us, then we need to identify with him. His destiny will be our destiny. He is on a mission from God, and it has all the semblance of a rocky road, but if his identification with us is to benefit our eternal salvation, there is only one place we can be, at his side. Jesus received the assurance of the Father's love and good pleasure at his baptism. With Brendan Byrne (*A Costly Freedom*, p 33) we can say that Jesus received the assurance of God's fatherly love not just on his own behalf but on behalf of all humanity, so that we, who are baptised into Christ and have received the Spirit, may call ourselves God's beloved sons and daughters in whom he is well pleased. We are challenged then to live up to our baptismal call, because we are sons and daughters in Christ in so far as we stay close to him. We need the Spirit's help that we may not fail the test. 'Do not put us to the test but deliver us from the evil one.'

2.4 Conversion

So how do we feel as people who wish to be better disciples of Jesus? We have experience of the blessings of being close to him, and sharing through him in our filial relationship to God our Father, and we have experience of our weakness and our failures. If the Son of God who has just been told how much the Father is pleased with him can be the next moment packed off into the desert for 40 days on no rations, we should not be surprised that God may permit life to treat us a little severely at times. The desert was the place where Israel was betrothed to the Lord in covenant love, as well as the place that tested their fidelity to the covenant, where they often failed the test. But Jesus did not fail. So if we find ourselves in the desert of isolation and feel lost, remember that the desert is also the place where God speaks tenderly to the heart of Israel and offers her comfort (Hosea 2:14: 'I will ... bring her into the wilderness, and speak tenderly to her'). May his tender love enable us to commit ourselves anew to the following of Jesus wherever it may take us.

3. Response

To make a personal response, read the text slowly and stop to pray with any phrase or verse that speaks to you.

In those days Jesus came from Nazareth in Galilee and was baptised by John. We give deepest thanks to God for his plan of salvation, for sending his beloved Son to be among us and embrace our sinful humanity. Thank you, Jesus, for being baptised with sinners in the Jordan, though you are like us in all things but sin. We are blessed, that you want to be part of us even though we are weak and sinful, inconstant disciples. Thank you, Lord, that every time we wish to turn, or return, to God to be healed you are with us. May we always wish to be with you.

You are my Son, the Beloved; with you I am well pleased. Lord, we rejoice in your splendid dignity as the Beloved Son of the Father, filled with the life and power of the Spirit. You are the one sent by the Father to fulfil his promises, the king like David. It will take us a long time to know what kind of king you wish to be, and maybe we have to keep rediscovering it. For you are also the Servant of God. Help us to learn from you how to rejoice in our dignity and yet be humble as servants. May we learn, as disciples and members of the church, by following you on the path to Calvary and to the Father's presence.

You are my beloved son/daughter. Lord, forgive the liberty of rewriting the Father's words as if they were addressed to any of the children of God baptised into the Body of Christ. Only through you, Lord Jesus, may we make such claims. We thank you for the gift of baptism that you made possible for us, that made us your brothers and sisters, children of the Father, brothers and sisters of all believers, members of the people of God. We are earthen vessels to hold such dignity. But how can we not rejoice in the dignity you have given us? Strengthen us, for without help we will give way in time of testing.

He was in the wilderness forty days, tempted (tested) by Satan. You, Lord, found strength in the wilderness to accept your mission and to resist Satan. Help us to know that our God is to be found in solitude and quiet. We pray in the name of your church, which is trying to renew her dedication to her mission in testing times, when many of her people have been unfaithful. We unite ourselves with all the people of the church and ask for healing for the church at this time, for a new outpouring of the Spirit upon the church. Lord, we ask pardon for the times your church sought glory before service, for the times we as members of the church have betrayed our trust. Heal and strengthen those who have suffered. We stand with you, Lord Jesus, on the verge of your great mission, with hope in the redeeming love of God, 'who so loved the world that he gave his only Son' (John 3:16).

4. CONTEMPLATION

Keep before the eyes of your heart the vision of Jesus emerging dripping from the Jordan, wiping the water from his eyes and ears, amazed at what he hears and sees. Tell him that we, like his Father, are very well pleased with him. Repeat with the Father, asking his pardon for adapting his words to Jesus: 'You are my beloved brother, with you I am well pleased!' And occasionally allow yourself to be addressed by the Father, and do smile and accept the compliment: 'You are my beloved son/daughter, with you I am well pleased.' Allow yourself to be affirmed, for you never know when you'll have a desert to cross.

The Kingdom of God is at Hand
(Mark 1: 14-20)

1. FAMILIARISATION

1.1 Getting to know the text (Mark 1:14-20)

The Good News of God

1.14   Now after John was arrested, Jesus came to Galilee,
      proclaiming the good news of God,

15   and saying, 'The time is fulfilled,
      and the kingdom of God has come near [is at hand];
      repent, and believe in the good news.'

Disciples – people catchers

16   As Jesus passed along the sea of Galilee,
      he saw Simon and his brother Andrew
      casting a net into the sea – for they were fishermen.

17   And Jesus said to them, 'Follow me
      and I will make you fish for people.'

18   And immediately they left their nets
      and followed him.

19   As he went a little further,
      he saw James son of Zebedee and his brother John,
      who were in their boat mending the nets.

20   Immediately he called them,
      and they left their father Zebedee in the boat
      with the hired men, and followed him.

1.2 Background

1.2.1 Jesus' first sermon: this is perhaps the most momentous sermon ever. In NRSV it has 19 words, in Greek only 15. Would that we all could be so profound and so concise. Since then, thousands of pages have been written about it. Those 19 (or 15) words are not necessarily the exact words which Jesus spoke, but there is general consensus that Mark has preserved the essential components of Jesus preaching, not just spoken here but often throughout his ministry. So we may presume that Jesus preached this message all round Galilee, eg in Capernaum, 1:21f, where they are astounded at his teaching, though no teaching is explicitly recorded, and in 1:39, 'and he went throughout Galilee, proclaiming the message in their synagogues ...'

1.2.2 'Now after John was arrested (lit. handed over)': This section begins with Jesus back in his own Galilee, deliberately coming to places where there are plenty of people, whereas John had called people to him in uninhabited places. The northern and western shores of the Sea of Galilee were heavily populated and the flourishing fishing industry attracted crowds. Mark begins 'after John was arrested' (by Herod Antipas who ruled Galilee as well as the east bank of the Jordan, where John was imprisoned). NRSV translation 'was arrested' misses the deeper meaning of the verb used by Mark, *paradothēnai*, the aorist passive infinitive of *paradidōmi*, I hand over. Mark used the same combination of verbs, *kērussō*, I proclaim, and *paradidōmi*, I hand over, to make a clear link between John's fate, handed over after his preaching (1:4, 14), the fate of Jesus (1:14, 9:31, 10:33f), who foretells that he will be 'betrayed (lit. handed over) into human hands, and they will kill him' (9:31), and the fate of disciples (13:10-11, 'the good news must first be proclaimed to all nations. When they bring you to trial and hand you over ...'). Preaching God's word meets opposition in each case.

1.2.3 'Proclaiming the good news of God': the 'beginning of the good news' has already been announced in 1:1 – there it is called 'the good news of Jesus' (meaning both 'about Jesus' and that Jesus is the good news). Now Jesus is about to proclaim its content, and it is called (the only time in the gospels) 'the good news of God'. It is appropriate, because we find Jesus normally focusing his preaching on the Father, rather than on himself. Already in the letters of Paul (some of which must have been read in the liturgical gathering of Mark's community) the word *euaggelion* ('good news' or 'gospel') was used without qualification to mean the Christian message about Jesus. After the resurrection the Christian community made Jesus the focus of its preaching, for they came to see more clearly that Jesus embodied the good news. The word *euaggelion* was originally a secular word for a message, but took on a religious meaning in Second Isaiah, with the verb *euaggelizomai*, I bring good news. The classical texts are

Isaiah 40:9 – close to the text about the voice crying in the wilderness, which is quoted in Mark 1:3 – Isaiah 52:7-10, and 61:1 – which Jesus read in Nazareth, according to Luke 4:18. Revealing background is Isaiah 52:7 (made into a popular folk hymn): 'How beautiful upon the mountains are the feet of the messenger who announces peace, who brings good news, who announces salvation, who says to Zion, "Your God reigns".' Now the messenger is the Son of God in person, proclaiming the nearness of the reign of God.

1.2.4 *'The time is fulfilled'*: the time has come for the fulfilment of all the prophecies (eg Second Isaiah fulfilled in a new way far beyond the return of the exiles from Babylon). The word for 'time' is *kairos*, the opportune or fitting time, as opposed to mere chronological time (*chronos*).

1.2.5 *'The kingdom of God has come near'*: the kingdom (*basileia*) of God is not a place or a territory, but the reign of God, which means that God is now proposing to act so that his reign may be established, and that people who accept God as king may be blessed by his saving love. How God proposes to establish his reign remains mysterious, but it is not going to be instantaneous or involve the immediate victory of God's power over all opposition and all people who oppose it. The verb translated 'has come near' is in grammatical terms the 'perfect' tense of the verb to approach, which in Greek gives a sense of what has been so accomplished as to be a present reality; eg 'It has stopped raining' refers to something that has already happened and which means that now we can walk out without umbrellas. Therefore is it translatable as 'the kingdom of God is at hand'. In some sense the kingdom is among us with the words and actions of Jesus, but in another and obvious sense it has not fully come, and will only reach its fullness with the coming of the Son of Man in glory at a time in the future which only God knows (13:32). For our present purposes the kingdom means that God's sovereign power is at work through Jesus, negatively, to set people free from all that would prevent them from accepting and submitting to the reign of God, in particular the power of Satan and the sinfulness that burdens humanity, which in Mark includes spiritual blindness and deafness and hardness of heart; and positively, to bless them with the gift of salvation and the promised life of the Holy Spirit. Everything that Jesus will say and do in the coming chapters will be pointing to the meaning of the kingdom.

1.2.6 'Repent and believe in the good news': the kingdom requires a human response of repentance (*metanoia*) and faith in the good news. John the Baptist has already called for repentance in preparation for the coming of the one we know now to be Jesus. *Meta-noia* means literally a change of mindset, the acquiring of a new set of values and a new lifestyle to match those values. The values of the kingdom will have to be learned by the disciples and by us. With repentance goes faith, which includes intellectual acceptance of what Jesus teaches, and trust in him and in the kingdom of God. Jesus asks us to believe in the kingdom now, and to learn about it gradually.

1.2.7 Calling disciples: Immediately we meet kingdom values. Those who respond to Jesus' proclamation will be called to have a close attachment to himself, and to be willing to spread the news of the kingdom to others. Jesus calls the brothers Simon and Andrew, who are fishermen, casting nets into the sea – such nets with weights may be thrown by wading into the sea or from a boat. The call is made with no preliminaries: 'Follow me and I will make you fish for people.' With no hesitation, they leave their nets and follow him. Similarly, the brothers James and John are called as they sit in their father's boat mending their nets, and they make the same prompt response. Mark notes that they leave their father with his hired men in the boat, so the Zebedee family has a thriving business. Some conclude that Simon and Andrew must be less well off, but this conclusion is not safe. Luke 5:3 says that Simon had a boat. Neither is it a safe conclusion to say that Jesus chose 'poor' fishermen as his followers. They were probably doing quite nicely, thank you, but they leave everything and follow him, apparently without knowing what they were getting into. (However, John chapter 1 says they had already met Jesus as disciples of John the Baptist.) Jesus shows a compelling confidence, sense of identity, and magnetism, which Mark will call *exousia*, authority (eg 1:22, 27). Mark lists three essential qualities of such discipleship: relationship with Jesus, readiness to promote his mission, and total commitment to his cause.

2. REFLECTION

2.1 Mystery

Look at the text to identify what is mysterious and wonderful. Jesus, filled with the Spirit, like the prophets before him, proclaims the coming of the kingdom as good news, with total certainty that he is speaking for God. Proclamation of good news gets us involved. Our minds raise a hundred questions, but there is no time for them. Instead, hearers (and readers) are asked to respond with faith and repentance. Live with your questions, put faith is this good news; allow your mind to be changed, turn to God, put aside sinful ways. Watch how the four fishermen, two sets of brothers, give instant response to Jesus' call: no job description, no terms and conditions, just come; and they leave everything and follow him. The reader may have two reactions: this is something big, I'd like to be part of it, and/or this is very demanding, it scares the dickens out of me! Are you ready to stay with it, and learn more about it as we go? You are already committed as a baptised Christian to following Jesus. Perhaps our lives could do with a bit of changing, and perhaps we need to think out more clearly what is involved by our being baptised into Christ. Take time to think about it, and read the passage again – slowly.

'Kingdom of God' is not a place or a nation, but the acceptance of God as king – my king, potentially king of all people, if only they 'repent and believe'. The beginnings of the kingdom come when people accept that God rules, and that his power directs their lives. We will find that his power is saving power, not compulsion. God brings about the kingdom; we just need to be receptive. Throughout the history of Israel God has been acknowledged as king. This new announcement through Jesus has to be more than just a call to accept the fact that God is king. God through Jesus his beloved Son must be beginning to bring about something new, that will affect our inner lives and relationships, something that will make us truly his people. Spend a little time thinking about what it means to you to say to God: 'You are my king', and 'Your kingdom come'.

2.2 Christology

Jesus in Galilee begins to act like 'the more powerful one', speaking with tremendous authority and drawing power. He is the bearer of good news from God, God's kingdom is at hand, and hearers are called to put faith in his message, and to change their lives. The most radical way to do that is to leave everything and follow him. His direct call to follow him tells us that Jesus believes the coming of the kingdom is tied up with his own ministry: following him is in some way submitting to the kingdom of God. This has deep implications for Jesus' identity. Scholars speak of 'an implicit christology': ie Jesus' actions and words speak to us about his role and relationship to God, even when he makes no explicit claims to be Messiah or Son of God. Jesus speaks of the kingdom of God (his Father), but he is completely confident that people will do what God wants by following him. Readers have already been told by Mark that Jesus is (Servant) Messiah and beloved Son of God, in whom God is well pleased. So we know that we are called by God to follow him. We must admire the first disciples who left their families and livelihoods at his call, without having any such clear understanding.

2.3 Discipleship

An essential part of this kingdom seems to be the gathering together in community with Jesus of people who are open to it, who are willing to believe, and to change their life. As well as being followers of Jesus, they have to spread the news so as to bring others into the community of Jesus: from being 'fish catchers' they are to become 'people catchers'. Jesus takes the initiative. They do not volunteer, he calls them. Rabbis in the time of Jesus had disciples, who learned from them how to become interpreters of the scriptures and the traditions that had been handed down. But they had to ask to become disciples. It will become clear later that there will be a wide circle of disciples of Jesus, but the inner core were those he chose and called. He called some who said no (the rich young man, 10:17-22), some who wanted to come he told to stay at home and spread the news there (the healed demoniac, 5:18-19). The essential ingredient is to be willing to do what Jesus asks.

Spend some time thinking about what it means to you to be a disciple of Jesus. Do you think you would have that 'jump to it' quality shown by the first four to be called? Do you find Jesus an attractive (irresistible) leader you would gladly follow? Do you think there are things keeping you back from following him as you would like to? Are you able and willing to try to identify the obstacles? Do you think they are insurmountable?

2.4 Conversion

We are called to 'repent and believe in the good news'. Blessed are those who have no hesitations or misgivings about believing in the good news. Resistance is fairly normal. The kingdom of God means that God is offering us many blessings out of sheer goodness and generosity. Something about this moment (*kairos*) in Mark's gospel speaks to us of the danger of missing the opportunity. God is going to do something life-changing for his people. His power is limited only in this sense, that it cannot work on those who do not open themselves to it. The kingdom may be near, but it cannot take effect in me unless I choose to respond. We ask the good Lord to take away all our negatives and fears that prevent us from accepting the kingdom (God's healing love). The new mind set that we need is precisely this readiness to believe in God's love for us and allow it to guide our lives. Each one of us may expect to have in our lives moments of conversion, some of which we may seize and treasure, some of which we may lose. Take a little time to look back over your life to identify such moments, experiences of God's movement in your lives which made a difference, 'calls' that you responded to or wish you had. The recently beatified John Henry Newman borrowed some religious books from a teacher as holiday reading when he was fifteen, and they became the seed of his lifelong passion to seek and teach God's truth. That was a kairos in his life. If we miss the kairos at a given time, is it gone for ever? Or is God always patiently calling us to be closer to him? Rather than contemplating past failures, it is better to put faith in the God of new beginnings and pray for the one thing necessary: openness to what God is offering.

3. RESPONSE

Make your personal response by reading the text again, stopping to pray with any word, phrase or verse that speaks to you.

Jesus came to Galilee, proclaiming the good news of God. Respond with gratitude to God for sending his Son to reveal the divine plan for our salvation and to call us to share in it. Out of God's goodness something wonderful is open to us if we are open to it. Pray for that openness. Pray for trust in the Lord's healing love, and determine to use the opportunity to begin again, or to deepen a relationship with God through Jesus that constantly needs to be rekindled.

The kingdom of God has come near (is at hand). Kingdom, reign, ruler, laws, regulations, taking orders – all this may have negative connotations for us. So, Lord, help us to work on our attitudes and assumptions that we may see the kindly offer of love and hope that is being made to us. Pray to see God as the 'good-news-God', who looks upon us with love, delights in us, not the 'I'm-watching-you-God' who is only interested in us when we do wrong. Help us to see that faith in a God who looks upon us with love and goodness is the beginning of a new adventure. The 'good news of God' means the 'news of God's goodness'. If you are carrying baggage from the past where the traffic warden God has been ever watchful to clamp your first wrong move, meet the God who sees far more good in you than you yourself know about and wants you to be fully alive. God's reign means his powerful, saving love in us and around us. Take a little time to relax and bask in his loving presence.

Repent and believe in the good news. The coming of the kingdom calls for our action as disciples ready to answer the call. Pray for the grace of true repentance, the kind that means changing your mindset from 'what's in it for me?' to 'what can I do to help?' Pray for understanding of what you can do personally and as a member of the People of God to witness to the kingdom, to welcome the reign of God in your own heart, then to co-operate with God in living by its values and building community. You may not be able to leave everything as the first disciples did, but there are many ways to be part of the great kingdom adventure. Pray to hear God's call to you in Christ, and for the grace to respond to it.

Follow me and I will make you fish for people. Jesus is the bringer of the kingdom, and asks us to follow him. So pray that you will be able to commit yourself to Jesus and seek to live in close relationship with him. Do not rule out a call to full-time following if your circumstances allow. Not everyone is called in the same way: his call will always find an echo in our deepest desires. So pray that your relationship with Jesus may grow, whether you feel called as Simon, Andrew, James and John, or as the healed demoniac in Gerasa was: 'Go home to your friends, and tell them how much the Lord has done for you' (5:19).

4. CONTEMPLATION

It is good to walk through life's journey with an awareness of God's loving power ('the reign of God') surrounding and guiding us. God is good, good to me and for me, and wishes me to do his will precisely that I may live a fuller and more graced life. Look back to our text and choose a phrase or sentence that carries a meaning for you and will continue to nourish your awareness of God's loving care around you: 'The kingdom of God is at hand', 'Believe in the good news'.

Authority in Word and Deed (Mark 1:21-31)

1. FAMILIARISATION

1.1 Getting to know the text (Mark 1:21-31)

Teaching in words

1:21   They went to Capernaum;
        and when the sabbath came,
        he entered the synagogue and taught.

22   They were astonished at his teaching,
        for he taught them as one having authority,
        and not as the scribes.

Teaching in action

23   Just then there was in their synagogue
        a man with an unclean spirit

24   and he cried out,
        'What have you to do with us, Jesus of Nazareth?
        Have you come to destroy us?
        I know who you are, the Holy One of God.'

25   But Jesus rebuked him, saying,
        'Be silent, and come out of him!'

26   And the unclean spirit,
        convulsing him and crying out with a loud voice,
        came out of him.

Reaction

27   They were all amazed,
        and they kept on asking one another:
        'What is this? A new teaching – with authority!
        He commands even the unclean spirits,
        and they obey him.'

28   At once his fame began to spread
        throughout the surrounding region of Galilee.

Simon's mother-in-law

29   As soon as they left the synagogue,
        they entered the house of Simon and Andrew,
        with James and John.

30   Now Simon's mother-in-law was in bed with a fever,
        and they told him about her at once.
31   He came and took her by the hand
        and lifted her up.
        Then the fever left her,
        and she began to serve them.

1.2 Background

1.2.1 *A typical 24 hours:* It is generally said that with this section and the next seven verses (ie altogether 1:21-38) Mark recreates a typical 24 hours in Jesus' Galilean ministry, centred on the Sabbath. We may assume that the pattern was to be repeated in many towns and villages throughout Galilee, as indicated in v 39: 'And he went throughout Galilee, proclaiming the message in their synagogues and casting out demons.' Mark gives us morning to morning, though the Jewish day stretches from sunset to sunset, not from midnight to midnight, as with us. The crowding around the door by the sick and possessed (v 32) comes at sunset, ie the end of the Sabbath and the beginning of the new day when it was possible to seek healing.

1.2.2 *The Synagogue:* Jesus made his 'headquarters' in Capernaum, near the north west corner of the Sea of Galilee. He would have to be invited by the local Rabbi or synagogue leaders to first read from the sacred scrolls on the Sabbath and then comment on the reading. That he 'entered the synagogue and taught' shows that he was already becoming known and gaining respect. You can see the remains of a large synagogue today in Capernaum, the upper part of white limestone built on black basalt foundations with lots of small basalt houses around. This suggests that a new (limestone) synagogue was built over the foundations of the basalt synagogue of Jesus' time. Not far away a modern church has been built over the remains of a church-like structure which may well have been originally the house of Simon Peter where Jesus healed Simon's mother in law.

1.2.3 *Teaching with authority:* Mark does not record as much of the content of Jesus' teaching as Matthew or Luke, but the vocabulary of teaching (Greek *didache*, teaching, *didasco*, I teach, *didascalos*, teacher) is actually used more often by Mark. In Mark it is normal for Jesus to be addressed as 'teacher' (*didascale*) by his disciples, whereas Matthew and Luke allow only outsiders (and Judas) to call Jesus 'teacher' or Rabbi. Mark does not tell us what he said, but we are to presume that he repeated, perhaps amplified the 'mission statement' that he made in v 15 (see Session 3). There he was said to 'proclaim', using the verb *kerussein*. But though disciples and witnesses are said to proclaim throughout the gospel, it is Jesus' messianic task to teach, so henceforth the teaching vocabulary is used of Jesus (*didasco* etc). Jesus' teaching made a deep impression in the synagogue – 'they were astounded at his teaching, for he taught them as one having authority, and not as the scribes'. The scribes were accustomed to cite other rabbinic experts and precedents to substantiate their teaching. Jesus speaks with total conviction in God's name and obviously believes he is giving God's message. What is more, he teaches by his actions also, not just with words. When he casts out the unclean spirit, the reaction is: 'What is this? A new teaching – with authority! He commands even the unclean spirits and they obey him' (v 27). So we are meant to deduce that his actions explain the meaning of 'kingdom of God' as much as his words. After all, actions speak louder than words.

1.2.4 Exorcism: So what does his action in the synagogue tell us about 'kingdom'? Exorcism plays an important role in Mark's gospel, for if the reign of God is to grow, the power of Satan has to be controlled and overcome. There are four graphic accounts of individual exorcisms (in addition to our present text, see 5:1-20, the Gerasene demoniac; 7:24-30, the Syrophoenician woman's daughter; and 9:14-29, the difficult demon that the disciples failed to drive out), as well as summaries of exorcisms, eg 1:32-34, following our present text. And the implications will be spelled out in 3:22-30 when the scribes from Jerusalem accused him of driving out demons by the power of Beelzebub; to which Jesus countered: 'How can Satan cast out Satan? ... If Satan has risen up against himself ... his end has come.'

Our modern minds are embarrassed about demon possession, and often try to soften it to a metaphor for illness. But Mark is mostly clear about the difference. His language for demon possession is very different from his language for healing. The unclean spirit takes over the person possessed, so that the person does not speak or act for himself, and is flung around vindictively. In v 24 of our text the man cried out, 'What have you to do with us (plural for demons in general), Jesus of Nazareth? Have you come to destroy us?' The man does not speak for himself. The demons have superior knowledge: 'I know who you are, the Holy One of God.' They sense the danger that Jesus presents for them, and try to curtail his power by revealing his name (identity). Jesus does not allow them to reveal his identity publicly and commands silence. It is unlikely that they suspect that he is 'Son of God' in the strict sense, but they fear his God-given mission and power. The coming of the kingdom means that God's saving power is at hand to save the possessed and all of us from the power of the Evil One. The Lord's Prayer (not in Mark) begins with 'Thy kingdom come' and ends with 'deliver us from evil (or from the Evil One)'.

1.2.5 The Reaction of the Onlookers: Mark uses very strong verbs for the reaction to both Jesus' words and the exorcism. 'They were astounded at his teaching ...' (v. 22); 'they were all amazed, and kept on asking one another, "What is this? A new teaching – with authority!"' (v 27) Astonishment, amazement – such words recur often to keep before our minds the newness and the power of what Jesus teaches. Even if what he says seems strange and mysterious, it is hard to resist words backed up with amazing deeds. After years of hearing the same texts it is possible for our ears to become dulled to the message, so we need to try to hear with fresh ears and allow the words to rekindle our awareness of the great thing that is happening.

1.2.6 Domestic Healing: After the heady events in the synagogue, Jesus and his new disciples went to 'the house of Simon and Andrew'. The excavated houses around the synagogue are very small, and this one also was home to Simon's wife and her mother. This house is traditionally the home base of Jesus and his disciples in Galilee, and was later turned into a small church for Christians. The first four disciples are privileged witnesses to many intimate moments in Jesus' life, and presumably they drew Jesus attention to the sick woman. Jesus quietly took her by the hand and raised her up, and the fever was gone, and she served them. Does this miracle also teach us about the kingdom, or is it just a favour to his friends? I suggest that Mark has carefully chosen actions of Jesus that teach us about the kingdom. In the synagogue Jesus acts with power and stern command. In the house he acts with tenderness, his gentle touch bringing healing to the sick woman. Mark uses two possibly theologically laden words: he raised her up (*egeirein*), the same word that is used for raising from the dead and for resurrection (NRSV lifted her up); and she served them (past continuous tense of *diaconein*, to serve, which later took on the special meaning of service to God and God's people, and later still gave its name to the order of 'deacon'). Healing miracles are symbolic of spiritual healing, which is the restoration of new life, and calls those thus en-livened to the service of Jesus and his followers. I am inclined to say then that this miracle also teaches us about how the king-dom grows. Both in Judaism and later in Christianity religion plays an important role in the worship and social interaction of public life, and in the life of the family. Jesus brings the powerful and tender love of God to the public life of the community and to the intimacy of the family.

2. REFLECTION

2.1 Mystery

The plan of God begins to be fulfilled. There is strangeness here, and power, and authority, and compassion. Mark hopes that the flow of the narrative will help us to get the message, for he doesn't take time to explain. Jesus' words astound his hearers with their power, assurance, and newness. The announcement of the coming kingdom of God must have been new to some of them, and it is big news. They know they are being challenged. It is enough to frighten the man with the unclean spirit, though he is only the vehicle for the spirit who controls him and speaks for him. The demon sees the implications: if what Jesus says is true, then it is bad news for Satan and his minions. He confronts Jesus, trying to pre-empt the danger by revealing his identity as the Holy One of God. But he cannot take the initiative from Jesus, who always refuses to allow his identity to be revealed by such dubious sources. So he commands, 'Be muzzled (a strong demand for silence) and come out of him.' The whole synag-ogue is amazed when the demon flings the man to the ground in a fit with a great roar, and with that final defiance, leaves him in peace and obeys the command of Jesus. The audience approves:

here's a real teacher, who backs his words with action. He talks about this kingdom, and there is an aura of authority and power about him, so perhaps God is working through him. They want to talk about it, and the news spreads through Galilee. And his new disciples bring Jesus home, and he raises up Simon's mother-in-law from her bed of fever. This time there are no words, just a gracious taking her by the hand and raising her up. And she is immediately so well that she begins to serve them.

Mark would like us to pay attention to his narrative and then reflect. What is going on? It is Jesus teaching about the kingdom of God in words and in actions. God's reign frees humans from the power of Satan. God's power is at work through Jesus to challenge Satan's kingdom. Those who hear and see are impressed: this is new, and with authority behind it. They are excited and spread the news. Having seen the power and authority of Jesus, the disciples also witness his gentleness at home in the healing of the woman they all know. Contrast the contempt of the demon(s) for the person who is possessed with the healing goodness of Jesus towards Simon's mother-in-law. That's the difference the kingdom makes. Power and tenderness, shown in synagogue and home, allowing the afflicted to be again full members of community and family. This is how the reign of God is to grow.

2.2 Christology

It is God's kingdom, but it is closely tied up with Jesus. It comes through him, is present where he is present. His is a magnetic presence, whether in the synagogues or the house. The worshippers in the synagogue react with astonishment and words of admiration: Jesus is a new kind of teacher, with such authority. The disciples say not a word, except to draw his attention to the sick woman. It is the unclean spirit who claims to know who he is. 'Jesus the Nazarene' (NRSV, 'Jesus of Nazareth'), then 'the Holy One of God'. Is the 'Nazarene' meant as a slight? People from Nazareth did not rate highly, if we accept Nathaniel's words in John 1:46: 'Can anything good come out of Nazareth?' The demon rightly fears, 'Have you come to destroy us? We know who you are, the Holy One of God.' He speaks in the plural, for demons in general. What is intended by 'the Holy One of

God'? Probably no more than that he is someone who carries God's power, though it could be a title for the Messiah. The demons are in the presence of supernatural power greater than their own. Jesus' strong words demonstrate that this is so. This power and authority impresses the observers; they can't stop talking about it. The news will draw a crowd to the house when the Sabbath is over at sunset (vv 32-34).

2.3 Discipleship

The first four disciples accompany Jesus back to Capernaum. V 21 begins 'they went', but then switches to the singular: 'He entered the synagogue and taught.' Reaction comes from unspecified observers, 'They were astounded' (v 23); 'They were all amazed' (v 27). We assume 'they' are the worshippers in the synagogue, but we may include the disciples, who leave the synagogue afterwards with Jesus and go to 'the house of Simon and Andrew' (v 29). This was the disciples' first experience of Jesus working miracles, so we rightly assume they were astounded and amazed like the rest of the congregation. In the house, the disciples have learned enough to believe that Jesus, who saved an afflicted man from the unclean spirit, might be willing to save a woman from sickness; they asked for nothing, merely drew the situation to Jesus' attention. They learned something more: they may have hoped that Jesus, who showed such commanding authority in the synagogue, would speak equally sternly to the fever and order it to leave the woman. But he quietly bends down (we may presume a smile), gently takes her by the hand and raises her up. She is instantly well, well enough to serve them. Perhaps a hint is given by Mark in v 31: 'The fever left her, and she began to serve them.' Literally it means that she helped to provide the Sabbath meal, but Mark's readers may discern a deeper meaning: that those who find themselves healed by the hand of Jesus, must become servants of Jesus and of his followers.

How have we experienced the power and tenderness of God that Jesus brings? In the healing and forgiveness of our sins? In the strength and support which sustain us in trouble and sorrow? In the joy and gratitude that can spring up in us when we join our community at prayer? When we join in our family celebrations and get-togethers?

2.4 Conversion

What would we have learned if we had been observers in these two incidents, like the four disciples? Firstly note that many of the participants were amazed and excited by Jesus' words and actions, but consider how many of them became committed to him? Interest and excitement are not enough if they do not lead to action, to service as the healed woman demonstrated. So there is a challenge to our routine practice of religion without mind and heart becoming engaged. We need also to have the humility to admit that evil, the desires and seductions of Satan, are constantly and insidiously undermining our spiritual lives, and that it is Jesus' power we need to raise us up, not our own.

Secondly, consider the need to hold in tension the two most striking qualities of Jesus at work, his authority and his tenderness. Have we built an overly sentimental picture of Jesus 'meek and mild', and favoured likenesses of him which support it? Have we forgotten the authority, power and courage he displayed here and will constantly need throughout his mission? The strong are gentle. Jesus' power and tenderness together teach us what he is like, and also what God our Father is like, and make the reign of God visible to us. And the other side of this is that any one of us, whether lay or cleric, who has authority over others, can only make God's reign visible by being both strong and tender, in the spirit of service.

3. Response

Make your personal response by rereading the text and stopping to pray about any word, phrase or verse that strikes you.

When the Sabbath came, he entered the synagogue and taught ... as one having authority. Lord, impressive teacher, man of conviction, prophet of God, we know you teach fulfilment, good news, kingdom, faith and repentance. You teach us also that words need to be allied to action. Forgive us when our words and our actions are out of sync. You show that God's reign means rescue for the possessed man, healing for the sick woman. Let the power of God rescue us from evil and the evil one; let the tenderness of God bind up our wounds and heal the hurts within us. We pray for strength where truth and right are at stake, we pray for compassion for those who are weak and suffering.

What is this? A new teaching – with authority. He commands even the unclean spirits, and they obey him. We pray for the growth of the kingdom, for the weakening of the power of evil and the evil one over humanity. We pray that the evil, cruelty and greed that mar the lives of many human beings, that still show the power of the kingdom of Satan, may be rooted out of the lives of God's people. We pray for all who are under the influence of Satan or of destructive habits, that they may meet Jesus and be set free. We pray that our young people may not fall under the influence of the current belligerent atheism, or of a destructive reliance upon drugs, alcohol, pornography, promiscuous sex or violence. We pray for the victims of sexual abuse that the hand of Jesus may raise them up. We pray for the church that God's people may face their failures and their strengths with humility and hope, that the Spirit may prompt a new vigour in our faith. 'Thy kingdom come, thy will be done.'

They told him about her at once. Tell him about all the people you wish to pray for. We know, Lord, that you cannot 'fix' for us all the things we bring to your attention. But it gives us strength to know that you are compassionate and that you are with us. We rejoice that you bring healing to families; we bring to you all the families who are troubled and burdened by bereavement, sickness, relationships growing cold or hurtful. We ask for a special blessing on the united, happy, life-giving families who are the hope of the community and the church and the world.

He came and took her by the hand, and lifted her up ... and she began to serve them. Raise us up, Lord, that we may serve you and serve your people. We pray for those mothers who serve their families so faithfully, and for all who serve in our parishes and communities, often without too much thanks. We experience so much love in our families, and too often, because we are human, so much hurt. Help us to be more open and vocal in our appreciation of our loved ones.

They were astounded ... they were amazed, and they kept on asking one another, 'What is this?' Identify with the onlookers for a moment. 'What is this?' for you. Pray for yourself, that your presence as an interested observer may be more than that. Pray for yourself, that this impressive man, one of us, but so much more, may heal you deeply, strengthen your commitment to him, renew and revitalise your spiritual life and your relationships, raise you up so that you may have pride in being a follower of Jesus, learning to serve him anew. Believe that the reign of God means an outpouring upon you – yes, you! – of God's healing goodness. Bask for a moment in the tenderness of our loving God, made visible by Jesus.

4. CONTEMPLATION

Walk with awareness of Jesus with us and in us, with all his authority and power, with the knowledge that God's reign of healing love is around us to sustain and uplift us. Walk with gratitude that we are so important to God that his love calls us to reflect the kingdom by our lives, and keep asking for the strength to try to make his love visible, in however small a way. Choose a text to remind us of his authority that challenges current wishy-washy attitudes: 'A new teaching – with authority!' And to remind us of the compassionate goodness that goes with his authority: 'He took her by the hand and raised her up.'

The Perfect Miracle (Mark 2:1-12)

1. FAMILIARISATION

1.1 Getting to know the text (Mark 2:1-12)

The house in Capernaum

2.1　When he returned to Capernaum after some days,it was
　　　reported that he was at home.

2　　So many gathered around
　　　that there was no longer room for them,
　　　not even in front of the door;
　　　and he was speaking the word to them.

Surprise for a paralysed man

3　　Then some people came, bringing to him a paralysed man,
　　　carried by four of them.

4　　And when they could not bring him to Jesus
　　　because of the crowds,
　　　they removed the roof above him,
　　　and after having dug through it,
　　　they let down the mat on which the paralytic lay.

5　　When Jesus saw their faith, he said to the paralytic,
　　　'Son, your sins are forgiven'.

Visible and invisible healing

6　　Now some of the scribes were sitting there,
　　　questioning in their hearts,

7　　'Why does this fellow speak in this way?
　　　It is blasphemy! Who can forgive sins but God alone?'

8　　At once Jesus perceived in his spirit
　　　that they were discussing these questions
　　　among themselves;
　　　and he said to them,
　　　'Why do you raise such questions in your hearts?

9　　Which is easier,
　　　to say to the paralytic, "Your sins are forgiven",
　　　or to say, "Stand up and take your mat and walk".

10　　But so that you may know

that the Son of Man has authority on earth
to forgive sins' – he said to the paralytic –

11   'I say to you, stand up and take your mat
and go to your home.'

12   And he stood up,
and immediately took the mat
and went out before all of them;
so that they were all amazed
and glorified God, saying,
'We have never seen anything like this!'

1.2 Background

1.2.1 Controversy stories: The section Mark 2:1-3:6 is usually identified by commentators as a series of controversy stories in which opposition to Jesus from scribes (legal experts) and leaders of the synagogues, mostly Pharisees, gradually grows until in the end there is a determination to destroy him (3:6). This unity of theme suggests that the section took shape before Mark composed his gospel, and that he incorporated it here without determining that these events happened strictly in this order or at this time in the ministry. The reader would do well to read the whole section, though we will concentrate only on a couple of the incidents. Our current section is 2:1-12, then comes 2:13-17, the call of Levi the tax-collector, which soon raises questions about Jesus eating with sinners; 2:18-22 raises the question of fasting and the newness that the kingdom brings (see Session 6); 2:23-28 raises questions about keeping the Sabbath, closely linked to 3:1-6, healing on the Sabbath. Jesus' goodness seems to provoke hostility, newness disturbs those who wish to preserve the established order. The scribes and Pharisees see Jesus as gratuitously provoking confrontation by permitting, nay, encouraging breaches of the traditions of the elders. Jesus seems to challenge pious conventions that do not put people and their healing first, that do not set people free from the guilt of sin and the imposed guilt that results from burdensome regulations. Be warned that reading the text looking at the controversies can obscure the good news in the section. The spiritual content is good news all the way, illustrating the meaning of the nearness of the kingdom announced in 1:15, the forgiveness of sins, the welcome for sinners who seek healing, the celebration that the presence of Jesus (the 'bridegroom') and his message should call forth, the joy that the sabbath is the very best day for God to give new life to his people.

1.2.2 Mark's editing of the paralytic incident: Mark links this incident to the cleansing of the leper (1:40-45) by having Jesus return to Capernaum after spending 'some days' in deserted places to allow popular enthusiasm to die down. As soon as his return is known, a crowd gathers around the door of 'the house' (presumably that of Simon and Andrew), and Jesus 'was speaking the word (the good news of the kingdom) to them'. The miracle occurs in the midst of his teaching, just as happened in the synagogue (Session 4), again stressing Jesus' teaching by word and action. There was little room around or in the small houses, so the crowd made it impossible to get in or out. The determination of the carriers who brought the paralysed man for healing is evident: they took time to carry him up to the roof (visualise little houses with an outside stairway leading to a flat roof, the 'extra room'), to find the tools to open the roof, and possibly ropes to let him down. Mark gives us just the result, and focuses on the healing rather than the family's reaction to the destruction of their roof, the noise, dust and disruption of Jesus' teaching. Surprisingly, Jesus firstly declared the paralysed man's sins forgiven, and then, to substantiate this forgiveness in the eyes of critics, he tells him to stand up, take his mat and go home. The reaction is amazement and praise of God.

Most commentators agree that Mark received the story substantially as he gives it, but many suggest that before Mark received it, a straightforward miracle story of physical healing (omitting the section between the two occurrences of 'he said to the paralytic', ie from the middle of v 5 to the beginning of v 11) was combined with a second story about forgiveness of sin. This is perhaps borne out by the sudden introduction of a new title for Jesus, 'the Son of Man', by the insistence that Jesus himself has power 'on earth' to forgive sins, not just power to declare that God has forgiven them, and by the reference to the scribes 'sitting' (their teaching position) in a little crowded room. A case might be made that we have little more that what is common enough in Mark, that he tries to bring out the deeper understanding of what originally happened, so as to convey the faith of the church. Anyhow, our need is to reflect on the text as Mark has given it, to see what he wishes us to realise about the meaning of the kingdom.

1.2.3 *Blasphemy:* Jesus is accused of blasphemy by the scribes at the beginning of his ministry (though under their breath). At the end of the ministry blasphemy will be the main accusation of the chief priests leading to the decision to bring Jesus to Pilate to ask for the death penalty (14:64). Blasphemy was disrespect of God's name (God's Being); claiming for oneself something that belongs only to God, like the authority to forgive sins, is an insult to God, unless, of course, God backs up the claim. Later Christian experience of the forgiveness of sin in the name of Jesus may have influenced the way Jesus' reply to the implicit criticism is worded: '… the Son of Man has authority on earth to forgive sins' (2:10). This leaves no doubt that in the text as it stands Jesus claims for himself the authority to forgive sins. Mark's readers would have had no difficulty with this, as the close relationship between the Father and Jesus had by then been worked out; but it was a big shock for the scribes, the guardians of the Oneness of God and the sacredness of his prerogatives.

1.2.4 *Sign of the kingdom at work:* 'Which is easier, to say to the paralytic, "Your sins are forgiven", or to say, "Stand up and take your mat and walk?"'(v.9) 'Easier' can only mean that the forgiveness of sins cannot be verified by onlookers, and so is in that sense easier. Jesus continues: "But so that you may know that the Son of Man has authority on earth to forgive sins" – he said to the paralytic: "I say to you, stand up …" (vv 10-11). When the man actually stands up and does what Jesus tells him to do, then the thing that is not 'easier', that has to be visible to be credible, has been seen before their eyes, and becomes a sign that the forgiveness of sins is also real. For how could God allow the physical healing in such a case, if the spiritual healing was not also divinely approved? The physical healing (wonderful in itself) becomes also a sign of the more wonderful spiritual healing. Some writers refer to the healing of the paralytic as 'the perfect miracle', since it involves healing of the whole person, body and soul, and even points to the total healing of the human being

61

that will be the resurrection. Until then, the healing of our bodily ills is not guaranteed (Jesus cured comparatively few of the sick people of his day), but spiritual healing, the forgiveness of sins, is available through Jesus to all who 'repent and believe in the good news' (1:15). Mark is enabling his readers to understand more about the reign of God at work among us.

1.2.5 'The Son of Man' (v 10): Volumes have been written about this title which is used frequently in the Gospels (Mark 14 times, Matthew 30, Luke 27, John 13), and not all that often in the rest of the New Testament or by early Christian writers. It is used mostly by Jesus himself, without explicit explanation, and seems to be Jesus' preferred title to describe his messianic mission (though this would be challenged by some commentators). Mark uses it only twice before the confession by Simon Peter at Caesarea Philippi that Jesus is the Messiah (8:29), upon which Jesus asks them not to use the title 'Messiah' and begins to refer to himself as 'the Son of Man' (8:31). Both the earlier references occur in this series of controversy stories (2:10 and 2:28), both with reference to Jesus' authority (over the forgiveness of sins and over the sabbath). The strangeness of the usage so early in the Gospel may be explained by the probability that this complex of stories predates Mark's composition, and there is no guarantee that they happened at the beginning of the ministry. It is not unusual for Mark to introduce mysterious sayings of Jesus which the reader has to accept in faith, awaiting explanation later. The main source for the title is Daniel 7:13-14 (there translated as 'one like a human being' by NRSV) which describes a vision of God enthroned in the heavens, to whom 'one like a son of man' comes and receives an everlasting kingdom. The literal meaning of 'son of man' is simply a human being (see the Irish idiom, 'every mother's son of you'), and represented in Daniel the people of Israel, who, after the attempt of the Syrian king Antiochus IV Epiphanes (175-164 BC) to suppress the religion of Israel with all its attendant suffering, will triumph through God's power and set up an everlasting kingdom. Later speculation, perhaps already known to some in the time of Jesus, gave this 'Son of Man' an individual messianic identity. The probability is that Jesus used this obscure messianic title until the nature of his messiahship was properly understood. It wasn't until Jesus was brought before the Sanhedrin, the Jewish supreme council, that he openly laid claim to the title Messiah (14:62); by then it was all too obvious that he was not going to lead a popular uprising against Roman rule. There are other aspects of 'Son of Man' that we will meet later in the Gospel, in particular its association with Jesus' passion prophecies, and with his triumph over death and exaltation by the Father.

2. REFLECTION

2.1 Mystery

Reread the text with the eyes of those who first experienced these dramatic events. Jesus draws a crowd around him by his teaching about the kingdom, and is unperturbed when a group of determined stretcher-carriers suddenly tear up the roof above him and lower a paralysed man at his feet. Jesus sees 'their faith' (of the carriers, but we cannot exclude the faith of the paralytic), does not do the expected thing, but declares that the man's sins are forgiven, calling him 'son', showing compassion. Eyebrows are raised by the scribes in the audience, there are nods and mutterings. Jesus feels his forgiveness of sins is being challenged, and offers to demonstrate the reality of his authority to forgive by commanding the man to get up and walk. This he does, and the invalid stands up, takes up his mat and walks out before their eyes. Not only is the audience amazed, but they give glory to God – a way of confessing that God is at work here through Jesus. The kingdom of God is at work, and it brings healing of body and of spirit. Jesus claims that he has authority as the bringer of the kingdom to forgive sins. So his call (1:15) to 'repent and believe in the good news' strikes us with new force. May we come to Jesus to be healed? What kind of healing do we need? The paralytic seems to have had more needs than his obvious one. Is the first need of each of us the healing of our spirits, of our inward dis-ease? Spend a little time reflecting on your needs, and on your willingness to come to Jesus for healing.

2.2 Christology

We see Jesus doing new things and giving himself a new mysterious title. Already we have had 'Messiah (Christ), the Son of God' (1:1), 'the more powerful one' (1:7), 'my Son, the Beloved'

(1:11), the proclaimer of the kingdom (1:14-15), the one who speaks and acts with authority (1:22, 27), the expeller of unclean spirits (1:25), the healer of the sick (1:31, 34), the healer of lepers (1:40-45). Now he is 'the Son of Man' with authority to forgive sins (2:10). Daniel 7:13-14 reads: 'As I watched in the night visions, I saw one like a human being (son of man) coming with the clouds of heaven. And he came to the Ancient One [ie God] and was presented before him. (14) And to him was given dominion and glory and kingship, that all peoples, nations and languages should serve him. His dominion is an everlasting dominion, that shall not pass away, and his kingship is one that shall never be destroyed.' The concept of God's people personified as this 'son of man' persecuted in the era of the Maccabees, offers to Jesus a connection to a messianic Son of Man who will suffer, but who through God's power will triumph over suffering when he seems to have failed. At this point Mark only introduces the title without explanation, and we can only guess how many of Jesus' original audience or how many of Mark's readers grasped the reference to Daniel 7. Live with it and keep it in mind. We are building up a picture of a powerful Messiah, and perhaps we with Jesus' disciples will be dismayed at his weakness later in the narrative. Now it seems he can do anything. Normally Jews had to go to Jerusalem and offer a sacrifice for the forgiveness of their sins, with the priests in Jerusalem officiating. Now someone who has not even asked for it receives forgiveness immediately through Jesus. This is impressive. Jesus is in trouble with the scribes, by their looks. But what can they say when the paralytic stands up at his word, a sign he offered to show that the forgiveness was real? What can any of us say, except to join in the onlookers' praise of God who has sent this deliverer from sins among us?

2.3 Discipleship

Identify with the disciples and look at the scene through their eyes. You're back in the house after being away for days, but the peace is over when a crowd gathers and presses into the house to hear Jesus speak. Scribes arrive, and perhaps you try to get them seats as befits their dignity. The scribes listen, exchange glances, say little. The inspectors have come for this teacher!

Watch the faces of Simon and Andrew as the roof disintegrates before their eyes and they are forced to reach out supporting hands to the man on the mat, suddenly dropped among them. Watch Jesus taking the intrusion in his stride. He looks at the carriers, presumably peering down through the roof, looks at the man on the mat, sees faith; and speaks with concern, 'Son, your sins are forgiven.' You are amazed! Is that what the man came for? You can see the knowing looks and whispers of the scribes. Jesus sees them too. He answers them before they can speak. Before their eyes he tells the paralysed man to stand up, take up his pallet and walk home unaided. And the man does just that! And it is to demonstrate that God is backing his authority to forgive sins. This is restoration to health in the deepest sense. What you have seen with your eyes shows that this man has the power to heal the human heart, which cannot be easily seen. He can change lives and direct us on a new path. You join in the praise of God with all the onlookers – and to be fair the scribes are impressed too, included for the moment anyhow in the universal amazement. The disciples' attachment to Jesus must be strengthened. Reflect for a moment on how your own attachment to Jesus is confirmed by this miracle of total healing.

2.4 Conversion

Identify with the paralysed man and with his friends who bring him to Jesus. Note their determination and 'their faith', which I think should not exclude the paralysed man himself. Firstly, how do we as disciples see our role in bringing others to Jesus? How determined are we? How full of faith are we? We can allow ourselves to be influenced by today's attitude that faith is a private matter, every person's own business. That is not thinking in Jesus' way. We cannot of course browbeat people into faith, but does our attitude say that we don't really think it is worth sharing? Invitation is always good, and our conviction that it makes a big difference to our lives may show that we have something worth sharing. Secondly, disciples should be grateful to those who have brought them to Jesus – it may be parents, teachers, friends, clergy, a long line of faithful people in the past. Thirdly, in today's world, we need to reflect on the terrible damage to others that can be done and has been done by disciples betraying positions of trust and responsibility. Pray for those who have been hurt. Pray that we may never become obstacles to other people coming to Jesus. For it doesn't take child abuse or something terrible to discourage others from coming to Jesus. We can do that by all kinds of carelessness and sins of omission, by not praying with our children, by cynicism, by careless or inappropriate language about God or church.

3. RESPONSE

Make your personal response by rereading the text, stopping to pray with any verse or words that strike you.

And he was speaking the word to them. Picture in your imagination Jesus in the house drawing people to hear him 'speaking the word to them' (2:2). Change the image to the people of God coming to church to hear the word of God. Think about your response to the word of God in church, or the response you are trying to make now. Pray earnestly for an attentive ear. Pray for those who preach the word.

They let down the mat on which the paralytic lay. Lord, was I ever as determined as this man and his friends to come to you for healing? What faith they had, what determination! We make so many requests to you, and we have often heard: 'God knows what we really need.' Jesus, you knew what this man really needed more than healing of his sickness. Give us what we really need, even when we do not know what it is. Help us to have the wisdom to come to you for healing, when we are weighed down, or have lost our inner peace. We seek healing for whatever kind of paralysis we suffer from, sometimes of our emotions (through fears, worries, habits, hang-ups), sometimes of our inner spirit (through worries about forgiveness, sins committed in folly or weakness, unhealed relationships, hurts that remain too raw to heal), sometimes it's physical, when we are unable to reach out to others through pride or stubbornness or lack of trust. We bring all our baggage to you, Lord, and lay it at your feet. Help us to make better choices: to be honest and sincere before you, Lord, and before our loved ones; help us to heal relationships that need healing with family, friends, colleagues, to break down barriers, not to hide behind them.

The Son of Man has authority on earth to forgive sins. We give thanks that you have come as a source of healing and forgiveness. We beg you to heal our spirits and renew us with your life. Son of Man, source of healing, you continue to offer forgiveness on earth through your church. Help us to know that our sins hurt our brothers and sisters too, and that we need to be reconciled with the church.

They were all amazed and glorified God. Father, we join in that praise. Lord Jesus, you have revealed to us your Father's love. You make the kingdom of God visible and tangible to us, and show us that it means the Father's love and forgiveness. Give us the faith to believe that God's love offers us complete and generous healing. May your generosity, your welcome, and your healing goodness inspire us to try to be better witnesses to you.

4. CONTEMPLATION

In moments of quiet, continue to let the image of Jesus the healer revolve in your mind. Let your conscious and subconscious mind rejoice in the knowledge that you are forgiven and loved. You do not have to be perfect or sinless for God to love you! He loves you in the midst of your struggle to be good, delights in you. Walk, work, play, sing and smile with that conviction. Choose a text from this story to help you to maintain that mindset: e.g., 'Know that the Son of Man has power on earth to forgive sins.'

SESSION SIX

Newness of the Kingdom (Mark 2:18-22)

1. FAMILIARISATION

1.1 *Getting to know the text (Mark 2:18-22)*

The question of fasting

2:18 Now John's disciples and the Pharisees were fasting,
and people (lit. 'they') came and said to him:
'Why do John's disciples
and the disciples of the Pharisees fast,
but your disciples do not fast?'

The bridegroom is here!

19 Jesus said to them, 'The wedding guests cannot fast
while the bridegroom is with them, can they?
As long as they have the bridegroom with them,
they cannot fast.

20 The days will come
when the bridegroom is taken away from them,
and then they will fast on that day.

New cloth to patch old?

21 No one sews a piece of unshrunk cloth on an old cloak;
otherwise, the patch pulls away from it,
the new from the old,
and a worse tear is made.

New wine needs new wineskins

22 And no one puts new wine into old wineskins;
otherwise, the wine will burst the skins,
and the wine is lost, and so are the skins;
but one puts new wine into fresh wineskins.'

1.2 Background

1.2.1 Mild controversy: In the sequence – forgiveness of sins, associating with sinners, fasting, breaches of sabbath observance – the one about fasting is milder, a genuine question seeking explanation, and the questioners are unspecified. The question was of interest to his original hearers, to the early

68

Christians, and to us. Note the greater hostility in the other controversies, building to a final resolve by the Pharisees to destroy him (3:6). Jesus answers the challenges with memorable pronouncements, which take a bit of thinking about: 'The Son of Man has authority on earth to forgive sins (2:10),' 'I have come to call not the righteous, but sinners (2:17),' 'The wedding guests cannot fast when the bridegroom is with them, can they? (2:19),' 'The sabbath was made for humankind, not humankind for the sabbath (2:27),' 'Is it lawful to do good on the sabbath, to save life or to kill? (3:4)' It seems to be Jesus' intention, and Mark's, in an oral culture where things did not immediately get scribbled on notepads, to give oral 'homework', memorable statements upon which people need to go on reflecting. This prepares us to look at the images in our chosen text, and indeed for the more developed imagery we will find in Jesus' parables.

1.2.2 *Fasting:* we need to distinguish between fasting prescribed by the Jewish law and voluntary fasting for special reasons. Jews were ordered to fast on the Day of Atonement (the 10th day of the 7th month). Zechariah 8:19 mentions a day of fast in the fourth, fifth, seventh and tenth months, apparently to remember the fall of Jerusalem in 587 BC, and a possible other is based on Esther 9:31. Fasting was for one day, and was normally a sign of mourning, though it could also be a sign of repentance. Voluntary devotional fasting was used in petitioning for God's favour or as preparation for important occasions or decisions. Moses fasted for 40 days on Mount Sinai, as Jesus did before his mission. In Jesus' time the Pharisees fasted regularly (see Luke 18:12 for the Pharisee who fasted twice a week) as a devotional practice. Jesus assumed that his disciples would fast (Matthew 6:16-18, 'Whenever you fast, do not look dismal ...'), but wished them to do so discretely, without public parade of their virtue. There is no evidence of prescribed fasting in the early church, though again they fasted in intercession and before important decisions. An early Christian document, the *Didache* (8.1), mentions fasting on Wednesdays and Fridays. It is possible that the disciples of the Baptist were fasting in mourning for their leader 'taken away from them' (v 20), or it is possible that both Pharisees and followers of John were fasting in intercession for the coming of the Messiah, and puzzled that the disciples of Jesus were not doing the same.

1.2.3 Who asks the question? In Mark and Luke (5:33) it is indefinite: 'They came and said to him'. In Matthew (9:14) it is 'the disciples of John' who ask the question. In all three the disciples of John are mentioned before the (disciples of) the Pharisees. Perhaps the episode originally concerned the disciples of John, who continued as a movement long after the death of the Baptist, their austere and ascetic founder. Their fasting would have been a sign of repentance and longing for the Messianic kingdom. By the time Mark gets the story they are linked to the Pharisees. Jesus is concerned not that they fast, but that they fail to recognise that the messianic kingdom has come, that its newness is an obstacle to them because it is not what they expected.

1.2.4 The wedding imagery: The imagery of the wedding feast occurs elsewhere for the fulfilment of the messianic promises (see Matthew 22:1-14, the parable of the wedding banquet, and probably also, though not so clearly Luke 14:15-24). Because fasting in Jewish usage was so closely aligned with mourning, Jesus uses the wedding analogy to stress that the kingdom is here and should be celebrated. Wedding guests cannot fast while the bridegroom is with them. (Mark repeats that for emphasis.) They will fast 'when the bridegroom is taken away from them' (v.20); this does not quite fit the wedding imagery, since normally the bridegroom stayed and the guests left! But it fits with the situation of the followers of John, who had been taken away from them, arrested and subsequently executed by Herod Antipas. The phrase may also be the first, hidden, reference to Jesus' death, though that would not have been understood by Jesus' hearers at the time. Jesus is still with his followers so they can only celebrate.

1.2.5 The bridegroom: probably in the original setting no one perceived any messianic significance in the term 'bridegroom'. In the Old Testament wedding imagery is used to symbolise messianic times, but the Messiah is never referred to as the bridegroom. That title is reserved for God the Father, the bridegroom of Israel. Jesus may have used it as a veiled reference to his messianic identity, and there is a possibility that the reference may have meant something to the Baptist's followers. In John 3:28-30 John the Baptist, questioned about the one that he baptised who is now gathering followers, says: 'I am not the

Messiah ... He who has the bride is the bridegroom. The friend of the bridegroom, who stands and hears him, rejoices greatly at the bridegroom's voice. For this reason my joy has been fulfilled.' Mark's Christian readers would certainly have seen the deeper meaning in the term. In the later Pauline writings and the Book of Revelation (see, eg Ephesians 5:25-33, Revelation 19:7-9) Jesus is seen as the bridegroom choosing his people and offering himself for them in fidelity and love, as God chose and loved the people of Israel. Mark probably intended this meaning, so it is right for Christian readers to identify Jesus as the messianic bridegroom in whose presence we celebrate.

1.2.6 Patching old garments: Mark 2:21 seems to focus on preserving the old garment; putting a new piece of cloth (not fully shrunk) on an old garment will only make it worse. The messianic kingdom is not something patched up, it is new. Matthew's text (9:16) follows Mark, but in Luke (5:36) the point is not the shrinking, but that you wouldn't destroy a new garment to patch an old one, and anyway the new cloth wouldn't match the old. Taken together, there is no desire to destroy the old, but the new just doesn't go with it. The implication is that the kingdom is new, and that it does not fit with old expectations or with devotional practices that are really manifestations of the old mentality, which fails to see the newness of what Jesus brings. It is possible, then, to see a link with the wedding imagery; the kingdom is something new, and it is not a time for mourning, but for rejoicing.

1.2.7 New wine: think of wineskins made of leather, which at first is pliable but eventually hardens and cracks, losing elasticity. If new wine not fully fermented is put into old skins, the skins will burst and the wine will be lost. New wine has to be put into new still flexible skins. Another picture to show why Jesus and his disciples are not conforming to the practices of the followers of John and the Pharisees. A new thing is happening, a new presence has arrived, and the old must change to embrace the new. It will be very sad if the genuine goodness in the old ways becomes so rigid and inflexible that it cannot see the good in the new, a perennial peril for good people. New wine in the Old Testament is a symbol of celebration, especially a symbol of messianic blessings. The new wine at the wedding feast calls for celebration of the presence of the bridegroom, and all are invited to join in the celebration. Though rejoicing is not the full picture (a time will come when the bridegroom is taken away), nevertheless Christianity is essentially and always, even in the midst of the stark reality of suffering and persecution, a celebration of God's saving presence among us, made visible by Jesus the bridegroom.

2. Reflection

2.1 Mystery

This section of the gospel is difficult, but to omit it would be to lose an essential aspect of the meaning of the kingdom. We have seen the power of the kingdom at work, and we have heard the call to repent. But perhaps we have not heard clearly enough the words 'believe in the good news'. The new thing we learn from this episode is the joy of the kingdom. God wishes us to be joyful, not just eternally, but now. Yes, life can be hard, and there is much suffering in the world, and we are called to follow a crucified saviour, but God's saving love is at work in this world, so that there is an essential element of joy and celebration in Christianity, a deep down gladness. We are in God's hands, and his plans are larger than we can imagine. We are invited to the wedding feast, we are clothed in newness of life, we are to propose toasts to God, to life and to love in the new wine of the kingdom. If we find religion a bit of a kill-joy, we need to open our minds to the newness. We can seek pleasure in many ways, some of them destructive, but the joy of the kingdom makes all other joys richer and more lasting. Reflect for a moment on how often we allow negative thoughts to get us down, and how we need to cultivate God-given optimism.

2.2 Christology

Jesus the Messiah is the bridegroom! If he is the bridegroom, then who is the bride? The New Testament answer is the church, the People of God (see above, 1.2.5). The title 'bridegroom' is a way of capturing important qualities of Jesus' relationship to his disciples: it implies choice on his part, love and the promise of undying fidelity. On the part of the disciple, it means saying yes to the call, the response of love, and the determination to be faithful followers of such a loving bridegroom. Israel was the

chosen bride of God, but was often unfaithful, needing forgiveness and cleansing from a compassionate God. Ephesians says
'Christ loved the church and gave himself up for her in order to
make her holy by cleansing her with the washing of water by the
word, so as to present the church to himself in splendour, without a spot or wrinkle or anything of the kind – yes, so that she
may be holy and without blemish' (5:25-27). We know all too
well that the church has not always been so wonderfully prepared for her nuptials. The church is made up of people, a mixture of good and bad within us, needing the forgiveness which
Jesus had won for her. In principle the People of God are holy –
Paul speaks often of 'the saints' or those 'called to be saints' in
the churches to which he writes (Eph 1:1, Col 1:2, Rom 1:7, 1 Cor
1:2,) – made holy not by their own efforts but by the grace of
God. To be worthy of the call to be the bride of Christ is a big
challenge, and of course the church does not always measure
up, nor do we as individuals. Remember that God was always
faithful to Israel and forgiving, and that Jesus is the image of the
Father, always faithful and always forgiving. 'For great is his
steadfast love towards us, and the faithfulness of the Lord endures forever' (Ps 117:2).

2.3 Discipleship

The disciples are again a passive audience in this excerpt, hearing new things, with how much comprehension, we do not
know. They at least, probably to their great relief, realise that
Jesus has a different outlook to the Baptist or the Pharisees,
more at ease with his God, less inclined to structure his response
to God in formal prescriptions and acts of piety, more joyful,
more grateful for the good things of life, more sure of the
Father's pleasure in his people and his great compassion. For
disciples there is the age-old dilemma: are we to work hard to be
worthy of God's favour though we never seem to get there? Or
are we to realise that no amount of work will perfect our humanity by its own endeavours and so rejoice in God's healing
mercy and goodness, become so truly grateful that life becomes
a place of greater shared happiness, awareness of the saving
love of God, which we may call the birthing of the kingdom of
God? The presence of Jesus brings this reassurance of God's

love for all his people, even and especially sinners. The bride-groom chooses the bride. Here we have an opportunity to make personal the tremendous blessing of being called through bap-tism to be the beloved of Jesus the bridegroom. Think back to our reflection on the baptism of Jesus (Session 2, 2.3): we may call ourselves the beloved sons and daughters of God. Now we add to that the call to be the beloved chosen ones of Jesus the bridegroom.

2.4 Conversion

Recall the words of Jesus, 'Repent and believe in the good news' (1:15). The two parts of the statement are important. Our love and fidelity as disciples are not always what they should be. We have sins for which we need to repent. Let us face up to them, take responsibility for them and bring them to God's healing. But do not stop there. Remember the second part: 'believe in the good news'. John's disciples accepted the need for repentance, but have not been able to go further and believe that with Jesus the kingdom is here. Part of repentance is the willingness to ac-cept forgiveness with a glad heart and to rejoice in the new life that forgiveness makes possible. God does not require us to be perfect in order to love us and bless us with his graces. Conversion should also make us missionary, eager to share the joy with others. The urge is the same as that recorded in 1 John 1:3-4: 'We declare to you what we have seen and heard so that you also may have fellowship (communion) with us, and truly our fellowship (communion) is with the Father and with his Son Jesus Christ. We are writing these things to you so that our (alt. reading, 'your') joy may be complete.' Mark's way of looking at things is often reflected and amplified in the Johannine writings. The Christian community, in close relationship with the Father and with Jesus, has more joy when others come to share that re-lationship. The disciples in Mark will not always reflect that close communion: there will be misunderstandings, jealousies and rivalries. As we have said, joy in the presence of the bride-groom is not the full story: it would be idealistic to think that we will face all the conflicts and crosses in life in a glowing ecstasy. There will inevitably be bad times, when we have to hang on to the conviction that Jesus is with us always. The truth is that, just as we have to work on human relationships, so we have to work on our relationship to Jesus. Most of us are not always ardent disciples: so we need to pray, and give ourselves time to read and reflect, so that our faith may be refreshed through the Holy Spirit. It is worthwhile to remember the famous statement of St Leo the Great (read in the Divine Office, Vol 1, p 186, on Christmas Day): 'O Christian, be aware of your nobility – it is God's own nature that you share. Do not then, by an ignoble life, fall back into your former baseness … Recall that you have been rescued from the power of darkness, and have been transferred to the light of God, the kingdom of God.'

3. Response

For your personal response, reread the text, and stop to pray with any of the words of images that appeal to you.

Why do John's disciples and the disciples of the Pharisees fast, but your disciples do not fast? Perhaps it's because through Jesus we are able to see God in a new way. Lord, we praise you for making us 'your disciples', chosen and loved, celebrating our identity as children of God, chosen ones of the bridegroom, clothed in the new garments of the kingdom, invited to drink the new wine of the kingdom at the wedding feast of the Messiah! We praise and thank you Father, for sending your Son out of love for us, making visible to us your everlasting love, bringing us deep joy.

The wedding guests cannot fast while the bridegroom is with them. We praise and thank the divine bridegroom for choosing us and for his love and fidelity towards his people. Lord, it cost you dearly to win our salvation, and we thank you from our hearts. But we know you acted out of love for us, and we feel loved and treasured, clothed and adorned in the grace of God, filled with the gifts of the Holy Spirit. You have invited us to the wedding feast! We pray for faith to believe that the will of God is for our good, and for faith that God sees with a longer and clearer vision than we do, and holds us always in his care.

As long as they have the bridegroom with them, they cannot fast. (Mark repeats this, so we may do so!) Note the plurals, guests. It is essentially about Jesus and his disciples, his community, the church. Pray to be able to reflect the joy of being part of the divine bridegroom's community. We know you want our joy to help to build community, the kingdom of God, not just our own. We pray for all Christians that the great joy of sharing the life of Jesus may bring us together and overcome our divisions.

The bridegroom is with them. Imagine the bridegroom choosing you (it is true!), asking you to be his beloved, promising to love and be faithful always, and to clothe you with gifts, the new garment of the kingdom, the new wine to celebrate this new thing. Just in case you think of yourself as being in an 'arranged' marriage, of someone else's choosing, now choose and say yes for yourself! Yes to the divine bridegroom, yes to a relationship of love, yes to being faithful for ever, yes to being very glad about it! And promise that if you ever find yourself inclined to be, or actually being, unfaithful, that you will return immediately to the one who loves you, and has given himself for you.

The days will come when the bridegroom is taken away from them, and then they will fast ... If Mark felt that this joy was possible in the straitened circumstances of his community, we pray that we will never lose that deep-down sense of who we are, the joy of being beloved children of God, the chosen ones of the bridegroom, even when hard times come. Lord, when we fast or have to deny ourselves for your sake, help us to do it with a smile, not with groans or to impress others. We pray that whatever suffering we are able to unite with yours, Lord, may be life-giving, through the power of your death and resurrection, the seed which dies to produce fruit (John 12:24).

4. CONTEMPLATION

Tiptoe through the starlight of your chosen-ness, and do not allow the awareness to be stolen from you. Remember your dignity, and walk in thankfulness. Keep a fresh mind, open to newness. Don't let them bury you until you're dead! Do not let the new wine be put (back?) into old wineskins. Keep saying: 'Wedding guests cannot fast while the bridegroom is with them'. The bridegroom is with you!

The Twelve (Mark 3:13-19 and 6:7-13)

1. FAMILIARISATION

1.1 Getting to know the text (Mark 3:13-19 and 6:7-13)
Here I bring together two related texts which Mark separates,
taking together the choice of the twelve and their mission.

The choice of the Twelve

3.13 He went up the mountain
   and called to him those whom he wanted,
   and they came to him.

14 And he appointed twelve,
   [whom he also named apostles],
   to be with him,
   and to be sent out to proclaim the message,

15 and to have authority to cast out demons.

16 So he appointed the twelve,
   Simon (to whom he gave the name Peter);

17 James son of Zebedee and John the brother of James
   (to whom he gave the name Boanerges,
   that is, Sons of Thunder);

18 and Andrew, and Philip, and Bartholomew,
   and Matthew, and Thomas, and James son of Alphaeus,
   and Thaddaeus, and Simon the Cananaean,

19 and Judas Iscariot, who betrayed him.

The mission of the Twelve

6:7 He called the twelve
   and began to send them out two by two,
   and gave them authority over the unclean spirits.

8   He ordered them to take nothing for their journey
   except a staff;
   no bread, no bag, no money in their belts;

9   but to wear sandals
   and not to put on two tunics.

10 He said to them, 'Wherever you enter a house,
   stay there until you leave the place.

11   If any place will not welcome you
        and they refuse to hear you,
        as you leave, shake off the dust that is on your feet
        as a testimony against them.
12   So they went out
        and proclaimed that all should repent.
13   They cast out many demons,
        and anointed with oil many who were sick
        and cured them.

1.2 Background

1.2.1 Sequence: After the series of controversy stories (2:1-3:6), Mark gives a summary passage (3:7-12): Jesus by the sea of Galilee is surrounded by great crowds, not only from Galilee but from all over the Holy Land and beyond, and they so press on him in the hope of cures that he has the disciples bring a boat so that he may teach from its deck. He cures many and demons again call out his identity and are silenced. Then we have the choice of the twelve (3:13-19), in which it is made clear that the twelve have two important roles (i) 'to be with him' and (ii) 'to be sent out to proclaim the message' (v 14). Mark will concentrate first on their 'being with him', and not until 6:7-13 are they sent out on mission. It may be helpful to us to reflect on both roles together.

1.2.2 Textual issues: there are some textual problems which in the end do not affect the meaning of the passages. In v 14 'whom he also named apostles' is missing from many manuscripts. Since 'apostle' is a noun derived from the verb *apostellein*, to send, which occurs at the end of the verse, the meaning is the same without the phrase. The twelve are to be sent out to proclaim the message. There is also doubt about the repetition of the phrase 'and he appointed twelve' (v 14) which occurs again, not in all manuscripts and with the inclusion of the article, in v 16 'and ('so' in NRSV) he appointed the twelve'. It could be done without, though the long sentence is complex enough, but the use of 'the twelve' again in 6:7 perhaps means it should be kept.

1.2.3 Choice of the twelve: Mark 3:13 makes us feel that the appointing of the twelve was a solemn messianic act of Jesus. He goes up 'the mountain', calls those whom he himself wishes, and they come to him and are appointed (vv 13-14). Luke does the same thing (6:12-16), and like Mark postpones the sending out until later (9:1-6). Matthew surprisingly has no solemn choice of the twelve, but presupposes it in 10:1: 'Then Jesus summoned his twelve disciples', before giving the list of their names and sending them on mission (10:1-15). Commentators differ on whether 'the mountain' refers to a specific mountain, similar to the mountain of the transfiguration, the mountain of the Sermon on the Mount, or the mountain in Galilee where the risen Jesus meets his disciples, or is just a general phrase meaning 'the hill country'. There seem to be echoes of the 'mountain of God', Sinai (*Horeb*), as a place of revelation or the place to meet God. The deliberate choice by Jesus is also emphasised: the twelve are called from a larger number; some of them have been called before – the two sets of brothers, Simon and Andrew, James and John, and the tax-collector Levi (2:14), if he is to be identified with Matthew (in Matthew 9:9 the tax-collector is named Matthew). But they with the others are now given their solemn appointment and mission statement. The choice is not their own, but that of Jesus. 'You did not choose me, but I chose you' (John 15:16).

1.2.4 The list of names: Some variations in the names of the twelve in the four places where they are recorded (also in Matthew 10:1-4, Luke 6:12-16, Acts 1:13) need not concern us here. Simon Peter is always first, Judas Iscariot is last (omitted in Acts). The three who most often appear as the inner circle are given new names by Jesus: Simon is called Peter (Mark gives no explanation – perhaps it was know to his community), James and John are called *Boanerges*, interpreted as 'Sons of Thunder'. A new name normally means a special role, but Boanerges seems no more than a friendly nickname. It may be that they were a little fiery in their youth: in Luke 9:54 they call for fire from heaven to punish the Samaritan village which refuses them hospitality, and were sharply rebuked by Jesus. We know that Peter the Rock had a lot to learn before he could begin to live up to his name, and we hope that Jesus' ability to see the potential in his chosen disciples in spite of their shortcoming still applies to us. Apart from these three, Andrew and Judas, the others play no individual roles in the gospel, and we know very little about them. But the number twelve is important: it symbolises the twelve tribes of Israel, named after the sons of Jacob, to be renewed in the messianic era. The divine plan is for Israel to be renewed and then for Israel to bring the message to the world.

1.2.5 Their mission: firstly they are to be with Jesus (3:14), a simple but profound expression. They are to be there to learn from him, from what he says and does. They have much to experience with him before they are sent out on their own. We will see the importance of their being by his side in 3:20-35, the new family of Jesus (see Session 8), and in chapter 4, where those, who are not constantly in his company to receive Jesus' explanations of the parables, find it difficult to understand, but those who are with him are given a chance to understand the mystery of the kingdom (4:10-12). Jesus will try to prepare them to be with him in his time of suffering and death, their time of testing. Disciples, including the twelve, are essentially learners, often slow learners, who fail in spite of having the best teacher. This gives us encouragement, for even though we are weak, he wants us to 'be with him', to grow in the knowledge of his will and to experience his presence. Their mission secondly is 'to be sent out to proclaim the message, and to have authority to cast out demons' (3:14b-15). In 6:7 he again gives them authority over the unclean spirits. Although there is no explicit mention of healing the sick, they in fact do this as well. Up to now it has been the authority *(exousia)* of Jesus that Mark has stressed (see eg. 1:22, 27 Session 4). Now the twelve are given the mission to use that authority in Jesus' name. They are to be sent 'two by two' (6:7), for mutual support and protection, and also because they are witnesses to Jesus, and two people are needed for valid witness in Jewish law. This is repeated in Acts where Paul and Barnabas go together, then Paul and Silas, Barnabas and John Mark and so on.

1.2.6 Instructions for the journey: They are to travel light, take no extras for themselves, trust in God and in the hospitality they are offered. No bread, no bag (for food), no coppers in their belt, only one tunic – dependent totally on the welcome they receive from the people. They are allowed to wear sandals and take a staff (Luke 9:3 allows sandals but not a staff, Matthew 10:10 forbids both). Scholars discuss the reasons why the traditions differ, and suggest that Matthew/Luke are here following the source that accounts for the material they have which is not found in Mark (known as Q from German *Quelle*, a source), and they think that it might be older than Mark's source here, representing a tougher line that was subsequently modified in the light of the experience of Christian missionaries. For it makes sense not to go barefoot on the rocky ground of Palestine where snakes may be encountered, and a staff for protection against wild animals (and wild men) was practical. Overall they have to be seen to depend on God and not their own resources, and when they are offered hospitality (probably a common thing in Jewish towns and villages) they were not to shop around for better conditions. Staff and sandals are more or less the recognised signs of wandering preachers, as they might be of pilgrims today, and the symbolism of the staff would be understood by those who were aware of the rich biblical tradition of God as shepherd of his people, a tradition into which Jesus fitted (we will meet it in 6:34, 'He saw a great crowd, and he had compassion for them, for they were like sheep without a shepherd'). It is fitting that those who are sent out with the authority of Jesus also witness to his care and compassion. Finally (6:11) where they are not welcome they are to depart with a sign – which was used by the Rabbis when they returned from Gentile territory to the Holy Land, shaking off the (gentile) dust from their clothing so as not to contaminate the sacred soil of God's land. Shaking off the dust from their feet is to be 'a testimony against them' (NRSV), but it could be translated 'as a witness to them', to make them think how they are missing the opportunity to be part of the kingdom of God.

1.2.7 Their experience: Summed up in two verses (6:12-13); they proclaimed that all should repent (no mention of the kingdom; either that is still reserved for Jesus, or it is implicit). They cast out many demons, and (not mentioned in their instructions, but surely implicit) they cured many sick people. The new thing, mentioned in the New Testament only here and in James 5:14, is that they anointed the sick with oil and cured them, a practice of anointing that has been continued by Christians ever since in the care of the sick. They will report back to Jesus on their experience in 6:30.

1.2.8 Implications for the church? We have come a long way from the simplicity of the first disciples sent out by Jesus. Our missionaries still have to travel light, but church leaders perhaps take Mark's permission to bring sandals and a staff a little too far. It is all blamed on Constantine. We hear regular calls for a more humble church, even calls for all ecclesiastical titles to be voluntarily relinquished. Of course, it is the heart that matters in the end, not the dress; the public display of piety without heart Jesus considered empty and self-defeating.

2. REFLECTION

2.1 Mystery

Review the text with the question: how does this text throw light on God's great plan for his kingdom? God's plan is to spread the news of the kingdom. Though Jesus is the one who proclaims and embodies the kingdom, we already saw hints of what is to come when the first disciples were called to be 'fishers for people' (1:17). Now in a solemn messianic act, Jesus goes up 'the mountain', and calls those whom he wills to form a group of twelve. It seems clear enough that the symbolism of the group of twelve is the restoration of the twelve tribes of Israel, called to be instruments of the kingdom. So the kingdom will first embrace Israel, as we would expect from the Messiah of Israel. We do not yet know how this will work itself out, but we know that Jesus has been reaching out to sinners and outcasts, and that God's intention for the renewed Israel will be broader and more inclusive than its leaders are able to conceive. There is as yet no hint that it will be Israel's task to bring the message to the Gentiles, though we do not find in Mark the restriction on the initial mission that we find in Matthew 10:5-6, 'Go nowhere among the Gentiles ... but go rather to the lost sheep of the house of Israel.' Indeed it is hard to envisage that the twelve would have dreamt of going anywhere else at this stage except to the Jews. They are to broaden the range of Jesus' presence, prepare the way for him, speak and act in his name, be his witnesses. The kingdom is growing, and we face the paradox that it is entirely God's work, but that God through Jesus wishes to enlist human endeavour in that work. This paradox is to keep witnesses of Jesus honest: it is never the witnesses who are important, but the message, the reign of God. Privilege indeed to be asked to help, to be chosen and empowered with the authority of Jesus himself – therefore the initial period 'to be with him' to learn how to be sent out.

2.2 *Christology*

We see in action Jesus the builder of the reign of God and the teacher who chooses, trains and forms his special witnesses in the work of building. Later in the gospel we will see Jesus seemingly exasperated by the slowness of the disciples' grasp of his identity and mission. But here we see his understanding and patience. We can almost hear him say: 'I have very difficult tasks for you to do, and I know how hard it will be for you; but I have chosen you, I know what you can be. First you have to stay close to me, be with me, listen to me, and believe deeply in the wonder of God's reign, his strengthening love for you and his love for all the people to whom I will send you.' It is Jesus' relationship with the God who spoke to him: 'You are my Son, the Beloved', which sustains him in his mission, and the presence of the Holy Spirit who came upon him at his baptism. Knowing he is God's chosen one, he chooses the twelve, and shares with them his mission to proclaim, to heal, to free the afflicted from the power of Satan. Asking them 'to be with him' before they go on mission is to allow them to form that relationship with him that will sustain them. He wants to share his urge to spread the good news with others, and to let them go out in confidence. But they have to be reliant on God's power, not their own, and their simple attire and dependence on the goodwill of others during their mission will be a sign to themselves and to others that they come in God's name and not their own. Can you picture this same Jesus choosing you, knowing your weaknesses and your potential, asking you to be close to him, asking you to think big about what you can do to spread the good news?

2.3 *Discipleship*

The emphasis here is on discipleship, full time discipleship, the twelve, the apostles, but also on all forms of discipleship. We do not know how aware they may have been of the implications of that moment of choice, whether they perceived then the symbolism of the renewal of the tribes of Israel, but it was an impressive moment for them. Being chosen always makes you feel affirmed; it can bind you for ever to the one who chose you. It can also go to your head and lead to illusions of grandeur, if you do not have the balancing self-awareness that promotes gratitude, humility, fidelity. They are to share in the work of this amazing Jesus, who had astounded thousands of people by his teaching, healings, power over evil. The first necessity is that they 'be with him', to have a close relationship with him, to listen and learn about his spirit, his life, his mission. If ever they forget that they need to be with him, and begin to have dreams of power or status for themselves, they will be in trouble. So they will be sent out after they have spent a good deal more time with him, and they are to bring his spirit with them by their trust in God, their simplicity of life, their lack of security based on possessions, even such basic possessions as food and drink, an extra tunic. They are to be like him, people with a mission, and that mission their only concern, to bring to God's people the good news of the saving love at work among them in Jesus who announces the reign of God. When you ask people to be as committed as that, you have to have high expectations of their ability to meet the demands, and also high tolerance for possible failures and wrong turnings: in short, the kind of demanding but compassionate love that Jesus shows. So how do they do? Initially well, amazed and excited at the successful results. Later they will meet greater obstacles, as they try to understand who Jesus is, and the deeper meaning of his mission.

Though we are not apostles, there is much for us to ponder. Jesus has a plan for us also, chooses us, sends us to share the good news and to work for the growth of the kingdom. We need to 'be with him', to develop our relationship with Jesus. This 'being with him' implies listening to his words, reflecting on them, trying to base our lives on them. It implies prayer for his help and guidance, openness to the Holy Spirit who inspired Jesus' own mission, and willingness to do what we can in our state of life to be his witnesses and bring good news and healing to others by our example. Faced with such challenges, it is consoling to remember that the twelve were 'ordinary' people, who might never have been heard of had Jesus not called them, that Jesus was able to see the best in them, and be patient with their attempts to understand and live by his wisdom. He will be as patient and compassionate with us. We probably need to ask ourselves how our way of living, what is nowadays called our 'lifestyle' (with more concern for the style than the life?), reflects the life and teaching of Jesus. What is he calling us to grow into or grow out of?

2.4 Conversion

It is a humbling but salutary thought that those who are sent out to proclaim the need for conversion will themselves be needing conversion as they grow in understanding of Jesus and his teaching. We know that even the inner circle, Peter the Rock and the Sons of Thunder, have a lot of becoming still to do, to overcome weakness and misunderstanding of the spirit of Jesus. And we know where the growing will be found: in bringing their failures and weaknesses to Jesus to find forgiveness and new strength. That is what we need to do: bring our known weaknesses and abject failures to Jesus for healing, and be open to the guidance of the Spirit in looking again at some of our 'certainties', rigidity, resistance to change, and fears that hold us back from becoming what Jesus sees we could be. In the wider context, the Church, in which there is so much good, wonderful concern for the truth of Jesus and the promotion of the kingdom of God, is 'semper reformanda' (always requiring to be reformed), needing to look always at Jesus and his commission to the twelve, a model for all future apostolate.

3. RESPONSE

Make a personal response by rereading the text and stopping to pray with any word, phrase or verse which strikes you.

And he appointed twelve ... to be with him ... Respond to Jesus' invitation 'to be with him'. Lord, help us to seek your presence, in our prayers, in the liturgy of the church, word and sacrament, in our families, in the community, in our attempts to pray with the scriptures. We know you want to live within us, and you give us the Holy Spirit to help us to be united with you, and with others. Lord, help us to pay attention to your presence in us. (I heard this quotation, don't know where: Jesus says to us: 'I am within you; are you?')

He appointed twelve, whom he also called apostles ... to be sent out to proclaim the message. Respond to his call to share the good news with others, to be witnesses. Lord, give us generosity and courage. Help us to feel privileged to be called to be part of your mission. Help us to live our baptism. Keep us close to you; the more we are 'with you' the better will be our witness. Help us to know that we witness by who we are, what we say, and especially by what we do. Help us not to be only Sunday morning Christians. Help us to be aware of the good and the harm we can do by our words and example. Lord, let us at least be known as people who do not belittle faith in you, or belittle others. Better, let us be known as people who speak gratefully of our faith, glad to be followers of Jesus, and who support and affirm those who are trying to be faithful.

He called the twelve and sent them out, with authority over the unclean spirits. Lord, your community is always going to need leaders, who are true to you and to your spirit. We pray that you will bless all Christian leaders, and raise up leaders who will be after your own heart. We pray for our church leaders that they may be very close to you, Lord, be true witnesses to your truth and truly build the kingdom of God. We know that in the present climate they need prayers more urgently. We know the temptation in times like these is to concentrate on 'maintenance', to be a steady pair of hands. We pray also for willingness to listen to the Holy Spirit and the courage to lead, to face what must be faced, deal with the wrong choices that have been made, and use crises as opportunities to go forward.

He called to him those whom he wanted, and they came ... We pray for vocations, for people who will answer the call of Jesus to bring good news to the poor, vocations to the priesthood and religious life; for a spirit of generosity that will prompt people to serve others who are in need, the poor, the sick, the elderly, the young, refugees and immigrants. We thank God for the healthy spirit of volunteering still to be found. We pray for grace to take up that symbolic staff that speaks of care for 'the sheep without a shepherd'.

4. CONTEMPLATION

The picture that stays with me is that of Jesus choosing disciples to be his hands and feet and voice in the spread of the good news, a particularisation of the bridegroom's choice of each of us. He is the source of power, love and goodness and he asks us to be with him to be nourished and sustained. Live with this picture: we can be with him in the course of our daily activities. He is within us: are we? The text to help us: 'He called those whom he wanted ... to be with him', and perhaps 'to be sent out'.

Jesus' New Family (Mark 3:19b-35)

1. Familiarisation

1.1 Getting to know the text (Mark 3:19b-35)

This text starts with Jesus' family having concerns about him and setting out to take charge of him. Meanwhile Jesus answers serious accusations by scribes from Jerusalem. When his family arrive, Jesus points to a new spiritual family.

Family concern

3:19b   Then he went home;

20   and the crowd came together again,
      so that they could not even eat.

21   When his family heard it,
      they went out to restrain him,
      for people (lit. 'they') were saying,
      'He has gone out of his mind.'

Accusation

22   And the scribes who came down from Jerusalem said,
      'He has Beelzebul,
      and by the ruler of the demons he casts out demons.'

Satan's house is under attack

23   And he called them to him,
      and spoke to them in parables,
      'How can Satan cast out Satan?

24   If a kingdom is divided against itself,
      that kingdom cannot stand.

25   And if a house is divided against itself,
      that house will not be able to stand.

26   And if Satan has risen up against himself
      and is divided,
      he cannot stand, but his end has come.

27   But no one can enter a strong man's house
      and plunder his property,
      without first tying up the strong man;
      then indeed the house can be plundered.

The eternal sin

28   Truly I tell you, people will be forgiven for their sins
     and whatever blasphemies they utter;

29   but whoever blasphemes against the Holy Spirit
     can never have forgiveness,
     but is guilty of an eternal sin'

30   -for they had said, 'He has an unclean spirit.'

The new family

31   Then his mother and his brothers came;
     and standing outside, they sent to him and called him.

32   A crowd was sitting around him;
     and they said to him,
     'Your mother and your brothers and sisters
     are outside, asking for you.'

33   And he replied,
     'Who are my mother and my brothers?'

34   And looking at those who sat around him, he said,
     'Here are my mother and my brothers!

35   Whoever does the will of God
     is my brother and sister and mother.'

1.2 Background

1.2.1 Mark's editing: Mark ties this section together by an A, B, C, B1, A1 pattern (called chiastic pattern); A (3:19b-21) is about his family, B (22) is a serious accusation, C (23-27) is the refutation of the accusation, B1 (28-30) is about the gravity of the original accusation, A1 (31-35) is again about his family. In this kind of pattern, the emphasis is usually on the central one (C), and on the last one (A1), ie on the plundering of Satan's kingdom, now that the kingdom of God has come, and on the new family which results. Let us look more closely at the series of events. Firstly Jesus comes to 'a house' (v 19b) or 'home' (NRSV), most likely the house of Simon and Andrew in Capernaum, his 'base' for the Galilee ministry. And as before he is surrounded by the crowd, so that normal mealtimes are impossible. In the common interpretation this message gets to his family in Nazareth (first mentioned here). They are disturbed and set out (from Nazareth to Capernaum) to take charge of him. The reason given is that either they heard others saying that Jesus was out of his mind (so NRSV) or they themselves were saying that (Mark's Greek is ambiguous, 'they were saying'). Meanwhile an even more serious accusation is made against Jesus by the scribes from Jerusalem, that he is possessed by Beelzebul (the ruler of the demons) and casts out demons by the power of Satan. Firstly, Jesus vehemently refutes the accusation of the scribes (vv 23-27). Then he returns to that accusation, calling it 'an eternal sin'. Then his family arrive outside the house and ask to see him, but Jesus does not go out to them, referring to a new family of those who do the will of God. His physical family stand 'outside', uncomprehending, those who are 'inside', listening, are his new family.

1.2.2 *Jesus' family from Nazareth:* It comes as a shock to those reared with great reverence for Mary the mother of Jesus to find that Mark seems to think that she and Jesus' relations in general had no understanding of his mission and seemed to think he was out of his mind, needing to be taken care of. Mark has nothing to say about Jesus' birth or his growing up in Nazareth. In 1:9 he is simply introduced as coming from Nazareth in Galilee. His personal family only appear in negative contexts: here in chapter 3, in chapter 6 one verse is given to them during Jesus' poor reception in Nazareth, 6:3: 'Is not this the carpenter, the son of Mary and brother of James and Joses and Judas and Simon, and are not his sisters here with us?' That he is called 'son of Mary' suggests that Joseph is deceased. In Catholic tradition the 'brothers and sisters' are seen as cousins. Some support for that may be derived from Mark 15:40, where Mark gives the names of some of the women who were present at Jesus' death: 'among them were Mary Magdalene, and Mary the mother of James the younger and of Joses, and Salome.' James and Joses are the names of two of the brothers of Jesus (6:3); their mother is called Mary, and it would be remarkable if this were Jesus' mother Mary, without that being mentioned. James and Joses were common Jewish names at that time, so many commentators dismiss the idea that they are the two mentioned in Mark 6:3. But I think this dismissal is too facile. Mark does not mention many names, and these must be names known to his readers, and at least the possibility that they are 'brothers' of Jesus with a different Mary as mother cannot be ruled out. Attempts have been made to avoid the embarrassment of Jesus relatives thinking he was out of his mind. The phrase translated 'his family' is an unusual *hoi par' autou* which would more naturally mean 'those sent by him', emissaries, but does seem to refer to the same people as v 31, 'his mother and his brothers came'. There is also uncertainty about who said Jesus was out of his mind: the Greek has 'for they were saying', rendered by NRSV as 'people were saying'. That is possible, but the natural subject of the verb is *hoi par' autou*, 'his ones'. Mark uses strong verbs: 'they set out to restrain (*kratêsai*) him', which practically means to seize him (though when they arrive, they send in merely a polite request to speak with him outside); and *exestê* is closer to 'he is mad' than merely 'he needs looking after' because he is missing his meals. So it is hard to escape the conclusion that Jesus' family thought Jesus was behaving very strangely, to say the least, and they wanted to take him home (virtually to end his mission). That is why Mark 'sandwiches' the accusation of the scribes between the two mentions of family. There are twin threats to end his mission, one by defamation, the other by taking him home. Both have to be dealt with.

1.2.3 What are we to make of this? I suggest two lines of thinking. Firstly, I imagine the family of Jesus were good Jews, deeply steeped in the traditions of their people, conservative in the best sense, very respectful of authority, of Rabbis, Pharisees and scribes, and the traditions they tried to safeguard. Mary and Joseph would have reared Jesus with great regard for the traditional values of piety, prayer, fasting and almsgiving. Now reports are coming back to them of Jesus challenging the authorities, offending the scribes, eating with outcasts and sinners, not observing cleanliness laws or the sacred sabbath traditions. You can imagine the local Rabbi in Nazareth shaking his head and suggesting that the family should take him in hand. Such conservatism finds it hard to accept the new, and the new wine of the kingdom did not come easily to the family of Jesus either. Good conservative people always find change difficult, then and now, because they rightly believe that what comes from God is sacred and perennial. The difficulty is in recognising how much comes from human endeavour to safeguard and surround the divine core of revelation even to the extent of obscuring it, concretising it in rituals, rules and regulations. Later James, 'the brother of the Lord', will be leader of the Christians in Jerusalem, still conservative, possibly finding Paul's mission to the gentiles hard to accept. I have a sneaking, unprovable, suspicion that Mark, writing for a gentile Christian community, still thinks the family of Jesus were always foot-dragging in their understanding of Jesus' mission.

Secondly, remember that at the time of Mark's writing, nobody to our knowledge was thinking deeply about the human origins of Jesus or the role of Mary. Matthew will write his infancy narrative from the point of view of Joseph; in Luke and John we find the beginnings of a 'mariology', thinking about the role of Mary. Those reared with a developed mariology sometimes tend to maximise Mary's understanding of the identity and mission of her son. The gospels are written with the benefit of hindsight and a rapidly developing christology, the understanding of Jesus as the unique, divine, Son of God. We have seen how this christology has been written into Mark's gospel, beginning from the first verse, and reinforced by the words from heaven at his baptism. The reader has this knowledge; the participants in the drama do not. We can assume too much from the words of the angel in Luke 1:32: 'He will be great, and will be called Son of the Most High, and the Lord God will give him the throne of his ancestor David.' No Jewess or Jew of the time had any concept of a divine Son of God, and the term for them meant a divinely appointed representative of God, like David and the kings of the Davidic line. It is more likely that Mary, like all the others in the drama, had to learn the hard way, reflective as she was about the word of God, and ready to say yes to God's plans as she perceived them. In this light it is not so shocking that she should be perturbed about the mixture of rumour and hostility to Jesus that she was hearing. Nothing of course prevents Mary and the other members of the family later coming to a much more complete understanding of the mystery. It would be going too far, as some writers have done, to conclude that Jesus repudiated his physical family including his mother. Jesus is not a repudiator; he is full of hope that those who fail to understand will be shocked or encouraged to think again and come to understand. Perhaps we should see a warning to all who would like to appropriate Jesus to themselves, and think that they alone understand his mission. The mystery is bigger than we are able to comprehend.

1.2.4 The New Family: His mother and brothers arrive (v 31) after he has dismissed the accusation of the scribes. Whether the altercation with the scribes took place in the house or outside we are not told, but by the time his family arrive, he is in the house with a crowd. The family remain standing outside, and send in a message calling him. This is relayed to Jesus, but he does not respond to them. Rather he uses the occasion to make a dramatic point; asking: 'Who are my mother and my brothers?' He looks around at those sitting in a circle about him and says: 'Behold (ide, see, imperative singular, used as an exclamation heralding a solemn statement – the NRSV 'here are'), my mother and my brothers. Whoever does the will of God is my brother and sister and mother.' Those who have come to listen to him, and presumably the group of disciples, are those who show willingness to receive and try to understand the message from God about the kingdom. They are 'inside', 'with him', while his mother and brothers remain 'outside'. This distinction may be taken up again in 4:11 (see Session 9), 'to those outside everything is in parables', while the disciples and 'those around him' (4:10) receive further enlightenment. This put Jesus' physical family firmly on the outside for now. Too much can be made of this, however. Jesus is making a general statement about what is necessary to be part of the new family. He is not necessarily saying that everyone in the room is 'inside' and everyone else is 'outside'. The whole section has set up the criteria for those who wish to belong: they must come to Jesus, listen to his message, repent and believe, show readiness to deepen their understanding of what Jesus is saying and doing, be ready to spread the good news, and not hinder it, for he is trying to explain the will of God to them. This does not exclude others who will meet the criteria, even the scribes who accuse him, and certainly his relatives, if they change their attitudes to his mission.

If we may dare to ask the question, why was Jesus abrupt with mother and brothers, that he could not give them a few minutes in private? The answer may be that he is asking disciples to leave family and home to follow him, and he can do no other himself.

1.2.5 Houses and kingdoms in conflict: Scribes from Jerusalem (presumably sent to see what Jesus is up to and report back) make the serious charge, offensive to pious ears, that Jesus is possessed by Beelzebul, the ruler of the demons (v 22), equivalent to Satan. Mark uses the imperfect tense, 'they were saying', indicating a continuous attempt to destroy Jesus' reputation. If the accusation is true, then Jesus is a fraud, being used by Satan rather than God. Jesus cannot let this challenge go unanswered and provides a scathing response 'in parables', ie similitudes, comparisons. If Satan casts out Satan, then his kingdom, his house, is divided, in conflict with itself, and cannot stand (a phrase repeated 3 times in Greek). It is not just the end of his kingdom, it is the end of Satan himself (vv 24-26). If Satan's house is being plundered, it must be by someone stronger than himself. The implication is that he, Jesus, is the stronger one, because he is acting in God's name, and the kingdom of God is destroying the kingdom of Satan.

1.2.6 The eternal sin, (vv 28-30): the sin against the Holy Spirit fits logically in Mark's sequence, but gives the impression of being clarified by later Christian reflection on forgiveness and the seriousness of the charge that Jesus is doing the work of Satan. The beginning is very positive, and made into a solemn statement, 'Truly I tell you'. Jesus has come to offer the forgiveness of sins, and that offer is open to all, even for the sin of blasphemy (insulting God or the things of God). Only one sin is unforgivable, blasphemy against the Holy Spirit, clarified by v 30, "for they said, 'He has an unclean spirit'." So it is the accusation that Jesus is possessed by Satan that is eternal, unforgivable. The listeners possibly, the Christian community certainly, knew that Jesus was filled with the Holy Spirit at his baptism, and that the Holy Spirit was guiding his mission. Therefore the accusation makes the Holy Spirit within Jesus into an unclean spirit. Apart from the offensiveness of such a claim (Jesus says even blasphemy may be forgiven) the mindset that makes such an accusation is closed to God's work and to the work of the Holy Spirit. This is the reason why forgiveness is not possible: so long as minds are closed, they will not allow themselves to be forgiven. They are making God's revelation to them impossible. God will not force closed minds to open. Resistance to the Holy Spirit in varying degrees is not something belonging to the past only, but is an ever present danger in the church as well as in the secular community. Much of the attack on faith in God in our own time is based on the conviction of the impossibility of the supernatural, of miracle, of revelation, and so God is not 'permitted' to reveal himself except in the natural, and we do not need God to explain what is natural! Mindsets closed to God do not accept revelation or forgiveness, indeed see no need for it.

2. Reflection

2.1 Mystery

As we have seen in the background notes, this section is full of shocks, paradoxes and strangeness. The virulence of the attack on Jesus by the Jerusalem scribes comes as a shock, remotely prepared for by the conspiracy between the Pharisees and the supporters of Herod Antipas to find ways to destroy him (3:6). Most puzzling is the attitude of Jesus' family, their apparent acceptance of the worst reports about him, and their decision to bring him home, unwittingly combining with those who wanted to destroy his mission. Jesus' trenchant reply clarifies for us again the inevitable conflict between the kingdom of God and the kingdom of Satan. Obstacles to the growth of the kingdom come not only from Satan, but from religious leaders who are supposed to be on God's side, and even from within the close circle of Jesus' intimates. The positive side is that Jesus remains immensely popular with the crowd, and that his clear exposition of the conflict gives them courage to resist the campaign of vilification from the scribes. Best of all, from the many who come to him, there will be the nucleus of the new family, those who hang on Jesus' words, keep contact with him, have faith in the reign of God, and so do the will of God. The invitation to be members of the new family remains open to all, then and now.

2.2 Christology

The one thing that stands out in this section is the Spirit filled drive of Jesus for the kingdom of God and for the mission God has given him. Nothing can deflect him from this pursuit. We do not meet here the conventional meek and mild Jesus, whom one scholar labelled 'the pale Galilean'. He speaks straight and clear, faces unjust challenges head on, determined not to let the religious authorities or even the love demands of his own family deflect him from his purpose. He is the anchor and the embodiment of the new family, of those whose life is given to the will of God. He is dedicated to the mission and the gathering together of this new family, the renewal of the people of Israel as symbolised already by the choice of the twelve.

2.3 Discipleship

We now have the twelve, a wider group from which they were chosen and a growing number of the crowd (not all of whom followed Jesus with the best motives) who could be termed 'the new family'. The twelve are learning from being with him that the mission does not always go smoothly, Jesus working wonders among enthusiastic crowds. There is also strong opposition, and courage and clarity are required to withstand it and continue to do the will of God. The twelve and the wider groups are doing the things that are necessary to qualify for the new family: be with Jesus, listen to him, believe in the good news, and be ready to share it, which Jesus sums up as doing the will of God. They are Jesus' brothers and sisters. We who propose to be his disciples know that all will not go smoothly for us either, and that we can provoke opposition just by trying to be disciples of Jesus. We need courage, and we will only get it from a close relationship with Jesus, listening and prayer, and trust in the power of the Holy Spirit. Ask yourself: where would you rather be than with him? Does anything else in the end give you more hope, or joy, or life?

2.4 Conversion

Verses 29-30 about the unforgivable sin come as a shock, until we remember that they come after the wonderful statement about forgiveness in v 28. 'Truly I tell you, people will be forgiven for their sins and whatever blasphemies they utter.' And the NRSV translation hardly does justice to the Greek text, which says literally: 'Truly I tell you that everything will be forgiven to the sons of human beings, their sins and blasphemies whatsoever they blaspheme.' There is no holding back – everything. Jesus has come to bring the Father's forgiveness to all humanity, and that is his hope and joy and mission. The healing compassion of

God, which we experience as the kingdom of God, is endless and all-embracing. The sin that is eternal, cannot be forgiven, is not unforgivable in God's eyes; it is operative only when the sinner is unwilling to receive the forgiveness offered, does not see the need for it, and closes his/her mind to reconciliation. 'Hardness of heart' is a common biblical concept for the condition of being impervious to the grace of God. It is the old biblical sin, sometimes superseded today by that other dangerous condition, total indifference. In the *Veni Sancte Spiritus* (Come Holy Spirit) we pray: '*Flecte quod est rigidum, fove quod est frigidum, rege quod est devium.* Make flexible that which is rigid, warm that which is frozen, rule that which is devious'.

3. RESPONSE

Make your personal response by rereading the text and pausing to pray with any verse or phrase that strikes you.

[They] were saying, 'He has gone out of his mind.' Lord, forgive your people both for lack of understanding and for deliberate insults offered to your Beloved Son. To avoid the truth, we have accused him of being bad or mad, leading people astray or suffering from cruel delusions. Jesus, you knew from early in your mission that goodness attracts opposition, that single-minded pursuit of God's will may be labelled as fanaticism or delusion. It is hard to see how your goodness, your healing and rescue from the power of Satan, can be seen as badness, how so clear and brilliant a mind, full of startling revelations, poetry of language, hope and joy, can be thought to be deranged! The charges have been there right through history, Lord, because people have cast about for any alternative to admitting that you are God's Beloved Son. In spite of detractions, Lord, you have been loved and worshipped by millions. We join our praise to theirs.

He has Beelzebul, and by the ruler of the demons he casts out demons. Attacks on religion and on believers from militant atheism we understand, but God grant that believers may not attack each other in his name. Lord, conflicts and divisions appeared among those who heard you preaching the good news. They seem to follow everywhere, in churches, parishes, families. We pray that we will not allow differences to drive us apart, we pray for healings of conflicts and divisions, which obscure and hinder the good news. You took time, Lord, and were firm and clear in refuting the accusation against you. We rejoice in the coming of the kingdom of God and salvation from the power of evil and the evil one. Help us to be firm, clear in our statement of the truth, and faithful to the Gospel. We pray that your people may not be led astray, but may hold firm to their faith in you. Holy Spirit, bind your people together 'that they may be one' (John 17:21).

People will be forgiven for their sins and whatever blasphemies they utter. We thank you for this promise, Lord, which gives us hope in our weakness. All our sins will be forgiven, even the foolish and bitter utterances of uncontrollable tongues against God and his goodness, which we make in anger and grief. Father, hallowed be thy name, thy kingdom come. Your kingdom offers healing and forgiveness, through your Beloved Son, who takes away the sin of the world. So forgive, Lord, the misuse of power and the betrayal of trust by so many clergy and religious, and the failures to deal with it openly and honestly. We pray for Jesus' healing for all who have been hurt by abuse and the failure to hear their cries for help. Show your compassion, Lord, to 'the sheep without a shepherd', who did not receive compassion from those who should have protected them. May the God for whom all things are possible deliver perpetrators of abuse from hardness of heart, that they may reach out in humility for forgiveness to the one who is ready to forgive even blasphemies against himself.

Whoever blasphemes against the Holy Spirit can never have forgiveness, but is guilty of an eternal sin. Lord, we know that you are ready to forgive all sins, for you are a God of life, and rejoice in everything you have made. We know the problem is the unwillingness of the human heart to admit the need for forgiveness and to ask for it. Lord, preserve us from hardness of heart. Open the minds of those who are closed to your message of healing because they refuse to admit that any supernatural revelation is possible, or that miracles can happen, or that you can make yourself known to us through your Son. We pray for those for whom great sorrow or loss or the suffering of the innocent may have turned the light of faith to darkness. We place them in your compassionate care, without whose knowledge no sparrow falls to the ground. We pray for those whose faith is weak, or who may be easily led astray by destructive criticism of faith. We pray that your good people may be open to the freshness of the Gospel, and the promptings of the Holy Spirit.

Here are my mother and my brothers. Whoever does the will of God is my brother and sister and mother. Picture yourself in the house in Capernaum sitting in the circle around Jesus as he talks about the kingdom and what it means to everyone. How do you feel as he stretches out his hand and says to you, 'Here are my mother and my brothers'? You are part of the new family of Jesus, the nucleus of the church. It is great to be seen as brother/sister of Jesus. Pray to realise also that family means brother and sister to each other; Jesus is creating family, community. Pray for a clear understanding of what Jesus is asking of us in the family: that we be 'with him', grow in knowledge of him and of the reign of God that he proclaims, listen to his word, be ready to share in building the community of faith, be open to others, open to the Spirit. Pray for your local parish community, for all who volunteer to help and share with others in that community.

4. CONTEMPLATION

Keep in your mind and heart the power of Jesus to protect his people: he is the stronger one who is able to plunder the strong man's house, to deliver us from evil and the Evil One, in whose presence we have safety and salvation. He is also the tender one who draws his people together into his family, making them his brothers and sisters. Keep these images alive in your heart. A text to carry with us: 'Whoever does the will of God is my brother and sister and mother.'

The Sower (Mark 4:1-12)

1. FAMILIARISATION

1.1 Getting to know the text (Mark 4:1-12)

We look at the parable (but not the explanation, vv 13-20), and Jesus' answer to his disciples' question about 'the parables'. I offer a re-translation of the difficult v 12.

Introduction

4:1   Again he began to teach beside the sea.
Such a very large crowd gathered round him
that he got into a boat on the sea and sat there,
while the whole crowd was beside the sea on the land.

2   He began to teach them many things in parables,
and in his teaching he said to them:

No growth

3   'Listen, a sower went out to sow.

4   And as he sowed, some seed fell on the path,
and the birds came and ate it up.

Quick growth that does not last

5   Other seed fell on rocky ground,
where it did not have much soil,
and it sprang up quickly,
since it had no depth of soil.

6   And when the sun rose, it was scorched;
and since it had no root, it withered away.

Growth that is choked

7   Other seed fell among thorns,
And the thorns grew up and choked it,
And it yielded no grain.

Abundant growth

8   Other seed fell into good soil
and brought forth grain,
growing up and increasing
and yielding thirty, sixty and a hundred-fold.

Conclusion

9   And he said, "Let anyone with ears to hear listen!"'

The mystery of the kingdom

10   And when he was alone,
       those who were around him along with the twelve
       asked him about the parables.

11   And he said to them,
       'To you has been given
       the secret (mystery) of the kingdom of God,
       but for those outside,
       everything comes in parables,

12   [NRSV] in order that
       "they may indeed look, but not perceive, (Is. 6:9-10)
       and may indeed listen, but not understand;
       so that they may not turn again
       and be forgiven."'

(12 My translation) so that
       they may indeed look, though fail to see,
       and indeed hear, though fail to understand;
       so they may never repent and be forgiven.

1.2 Background

1.2.1 The parables section, 4:1-34: In this section Mark has brought together a series of related parables of Jesus: first the sower (vv 1-9), then Jesus' answer to a group of disciples who ask about the parables (vv 10-12), followed by an explanation of the sower to the disciple group (vv 13-20). From v 21, Jesus speaks to unspecified groups, most likely to the crowd of vv 1-9; firstly some parabolic sayings related to the theme of the parables (vv 21-25), then two parables about growth, specifically related to the kingdom of God (vv 26-32). In conclusion Mark returns to Jesus' use of parables (vv 33-34). I recommend you to read all this material, but we will not be able to deal with it all in detail, so I have chosen the above text, the parable of the sower, and the words of Jesus to his disciples about the parables, which, though difficult to interpret, are vital to our understanding.

1.2.2 The parable and its explanation: It is not often that Jesus offers a detailed explanation of one of his parables, even to the inner group of disciples. Not every commentator believes that the explanation in vv 13-20 really comes from the lips of Jesus, because there is a slight shift of emphasis, and each point in the parable is explained, which used to make the experts very suspicious. Why? Firstly, because then it becomes more like an allegory than a parable. A story-parable (parables can also be graphic images, one-liners, riddles: eg 3:23-27, 4:21-25) is a true to life story with an important main point to make, and the interpretation of the parable depends on getting that main point correct. Careful reading and reflection should be able to elucidate the main point without the need of a 'key' or explanation. An allegory makes a whole series of points, with nearly everything in it standing for something else, so it becomes important to have the correct 'key', or the allegory will not be understood (see Matthew 13:24-30, the weeds among the wheat, and the 'key', 13:36-43). Jesus normally used story-parables, not allegories, therefore we don't often get explanations. The early Christians are thought to have loved allegories, or at least been tempted to turn parables into allegories in their understandable attempts to apply them to different situations in the life of the church. The explanation of the parable of the sower (vv 13-20) looks a bit like an 'allegorising' of the parable, making a whole series of points (the birds represent Satan, the different soils represent people who hear the word, rocky soil represents persecution etc.). It was thought during a large part of the 20th century that Jesus did not do that sort of thing. Nowadays commentators are not so sure (a) that a parable always has only one central point to make, and (b) that Jesus never used allegory. So it is not impossible that the explanation actually comes from Jesus, perhaps from a different occasion. But the parable can stand on its own, and to include vv 13-20 would give us a very long text.

 1.2.3 A parable about the kingdom: The whole section, 4:1-34 is really about the kingdom of God. This is not explicitly stated in the parable of the sower (4:3-9), but is made clear in v 10, when the disciples ask Jesus 'about the parables', and he said. 'To you has been given the secret (or mystery) of the kingdom of God ...' Two other parables in this same section about seeds growing are explicitly told to illustrate the kingdom: vv 26-29, 'The kingdom of God is as if someone would scatter seed on the ground ...', and vv 30-32, 'With what can we compare the kingdom of God, or what parable will we use for it? It is like a mustard seed ...' So it is clear that the parable of the sower is about the kingdom of God, which up to now has been explained more by Jesus' actions than by his words. We have seen in chapters 2 and 3 many different reactions to Jesus' proclamation of the kingdom, some enthusiastically for him, some curious, some looking for healing, others puzzled by his actions, some totally against Jesus to the point of accusing him of being possessed. How do we understand these totally differing reactions? There was also an expectation that the coming of the kingdom of God would be a much more instantaneous event, a once-and-for-all sorting out of the wicked and exaltation of the just. But Jesus says, 'Those who are well have no need of a physician, but those who are sick; I have come to call not the righteous but sinners' (2:17). The parable of the sower will attempt to give the beginnings of an explanation for these paradoxical things, as will indeed the whole section.

1.2.4 The sower: visualise fertile ground surrounded by a hard path, with patches of poor, shallow soil, and patches of scrub that could not be easily eliminated. Seed is sown on four types of ground, and the resulting growth described. Firstly, seed that falls on the hard path is eaten by birds, so it is lost. Secondly, seed that falls on the shallow, rocky soil does indeed grow, the first to appear, but it is soon scorched by the sun and dies. Seed that falls in the thorny parts grows well enough, but so do the thorns, and the thorns have long-established roots and they win; the growth is choked. But the seed that falls on good soil with no obstacles grows and flourishes; the growth is abundant, the harvest beyond expectation. Jesus says: 'Let anyone with ears to hear listen.' That suggests that the meaning should be clear enough to those who really listen and think. We are talking about the growth of the kingdom of God, and the reception that it receives from those who listen to Jesus. The key point is reassurance that the kingdom will have magnificent growth is spite of the obstacles to growth. Though God is all-powerful, and the kingdom of world-shattering importance, its growth depends on the reception it finds in human hearts. This is the first great paradox. God will not force his kingdom-blessings on anyone who refuses to accept them. Jesus, sent by God and filled with the power of the Spirit, has been given no power to force his message upon anyone who has no ears to hear. Free response to the kingdom is of paramount importance. The second paradox is that in spite of the obstacles which human lack of receptivity throw up, the kingdom will come in abundant measure, for it is God's kingdom. Set yourself down in Galilee at that time: ask yourself does this reassure you? Looking back over the preceding chapters, you can see that there has been some total resistance; there have been enthusiastic beginnings, which did not last; there have been people who failed to understand, or who came for the wrong motives, whose attention was soon diverted when their initial curiosity was satisfied. And there have been those who have left everything and followed him. In which category of receptivity do you see yourself? And are you always at the same stage, or can you grow from one stage to another, or even revert to a former stage?

1.2.5 Is the ' mystery of the kingdom' only for some? We are now in difficult territory (vv.10-12), with no assured agreement among commentators. If you wish to omit vv. 10-12 and concentrate for your prayer purposes on the parable, you may omit this section and the following two. If you wish to study further, I refer you to the commentaries, eg M. Mullins, pp 131-140. I will state my reasons for following the line that I take, admitting that it is open to challenge! I wish to deal first with v 11, and then with v 12 in 1.2.7. The picture we are given in the introduction (4:1-2) is of a huge crowd gathered around Jesus on the lake shore, so that Jesus (presumably with his immediate disciples) sat on a boat on the lake from which he taught them 'many things in parables'. After only one parable, Mark diverts to Jesus speaking alone to 'those around him with the twelve' (v 10), who ask him about the parables (plural). So Jesus' words that follow (vv 11-12) are more generally applicable than just to the parable of the sower. He then explains the sower parable to them, and later seems to be teaching the crowd again from the boat (from v 21). V.11 reads, 'To you has been given the mystery (NRSV secret) of the kingdom of God, but for those outside, everything comes in parables.' Firstly, I much prefer to translate the Greek *mustêrion* as mystery rather than secret. A secret is something that may be revealed and once heard, it is known. A

mystery in its religious sense is something that can only be revealed to us gradually, that we can learn about and experience
but never understand completely, for it is a divine reality. This
'mystery of the kingdom of God' is revealed to the disciples but
apparently withheld from 'outsiders'. Does Mark believe that it
is the divine will to reveal the mystery to some and withhold it
from others? V 12 is understood by many to say just that (see
1.2.7). We must stand humbly before the mystery of the divine
will, but I will tell you what I think, for what it is worth. If we remember what has been happening up to this point in the
Gospel, what is happening now, and what will continue to happen, we will see that the simple answer is no, Mark does not believe that Jesus wishes to withhold knowledge of the mystery
from anyone. Jesus has been speaking openly to all who will listen, 'for that is what I came out to do' (1:38). The only difference
lies in people's response, as the parable makes clear. He has indeed chosen a group of special disciples, but only from those
who have responded positively to him, and answered his call,
and they are chosen from a greater number of disciples. Their
task is 'to be with him and to be sent out to proclaim the message' (3:14), not to conceal it. Mark makes it clear that the mystery is given not only to the twelve, but to a wider group, 'those
who were around him along with the twelve' (v 10). They are
precisely those who are interested enough to come and talk to
Jesus about his teaching, who are willing to learn, who stick
with him and are most receptive. They represent others who are
and will be receptive. The outsiders are those who are negative
or sceptical or totally opposed to him. For them 'everything
comes in parables' not to keep them outside, but to give them
something to remember, to reflect upon and be challenged by, in
the hope that one day they may decide to learn more and become insiders. In 4:21-25 Jesus emphasises that nothing is to remain hidden, but all is to come to light; 'For there is nothing hidden, except to be disclosed, nor is anything secret (*krupton*), except to come to light. Let anyone with ears to hear, listen.' Some
things will be kept 'secret' for a while, precisely the identity of
Jesus as Messiah, for if it is too soon revealed, there may be a reaction of popular fervour to declare him king and challenge the
Romans. But it will be declared publicly by Jesus when the time

comes. In the conclusion to the section, 4:33, Mark says that Jesus 'with many such parables ... spoke the word to them, as they were able to hear it'. Again the emphasis is on the receptivity of the hearers; if they are receptive to it, they are given more. All of this helps us to interpret vv 11-12 correctly.

1.2.6 What is this mystery of the kingdom? The mystery is God's plan to bring about his reign over human hearts through the mission, passion, death and resurrection of Jesus. Immediately we realise that it cannot be given as a once-off teaching to disciples at this stage of the mission, no matter how receptive they may be. It is something they can only appreciate by remaining in the presence of Jesus during the remainder of his mission and through his death and resurrection. Up to this point the disciples have received only obscure hints of what is to come, and are not able to understand the depth and strangeness of the mystery. There will be a long hard road to follow before they get there. But they are doing the right things: staying in the presence of Jesus, listening to his words, asking for help to understand. Understanding of the mystery was difficult for the members of Mark's community: Mark is also speaking to them, since they are facing persecution and danger, even danger of death, and they need to remember that following Jesus is taking up the cross and following him (8:34). We too need to grow into that mystery, and often it is only in times of crisis that we have to face up to the demands of our faith in Jesus. Part of our purpose in this journey through Mark's Gospel is to learn with the disciples as they learn, often painfully.

1.2.7 Verse 12 and Isaiah 6:9-10: Mark's intention in quoting (loosely) Isaiah 6:9-10 is one of the most difficult problems in his gospel. Mark's quotation is not close to the Hebrew text or to the Septuagint (LXX) Greek translation, and is closer to an Aramaic commentary on Isaiah (of uncertain date). Matthew at this point (13:14-15) quotes the LXX text in full, while Luke (8:10) gives a brief 'so that looking they may not perceive, and listening they may not understand'. Isaiah 6:9-10 is part of the 'call narrative' of the prophet; God is sending Isaiah with a message for the people. The Hebrew text says that God said to Isaiah, "Go and say to this people: 'Keep listening, but do not comprehend; keep looking, but do not understand. Make the mind of this people dull, and stop their ears, and shut their eyes, so that they may not look with their eyes and listen with their ears and comprehend with their minds, and turn and be healed.' The first question you ask is, would God be sending a prophet to speak to the people in order that they would not listen and would not be forgiven? That would seem to be a strange and contradictory thing for God to do. It is possible that the text is about the result of the mission: in spite of some promises and some success, the kingdom of Judah as a whole did not repent for long and was destroyed by the Babylonians in 587 BC. The text of Isaiah, originally belonging to the early 8th century BC, was possibly reused, maybe even adapted, at that time to show that God always knew that the people would not listen and that his providence governed even the destruction of Jerusalem and the exile. It is possible that Mark is working on the same lines: that Jesus knew that the leaders and the majority of the Jewish people would not believe in him, and that similarly God's providence would be able to embrace that refusal. But that is very conjectural, and depends on a very literal interpretation of Mark 4:12 as a purpose clause, meaning that the intention of Jesus in using parables for 'outsiders' was in order that they would not understand and be saved. That does not seem in the least like the Jesus presented to us so far by Mark. There are at least two other possibilities. (1) The Greek *hina*, translated 'in order that' –its normal meaning in classical Greek – may also, in the common (*koine*) Greek of Mark's time, be used for a result as well as a purpose, and be translated 'so that' meaning 'with the result that'. This entails taking the second 'so that ... not' (Greek *mêpote*) also as result rather than purpose. Hence my alternative translation of v 12, which implies that, even though Jesus will give the leaders of Judaism and other 'outsiders' every chance to hear his message, their lack of receptivity will result in their being unable to understand the mystery of the kingdom, because the message will fall on stony ground. (2) An attractive possibility is that the text of Isaiah is deliberate irony, a persuasive technique uses by the prophets to excite the curiosity of the listener, using words with the opposite meaning to what they really intend, 'I will speak to you but you will not listen, and so you will miss a great opportunity' is meant to provoke the hearers to listen attentively. G. Ernest Wright (*Isaiah, Layman's Bible Commentaries,* SCM 1964, p. 36) says: 'The words in verses 9-10 must be understood to be purposive hyperbole which has the aim of shocking people to pay attention. The words are ironical.' Mark's Jesus therefore may be intending the words to be taken in a similar ironic way, as 'purposive hyperbole', deliberate over-exaggeration, recognizable to his hearers as such, aimed at catching the attention of the audience and desiring nothing more than their conversion. The difficulty with this approach is that irony depends to an extent on tone of voice, and is more difficult to demonstrate conclusively from a written text. But it seems to me that there is enough evidence of Jesus' intention from the whole context to justify the acceptance of one or other of these approaches to avoid the dire conclusion that Jesus gives a message to some people that he intends them not to accept. What it is, though, is a warning to those who harden their hearts and will not listen to the Spirit, in every age, including our own.

2. REFLECTION

2.1 Mystery

'The mystery of the kingdom of God' is a central concept not just of this section but of the whole Gospel. It 'has been given', i.e., revealed by God to 'those who were around [Jesus] along with the twelve'. There we have concepts for reflection. 'Mystery' means that we get a little of it now, and know that we will have to go on paying close attention to Jesus to learn more; and that though it may be difficult to learn, indeed needs to be lived to be learned, it is wonderful to know and to be part of! What we learn is that its growth may be invisible, slow and subject to many setbacks, but the growth is certain, unstoppable, copious. Because it is God's loving plan of salvation working in us and around us, the warmth of his love, the strength of his Spirit, the life-giving power of the Beloved Son. 'Kingdom of God' helps us to remember that it is God and God alone who makes the growth possible, though he looks to us to be receptive soil. 'Unless the Lord build the house, those who build it labour in vain' (Psalm 127:1). By extension we may think about the renewal of the church. The revelation of the mystery of the kingdom of God is never just a matter of personal spirituality, but is made to those who are asking the question: 'What does it mean to be part of the family of Jesus, his community, his church?' The church, like the different soils in the parable, is made up of people who are in varying ways receptive or unresponsive to the message. We have to include all of them in a vision of what it is to be church, which is why church renewal is never a quick fix, but requires deep ploughing and preparation of soil. But there is this: seeds are meant to be sown, and seeds have a built-in drive towards growth. The growth of the kingdom is certain, but seeds die in the process, as Jesus so richly exemplified. 'Unless a grain of wheat falls into the earth and dies, it remains just a single grain; but if it dies, it bears much fruit (John 12:24).'

2.2 Christology

From his boat-pulpit Jesus teaches all who will listen. Like the sower in the parable, he is profligate, allowing the seed to fall on all parts of the field in the hope that no source of growth will be missed. Quietly afterwards he is willing to explain further to those who wish to know more. When he tells them that the mystery of the kingdom of God will be revealed to them by God, implicit in what he says is that the mystery is very closely bound up with himself and his mission. It is precisely to those who wish to know Jesus and his teaching and who seek his presence that the mystery is revealed. Jesus is the revealer of the Father and the kingdom. As the seed grows quietly, so is the teacher patiently seeking disciples and teaching them, in preparation for the decisive moment when the mystery will be revealed in his death and resurrection. We will try to follow the disciples in their learning process with its highs and lows throughout the Gospel. Knowledge of ourselves and of our role as his disciples comes from close contact with him in word and sacrament, and all renewal in the church will be based on the renewal of hearts and minds that comes from allowing Christ to live in us.

2.3 Discipleship

It is plain then that commitment to Jesus is essential for those who would learn from God the mystery of the kingdom. Disciples are 'learners'. We noted that the words of Jesus in 4:10-12 are in answer to their enquiries 'about the parables', ie a more general situation than merely the explaining of the sower parable. The revelation of the mystery will not be a once off, but a lengthy process, which will demand fidelity in the disciples in spite of all opposition. There will be set-backs, most clearly seen in the progress of the twelve, some of whom will be in peril and one lost. The quality of our discipleship is being challenged here. We realise that though we may have known Jesus for many years, we are not the finished article, but have much learning to do and much repentance. We need to grow, be more receptive, open to newness and to change. Growing close to Jesus, learning his mind and being open to the Holy Spirit is the beginning of renewal for the church in its present crisis. To many people's dismay, renewal that is worthwhile and lasting is a slow process, never instantaneous. But quick results, changes which only affect externals and procedures will not produce real growth if hearts are not changed first. Some are perhaps rightly afraid that renewal will in the end be seen only in the spiritual growth of individuals, lacking that church dimension that is also demanded. By their fruits you shall know them. Spiritual growth must also be reflected in ways of being church, ways of making our institutional embodiment of life in Christ more consistent with the gospel. However, each of us must start with asking ourselves... 'What sort of soil does the message of Jesus find in me?'

2.4 Conversion

Conscious that any one of us at any given time may be that too-trodden path where even dandelions fail to grow, the shallow soil where weak enthusiasms have no strength or heart to realise their potential; conscious that our fervour is constantly cooled by distractions, the business of life, the making and getting of money, the everybody's-doing–it conformity to lowered standards, we know that conversion is an ongoing process for all of us. To become that good soil where the word of God may find a gracious reception, we must plough up the stony ground, dig deep and remove the thorns whose roots keep reproducing the same failings within us. If we can do that as individuals, then we have a chance to do the same as a group, as a community, a parish, a diocese, a church. It is possible to see the words of v 10, 'those who were around him along with the twelve' as a pattern for the laity and the hierarchy in the church coming together around Christ to listen, learn and work together more openly and more fruitfully than before. We need lots of individual and community prayer for the guidance of the Holy Spirit. Can we doubt that some of the systems and procedures in the church have hardened into stony ground for those who hope to redis-cover the optimism and hope of the era of Vatican II, who seek an honest re-embracing of the long acknowledged dictum that the church is always in need of reform? We need to pray together for courage, honesty and openness to the Spirit, so that the church may speak and act clearly as the sign or sacrament of the mystery of the kingdom of God.

3. RESPONSE

Make your personal response by rereading the text, pausing to pray with any verse or phrase that strikes you.

'A sower went out to sow.' Divine Sower, who sows the word of God, the message of good news about the kingdom of God, open our hearts to your word. You are a prodigal sower, cover-ing everything that might possibly give growth, like the 'fiddle' sowers of my youth who sprayed seeds far and wide. But you bring us a message from a prodigal Father, and like the Father, you sow in abundance. We are the often ill-prepared soil on which the growth of the kingdom depends. We pray that we, as individuals and as church, may be better soil to allow God's reign to be active in our lives, in our relationships, in our social and ecclesial structures. Help us, Lord, to allow the reign of God to grow in our lives, in our relationship to family members, col-leagues, friends. (Abraham Lincoln is reputed to have said. 'I don't like that fellow! I must get to know him better.') Help us to be more involved in our parishes and communities, to join in prayer together for the growth of the kingdom.

Some seed fell on the path, and the birds came and ate it up. Other seed fell on rocky ground ... Lord, forgive the hardness of heart that allows the seed you lovingly sow to be wasted. Perhaps, Lord, the waste is part of your love story for us, like the feeding of the multitude, the water becoming wine at Cana, providing an abundance for everyone, with plenty left over. You ask us for generosity in response. 'Give, and it will be given to you. A good measure, pressed down, shaken together, running over, will be put into your lap; for the measure you give will be the measure you get back (Luke 6:38, cf Mt 7:2).' You call us to be generous, yet our temptation is to settle for shallowness, resenting challenges to participate more, to learn more, to pray more, to grow into an adult faith. Lord God, make us alive, deepen our faith, widen our hearts, open our eyes and ears to the mystery of the kingdom, to the Saviour who makes your love visible to us.

Other seed fell among thorns, and the thorns grew up and choked it, and it yielded no grain. Pray about the thorns that choke your growth. What are the particular 'thorns' in your life that need to be dug out? 'The cares of the world, and the lure of wealth, and the desire for other things come in and choke the word' (4:19). Lord, forgive and heal the discontent within us, the lack of satisfaction with what we have, and illusory happiness that seems to lie in a new job, a new car, a new me, made-over in the likeness of the up-to-date woman or man. Lord, help us to focus on the blessings we have, your living presence within us, the gifts of your Spirit.

Let anyone with ears to hear, listen. We pray that not only individuals, but the whole church may listen to where the Spirit of God is leading us in these times. We pray with and for the church, uniting ourselves to everyone in the church who is praying humbly for the guidance of the Spirit, that the people of God in all their diversity may be enabled to respond fully to the Gospel. We pray that the current spirit of openness, the listening 'upwards' as well as 'downwards' may open up new possibilities for life and growth in the church. Lord, pour out your Spirit upon your whole church that your church may become a stronger sign of the kingdom.

To you has been given the mystery of the kingdom of God. Lord, help us to know you and the power of your life, death and resurrection. Help us to be 'with you', to hear your word, learn from you, and grow in your friendship and love. Thank you for your generosity and goodness. Forgive us for the times when we are stony ground or allow our following of you to be choked by the thorns that grow in our lives. We know that nothing is really good for us without you.

4. CONTEMPLATION

Try to take from your prayer an awareness of the great blessing we have received: 'To you is given the mystery of the kingdom of God'. The mystery is 'Christ in you, the hope of glory' (Col 1:27). A suggested phrase from our text to keep in mind as a way into the thoughts and hopes we may have experienced: 'seed fell into good soil and brought forth grain'; or 'to you is given the mystery of the kingdom.'

Multiplication of Loaves (Mark 6:30-44)

1. FAMILIARISATION

1.1 Getting to know the text (Mark 6:30-44)

A crowded deserted place

6:30　The apostles gathered around Jesus,
　　　　and told him all that they had done and taught.

31　　He said to them: 'Come away to a deserted place
　　　　all by yourselves and rest awhile.'
　　　　For many were coming and going,
　　　　and they had no leisure even to eat.

32　　And they went away in the boat
　　　　to a deserted place by themselves.

33　　Now many saw them going and recognised them,
　　　　and they hurried there on foot from all the towns
　　　　and arrived ahead of them.

Sheep in need of nourishment

34　　As he went ashore, he saw a great crowd,
　　　　and he had compassion for them,
　　　　because they were like sheep without a shepherd;
　　　　and he began to teach them many things.

35　　When it grew late, his disciples came to him
　　　　and said: 'This is a deserted place,
　　　　and the hour is now very late;

36　　send them away, so that they may go
　　　　into the surrounding country and villages
　　　　and buy something for themselves to eat.'

37　　But he answered them:
　　　　'You give them something to eat.'
　　　　They said to him: 'Are we to go
　　　　and buy two hundred denarii worth of bread,
　　　　and give it to them to eat?'

38　　And he said to them:
　　　　'How many loaves have you? Go and see.'
　　　　When they had found out, they said:
　　　　'Five, and two fish.'

The feast of plenty

39 Then he ordered them to get all the people
    to sit down (recline) in groups on the green grass.
40 So they sat down in groups of hundreds and of fifties.
41 Taking the five loaves and two fish,
    he looked up to heaven, and blessed (said the blessing)
    and broke the loaves, and gave them to his disciples
    to set before the people;
    and he divided the two fish among them all.
42 And all ate and were filled;
43 and they took up twelve baskets
    full of broken pieces and of the fish.
44 Those who had eaten the loaves
    numbered five thousand men.

1.2 Background

1.2.1 Context: Chapter 6 began with Jesus' visit to Nazareth (6:1-6), where he was amazed at their lack of faith, so that Mark says: 'He could do no work of power there.' This is followed by the sending out of the twelve (6:7-13), which we looked at already (Session 7). Then speculation about Jesus' identity comes to the ears of Herod Antipas, and that leads to the story of Herod's extravagant banquet and the execution of John the Baptist (6:14-29), which previews the fate of Jesus himself. Next is our passage, at the beginning of which the 'apostles' (so called here by Mark, otherwise disciples or the twelve) return and report to Jesus on their mission (6:30). Jesus tries to take them away quietly 'on retreat', but the crowd frustrate his intention. Jesus looks on this crowd with compassion, as 'sheep without a shepherd', and gives them a different kind of banquet, feeding them in two ways: by teaching (v 34) – at length, though Mark gives no content – and then, after some dialogue with the disciples, by giving them an abundant feast from minimal resources, a sign of God's promised rich pasturing of his sheep in messianic times (vv 35-44). We will see that the next episode, Jesus walking on the water (vv 45-52) is very closely related to the feeding of the crowd. Mark unusually gives no reaction from the crowd or from the disciples after the feast, but after the walking on the sea, he seems disappointed at the disciples' puzzled response

('utterly astounded'), which he attributes to their lack of understanding of the meaning of the feeding of the multitude (vv 51-
52).

1.2.2 Political implications? At the beginning of the following
episode, the walking on the water, we will see, through comparison with John's account, that Jesus takes steps to forestall a
nationalistic reaction from the crowd after the feeding miracle.
This reaction is widely acknowledged, but some commentators
also postulate a prior plot to appoint Jesus as 'king' when he arrived off the boat. The evidence for this is scanty. Mark states at
the end of the feast that five thousand men (*andres*, males) were
fed (Matthew in the parallel passage, 14:21, adds 'besides
women and children', though the Greek *choris gunaikôn kai
paidiôn* could possibly be translated 'there were no women and
children'. This is the only miracle recorded in all four gospels,
and remarkably all four mention 5,000 *andres*, males; none uses
the inclusive Greek word *anthrôpoi*. So some see this crowd as all
males, gathered from all the (surrounding) towns, intent upon
the business of making Jesus leader of their nationalist aspir-
ations, with no women and children allowed to be present. The
arrangement of the crowd later into groups of hundreds and
fifties (v 40) could possibly be seen as a reference to military
structures in Israel's history, but that is negated by the description of the groups in Greek terms *sumposia* and *prasiai* (literally
gatherings for a meal/drinking party arranged like garden beds
in rows). The military hypothesis does not fit well with the narrative as it develops. The crowd is seen by Jesus as 'sheep without a shepherd' and they allow Jesus to teach them well into the
afternoon, permit the disciples to arrange them in groups for a
meal, and accept the food given, and the collection of the left-
overs. So the movement to 'take (Jesus) by force to make him
king' (John 6:15) seems much more likely to have been a spontan-
eous reaction to the miracle of the loaves seen as a messianic
banquet, rather than a pre-planned concerted action.

1.2.3 Links backwards and forward: The early Christians used
the language of their Bible (what we call 'The Old Testament'),
and the language of their liturgical gatherings in their narratives
about Jesus. The account of the feeding has a rich variety of references to the scriptures, and forwards to the Christian celebra-

tion of the Eucharist. Firstly we have the imagery of a deserted place, mentioned three times, recalling the experiences of the Israelites in the desert, and Jesus own experience in the desert (1:12-13) – the place of testing but also the place to find God. The exact location of this deserted place is uncertain, though Luke 9:10 says they went to (towards?) Bethsaida, a town on the north eastern shoulder of the Sea of Galilee, east of the inflow of the Jordan river, and significantly, in the tetrarchy of Herod Philip, not of Herod Antipas. Luke however also refers to a 'deserted place' (9:12), and the disciples want to send the crowd away to villages and countryside to get food, so they cannot have been in the town of Bethsaida. The most likely setting is somewhere near the shore, further west of the inflow of the Jordan, an uninhabited place rather than a desert ('green grass' Mark 6:39). The traditional site, Tabgha, is actually a place of springs, and an ancient mosaic found in a church there has a famous depiction of a basket of loaves with two fish beside it. But Mark evokes the atmosphere of the desert and the feeding with manna, though there is no explicit mention of manna. There is some evidence of an expectation that the Messiah would repeat the miracle of the manna, hinted at in John 6:31f. In the background also is Elisha's miracle of feeding in 2 Kings 4:42-44, 20 barley loaves to feed 100 people, with some left over. But the strongest evocation is of the shepherd theme, God as shepherd of his people, who entrusts the shepherding to the leaders of the people, though they often fail to take care of their charges. Jesus' compassion for the crowd, who were 'like sheep without a shepherd' (6:34) echoes Numbers 27:17, where Moses is told by God to climb a mountain and view the Promised Land, which he himself will not enter. Moses then begs God to choose a new leader so that: 'The congregation of the Lord may not be like sheep without a shepherd.' The theme is prominent in the great prophets, especially Ezekiel. Read Ezekiel chapter 34:1-16. 'As I live, says the Lord God, because my sheep have become a prey ... and because my shepherds have not searched for my sheep ... I myself will search for my sheep ... I will rescue them from all the places to which they have been scattered ... and will bring them into their own land, and I will feed them on the mountains of Israel ... I will feed them with good pasture ... I myself will be the shepherd of my sheep' (8-15). God is now doing this shepherding through Jesus, who nourishes the sheep with his teaching and then with a meal, the messianic fulfilment of the promises of God to gather together and nourish his sheep in messianic times.

These are some of the main links looking backwards. Looking forward, there is fairly widespread agreement that this meal symbolises the Eucharist. If that would be too difficult for the original participants to understand, there is no doubt that Mark's readers would see in the gestures of Jesus as he took bread, said the blessing, broke the bread and gave it to the disciples to distribute to the crowd, the familiar actions of Jesus at the Last Supper, actions repeated in their liturgical gatherings. Indeed, the liturgical pattern, teaching (the word) followed by sharing of the bread of life, developed at length in John chapter 6, already implicit in Mark, has been continued by Christians down through the years. Looking further forward, the miracle is symbolic of the banquet in heaven to which all God's people will one day be invited.

1.2.4 Making 'sense' of the miracle: the disciples take the common sense approach with regard to 'shepherding' the crowd, asking Jesus to send them away as the afternoon wears on, so that they could find food to buy in the country houses or the local villages. When Jesus says feed them yourselves, they point out that it would be hopelessly beyond their means, and that their own food supply (meagre enough for even themselves as they set out on a retreat to a deserted place) amounts to five loaves and two fish. We either believe that Jesus fed the crowd with the five loaves and two fish, ie miraculously, or seek some rational explanation for the ample sufficiency of food which suddenly appeared. This trend began with rationalists who believe that miracles are impossible, and some rational explanation has to be found for everything that happens. But you will also find in some good believing Christian commentators the 'rational' explanation that Jesus and the disciples gave an example of generosity in dividing what they had with others, and many people who had brought provisions with them began to do likewise, everyone prompted to generous sharing by the example of Jesus, and lo! there was plenty for everyone and lots left over.

Some propose this as a greater miracle, getting people to be ready to share with others in trust and love, as God wants us to. It goes to show how good intentions can lead you astray, if you are not careful. From the beginning, we have been trying to pay close attention to the words which Mark uses and the meaning which he intends. We are not entitled to read our own meaning into the text, with no evidence. Read the text again: everything in it points to this being an example of God's generosity, God's abundant giving as a sign of the coming of the kingdom. The blessings of the kingdom are from God, not from human resources. Mark (and the other evangelists who record it) intends to tell us about the miraculous generosity of God, who can take a few meagre resources of human beings, and turn them into overwhelming plenitude, enough for everyone and plenty left over. John, recording the wedding at Cana (John 2:1-11), gives the same message: Jesus, when human resources fail, provides an abundance of wine of the highest quality, but as a sign (v.11) of the blessings that will come in the 'hour' of Jesus' death and resurrection. Mark is celebrating God's fidelity to his promises to shepherd his people, feed them on rich pasture through the Beloved, Jesus the Messiah, who is full of compassion for the people. It may be helpful to look on the miracles of Jesus as 'the love of God made visible in Christ Jesus our Lord' (Romans 8:39, Jerusalem Bible translation).

1.2.5 How many multiplications of loaves? Mark and Matthew have two, Luke and John only one. Commentators speak of 'the bread section' in Mark, 6:32-8:21, where bread is frequently mentioned, sometimes with a symbolic meaning (not always understood by the disciples). The first miracle of the loaves is in a Jewish setting, with five loaves and two fish, 5,000 men, and twelve baskets of food left over. The second miracle (8:1-9) mentions seven loaves (and later 'a few small fish'), 4,000 people, and seven baskets remaining over. These numbers seem to many to indicate a Gentile setting for the second miracle, so that two cycles of incidents are suggested, the first in a Jewish setting, the second cycle in a Gentile setting, pointing to the broadening out of Jesus' mission to include Gentiles. There are two parallel sequences, feeding, sea-crossing, dispute with Jewish leaders, teaching, healing (see eg Mullins, pp 184-5). Most commentators are agreed that historically there was only one miraculous feeding, which came to Mark (and through him to Matthew) in two versions with slightly different details, one from a Jewish-Christian community, the other from a Gentile-Christian community. Mark then used them to indicate that Jesus had come to bring salvation to Jews and Gentiles, and intended them to be fed with bread together, the bread of the eucharist. An argument for there being only one multiplication is that when Jesus suggested feeding the crowd themselves in the second account, the disciples raised the same objections as before, and seemed to have no knowledge of a previous miraculous feeding (8:2-4).

2. Reflection

2.1 Mystery

In this text we are able to see a whole sweep of God's plan for the kingdom. The feeding of 5.000 men in the deserted place is a sign of the fulfilment of so many hopes for Israel, a sign of the continued nourishing of the people of the new covenant with the word of God and the eucharistic banquet, and a preview of the goal which will be the completion of all God's plans, the heavenly banquet in the fullness of the kingdom. The driving force of the whole plan, despite the setbacks that come and will come from human incomprehension and human wickedness, is not God's mighty power or judgement, but God's compassion, made visible in Jesus. The reign of God is a reign of love. The disciples will be blamed for their slowness to understand the mystery, which is to be gradually revealed. Spend a little time thinking about the fullness of life that we have received, luxuriate in being chosen and loved, richly fed by God, with a wonderful destiny, though we may be frail and subject to the setbacks and disappointments of life. There is a deliberate echo of the 23rd Psalm in the reference to the green grass on which the people recline for the bread to be distributed: 'The Lord is my shepherd, I shall not want. He makes me lie down in green pastures.'(Ps 23:1-2).

2.2 *Christology*

We are used to the title 'the Good Shepherd' being applied to Jesus, from the Gospel of John. The Good Shepherd throughout the Old Testament is of course God, as we see from Ezekiel 34 (1.2.3). Jesus, addressed as 'my Son, the beloved' at his baptism in the Jordan, is the visible expression of God's care, nourishment and guidance embodied in the word 'shepherd'. The actual word 'shepherd' is only used twice in Mark, in our passage here (6:34), and after the Last Supper on the way to Gethsemane, again in a quotation from the Old Testament (Zechariah 13:7), when Jesus prophesies that the disciples will desert him: 'I will strike the shepherd, and the sheep will be scattered.' They will be like sheep who scatter in panic when their shepherd is attacked. Though Mark does not explicitly call Jesus shepherd, he certainly casts Jesus in the role of the messianic shepherd of his followers and disciples. In our passage he firstly shows his concern for the twelve (vv 31f) after their return from the mission. With hardly time to talk to Jesus or even to eat because of the crowd, they need a period of quiet and reflection, so Jesus takes them to a quiet place to rest. Their privacy only lasted for the length of the boat journey. But it surely helped. The first time I crossed the sea of Galilee on a boat with a group of pilgrims, our temporary shepherd-leader said: 'You have time to read St Mark's gospel before we reach the shore.' And we had.

Jesus then shows his patience and compassion when the crowd meet him as he disembarks; he teaches them and feeds them in what seems to be a very deliberate messianic act, with an implied answer to the question that has been in the air: 'Who then is this, that even the wind and the sea obey him' (4:41, and see also the speculation in 6:14-16). Though the disciples may have failed to draw the conclusion, perhaps the crowd did, though not in the way Jesus wished, and Mark certainly hopes his readers will draw the right conclusion.

2.3 *Discipleship*

As we saw, the twelve reported back to Jesus, and he tried to take them away for a while to a deserted place, but the plan did not work out fully. They are invited by Jesus to take part in his shepherding of the people, to give up their scanty supply of

121

food in trust, and to distribute the bread to the crowd arranged in rows on the grass. The gift of plenty comes from God; some part in the divine shepherding of the people is given to human workers. The strange thing is that no reaction or response of the disciples is recorded at the end of the miracle. At that stage, although it seems likely there was some reaction from the crowd, who, according to John 6:15, wanted to take Jesus by force and make him king, the disciples do not seem to have drawn the kind of conclusion Mark would have expected. In this whole 'bread section' 6.32-8:21, the disciples' slowness to comprehend is repeatedly highlighted. At the end of the walking on the water, they again failed to draw a proper conclusion, 'for they did not understand about the loaves, and their hearts were hardened' (6:52). They, who were at the heart of the action and cooperating in it, did not apparently see it as a messianic action and draw the proper conclusion. Therefore they did not draw the conclusion about the walking on the water either. Either you can be disappointed or consoled by the disciples' slowness, even hardness of heart! It seems that Mark is trying to get his contemporary readers to have stronger faith in the face of possible persecution. We also should know better, for we readers have been privy to information about Jesus' identity that the twelve did not have, the words of the Father from heaven: 'You are my Son, the Beloved' (1:11). But we know that our faith can waver; if we do not suffer from hardness of heart, we often enough approach indifference of heart, and need to take Jesus' advise to go away with him to a quiet place and pray.

2.4 Conversion

This is the beginning of a section which reflects Mark's disappointment with the disciples, disappointment later voiced by Jesus himself (8:17-21): their understanding does not mature in relation to what they see and hear. Their hardness of heart is reported only after the next episode, but its root cause is that 'they did not understand about the loaves' (6:52). Mark in his own enigmatic way does not clearly state what they should have concluded from the miracle of the loaves, but it seems that the clearly messianic intent of Jesus' action should have led them to recognise the Messiah in their midst. Jesus is asking them to see and hear more attentively, but he needs them to come to their own profession of faith, not to put it on their lips for them. The mystery of the kingdom, already being revealed to them (see 4:11), is so closely related to the person of Jesus, that they need to be 'with him' (3:14), hang on to his words and think about his actions, if they are to come to the mindset that will allow them to confess stronger faith in him and total trust in him. The kingdom of God is being revealed as a kingdom of compassion, generosity, healing and rescue from the power of Satan, all this the free gift of a generous and liberating God whose reign Jesus proclaims. Openness of heart to this God and to Jesus who reveals him is required not just of the original disciples, but of each of us. The miracle of the loaves reveals our great need as shepherdless sheep to be fed by God's word and by the divine gift of lifegiving bread.

3. RESPONSE

Make your personal response by rereading the text, pausing to pray with any verse or phrase which strikes you.

Come away to a deserted place all by yourselves and rest a while. We have this lovely personal invitation from Jesus to his disciples, to come away to a place of quiet to be 'with him', to listen to his words and find food for our souls. Just place yourself in his presence and be grateful for his invitation, and the compassion and generosity he shows for the multitude. Use words if necessary.

He had compassion for them, because they were like sheep without a shepherd. Contemplate the compassion of Jesus. Looking for a quiet place he found a crowd, but responded with patience and love to the needs of the 'sheep without a shepherd'. Pray for compassion, understanding of the feelings and needs of all who fill your life, especially those closest to you, even the noisy and demanding ones.

You give them something to eat. Lord Jesus, you wish to involve your disciples in the work of shepherding the sheep: but they need to learn to do it your way, and not their own. Your way is more generous and trusting and risky – for you ask us to give away our own five loaves in trust. Lord, help us to be involved in the care of your people. We often feel overwhelmed by the many needs, feeling that our paltry resources and talents can achieve little. Help us to believe that we each have something to give; help us to put our few resources into your hands, that you may make something of them! We may find that in the end we have more than we started with, even if the in-between time may be difficult.

He began to teach them many things ... He ordered them to get all the people to sit down (recline) on the green grass. Good Shepherd, you feed the hungers of your people, first with your word you feed the hunger for 'more than bread', and then the hunger for food. Lord, fill the empty spaces within us. 'My soul thirsts for you; my flesh faints for you, as in a dry and weary land where there is no water' (Ps 63:1). You might like to use Psalms 23, 42 or 63 for your prayers.

He looked up to heaven, and said the blessing (NRSV 'blessed'), and broke the loaves, and gave them ... We pray in gratitude for the gifts of God. We bless God with Jesus for the food for soul and body that he gives us. We pray that we may treasure the eucharistic gathering of God's people, our greatest thanksgiving to God in union with Jesus. We pray for grace to be thankful and to live with a eucharistic mind-set, blessing God for his eternal care for us.

And all ate and were filled. We pray that God's people may be united, all fed by the same word and the same bread. We pray for unity among us, in our communities, among all the baptised, among those who receive the bread of life. Lord, we come together is a sign of unity, but we know the unity is very imperfect; let our very gathering be a prayer for unity. Lord, we are one, make us one. 'Grant that we, who are nourished by his body and blood, may be filled with his Holy Spirit, and become one body, one spirit in Christ' (Eucharistic Prayer III).

They did not understand about the loaves, but their hearts were hardened (borrowed from 6:52). Lord, we know that the thing that keeps you at a distance is our hardness of heart. We know it puts distance between ourselves as well. It is a terrible thing to see the shutters go up between couples, who began by being in love, hearts hardened. We pray that it never affects our relationships with loved ones, family or friends, and especially our relationship with you, Lord. Lord, give us openness of heart. Free us from anger, resentment and the bitterness that turns our hearts to concrete. Give us hearts of flesh.

4. CONTEMPLATION

It would be good to bring with us after our prayer the feeling that we are marvellously nourished and cherished by God through Jesus, who feeds us with word and sacrament. Walk in his presence and be thankful. Choose a phrase to remember. Suggestions: 'He had compassion for them, for they were like sheep without a shepherd.' 'He looked up to heaven, said the blessing, broke the loaves, and gave them ...' 'And all ate and were filled.'

SESSION ELEVEN

Walking on Water (Mark 6:45-52)

1. FAMILIARISATION

1.1 Getting to know the text (Mark 6:45-52)

Separation

6:45   Immediately he made his disciples
get into the boat
and go ahead to the other side, to Bethsaida,
while he dismissed the crowd.

46   After saying farewell to them,
he went up on the mountain to pray.

Mysterious reunion

47   When evening came, the boat was out on the sea,
and he was alone on the land.

48   When he saw that they were straining at the oars
against an adverse wind,
he came towards them early in the morning,
walking on the sea.
He intended to pass them by.

49   But when they saw him walking on the sea,
they thought it was a ghost and cried out;

50   for they all saw him and were terrified.
But immediately he spoke to them and said
'Take heart, it is I; do not be afraid.'

51   Then he got into the boat with them
and the wind ceased.

Reaction

    And they were utterly astounded,

52   for they did not understand about the loaves,
but their hearts were hardened.

1.2 Background

1.2.1 *An epiphany:* This text is a manifestation by Jesus of God the Creator's power over nature, specifically over the water, which in its unruly power is a symbol of chaos; and also a manifestation of Jesus' own sharing in that power of God. The

126

disciples labouring on a difficult sea passage see Jesus treading on the chaotic waters. Such a manifestation of divine power is called an epiphany (from the Greek *epiphanein*, to show forth). The incident is recorded in Mark, Matthew (dependent on Mark?), and in John (independent), in each case joined to the miracle of the loaves. By delaying the disciples' reaction to the loaves until after the walking on the water, Mark seems to say that they are mutually illuminating, that they both show God's power over nature, and reveal the identity of the one through whose agency they take place. Mark is disappointed that the disciples failed to draw any conclusion about the identity of Jesus.

1.2.2 Context: All the episodes in the 'bread section' are interconnected. Three related crossings of the sea are recorded, two of them in this section. Firstly, the calming of the storm (4:35-41) raised the question: 'Who then is this, that even the wind and the sea obey him?' The walking on the sea raises the same question, though the answer is not understood by the disciples. The crossing in 8:13-21 has an animated discussion on the disciples' lack of insight about the miracles of the loaves, ending in the question of Jesus: 'Do you not yet understand?' We need to look at the walking on the water, because it is closely attached to the miracle of the loaves, and because there are big questions of interpretation involved; and we will examine the dialogue between Jesus and the disciples in 8:13-21 (Session 12) in the hope of finding some answers to the mystery of the person of Jesus.

1.2.3 Geography: Mark, or the tradition he inherited, does not seem to have had much 'hands on' knowledge of the geography of Galilee, and it is very hard to follow the indications he gives. Jesus sent the disciples to (towards?) Bethsaida, which was away to the east of where the miracle of the loaves happened; that we will see makes some sense, as it was outside the territory of Herod Antipas, who had executed the Baptist. But after an evening and most of the night rowing against a headwind, they were nowhere near the known Bethsaida (Julias), and they eventually land at Gennesaret (6:53), which is close to where they set out. Some postulate another unknown Bethsaida on the north western shore, for which there is no evidence, though it would fit Mark's directions better. We do not need to concern ourselves too much with the geography, except that it would indicate a very severe headwind if they spent so much time rowing the boat without getting very far, totally off course. Most of the commentators insist that Jesus did not need to 'rescue' the disciples, as was the case in the storm-stilling in chapter 4, because Mark seems to wish to emphasise only the epiphany of Jesus. I think they make too little of the severe conditions and the disciples' inability to make their rendezvous with Jesus, and maybe in an earlier stage of the tradition, the idea of rescue was more prominent.

1.2.4 Biblical references in the narrative: We read the text differently when we begin to appreciate the scriptural references in the language Mark uses. Jesus goes up the mountain to pray: raising many biblical memories of Moses and Elijah meeting God on the mountain, the place of revelation. Strange things happen when Jesus goes up a mountain, as in the transfiguration (Mark 9: 2-8); Jesus' oneness with God and his sharing in divine power are most apparent. By dusk 'the boat was out on the sea' (v 47), literally 'in the middle of the sea'; perhaps Mark here also intends to suggest a parallel with the Israelites rescue by God through the sea in the exodus from Egypt, for the Israelites and the Egyptians are frequently said to be 'in the middle of the sea' in Exodus 14 and 15 (8 times in Septuagint [LXX] Greek translation). Seeing the disciples 'being tortured' (*basanizomenous*, v 48) at the oars, 'about the fourth watch', i.e., around 6 am (NRSV 'early in the morning'), Jesus comes towards them 'walking, *peripatôn*, on the sea'. In biblical texts, God the creator is the only one who has control over the waters of chaos, 'who alone stretched out the heavens and trampled the waves of the sea' (LXX, Greek translation, 'walking, *peripatôn*, on the depths of the sea', Job 9:8). Job 38:16 reads: 'Have you [Job] entered into the springs of the sea, or walked (*peripateo* again) on the recesses of the deep?' A few other references out of many: Psalm 77:19f (=LXX 76:20), 'Your way was through the sea, your path, through the mighty waters; yet your footsteps were unseen. You led your people like a flock by the hand of Moses and Aaron' – referring to the rescue of the Israelites escaping from Egypt through the sea. Compare Isaiah 43:16: 'Thus says the Lord, who makes a way in the sea, a path in the mighty waters.' Mark, by using the same wording as in Job, implies that Jesus' walking on the water is a manifestation of his sharing in the power of God over the waters of the deep, something Mark expected the disciples to be prepared for after his stilling of the storm in the previous sea crossing (4:35-41). But how could you be prepared for something like this? The disciples, seeing the figure on the sea in the dim light and spray, are terrified, thinking it must be a ghost, and cry out in alarm. The difficult clause, 'He intended to pass them by (v 48),' may also have important biblical background, and we will discuss it later (1.2.5). Matthew 14:25, the parallel passage, omits it. Jesus immediately speaks to reassure them in very biblical language: 'Take heart, it is I; do not be afraid' (v 50). This is the reassuring language of God in the Old Testament to prophets and people called to undertake difficult tasks. Read, eg, Isaiah chapters 41 and 43, full of God's reassurance to the people in exile: 'For I, the Lord your God, hold your right hand; it is I who say to you, 'Do not fear, I will help you' (Isaiah 41:13). The striking thing is that Jesus uses the words of God in the Old Testament as his own, giving the reassurance in his own name. It will be some time before the disciples realise the implications of that. Then Jesus gets into the boat and the wind dies, without any words from him. The disciples' reaction is one of utter amazement. They do not get the message, Mark says, because they did not understand about the loaves, and they are accused of that hardness of heart which is impervious to God's revelation.

1.2.5 'He intended to pass them by': This text, instead of being a puzzle, perhaps really illuminates the meaning of the whole story. The verb, to pass by, Greek *parerchomai*, is used in those extraordinary visions of God to Moses and Elijah on Mount Sinai. In Exodus 33:18 Moses asks to see the glory of the Lord, and God agrees: 'I will make all my goodness pass before you, and will proclaim before you the name, The Lord ... and while my glory passes by I will put you in a cleft of the rock, and I will cover you with my hand until I have passed by ...' (Ex 33:19-22). The promise is fulfilled in Ex 34:6, 'The Lord passed before him, and proclaimed, The Lord, the Lord, a God merciful and gracious ...' Elijah, fleeing from Jezebel, comes to Horeb (*Sinai*), and is instructed by the Lord: 'Go out and stand on the mountain before the Lord, for the Lord is about to pass by' (1 Kings 19:11). He then has his famous vision, where the Lord was not in the wilder forces of nature, but in the 'sound of sheer silence' (19:12 NRSV). In all these cases the LXX uses the Greek verb *parerchomai* for 'pass by', the verb used by Mark. So Jesus intended, not just to go ahead of them, but to manifest his true nature to them, a true epiphany, as God himself let his presence be manifested on the sacred mountain. This is reinforced by the use of the words: 'Take heart, it is I' (Greek *ego eimi*, which can be translated as 'It is I', a normal greeting/identification, or as 'I am', which is the LXX Greek for the sacred name of God revealed to Moses, 'I am who I am' Ex 3:14). If Mark meant us to take the words as 'I am', rather than 'It is I', then Jesus is displaying to his disciples his oneness with God and claiming the divine name for himself. It has long been accepted that John's Gospel uses the sacred 'I am' for Jesus, and we can be pretty certain that John in the parallel text, 6:20: 'It is I/I am, do not be afraid,' intends the ambiguous phrase to be taken as 'I am', though he does not have any corresponding words about 'passing by'. If we accept all this, Jesus is being revealed as more than human, transcending even the expected Messiah, one who has power over nature like God himself. See eg M Mullins' Commentary, pp 193-5.

This attractive theory adds to the whole 'epiphanic' character of the episode. It is a real difficulty that the verb 'to pass by' in Mark is transitive (to pass by them), used with an object like this nowhere else in the Gospels. In Exodus and Kings the verb is intransitive, either used absolutely or with a prepositional phrase, (*proteros sou, pro prosôpon autou*, before you, before his face, Ex 33:19, 34:6). So you will find authors who go with the NRSV translation in its natural meaning, 'He intended to pass them by,' and explain it as Jesus intending to lead them to the shore, happy with the parallelism with the Exodus escape of the Israelites. Then you have to say that, when Jesus realised that the disciples were terrified, he got into the boat instead to reassure them. The decision is complicated by the obvious fact that Christians after the resurrection, and Mark's readers whose faith Mark is challenging, were able to see more in the words and actions of Jesus than was possible at the time, and could read more into the words *ego eimi*, 'I am', than the disciples on the boat, who would more likely have understood it as, 'I am Jesus, do not be afraid.' Their response, 'they were utterly astounded', makes sense enough in the circumstances, though Mark would be very disappointed if that was still the response of his first readers, (or of us), who should understand about the loaves, unlike the first disciples. The response which Matthew puts on the lips of the disciples (Mt 14:33), 'And those in the boat worshipped him, saying, 'Truly you are the Son of God,' bears all the imprint of a post-resurrection confession of faith.

1.2.6 What is the meaning of this strange episode? I ignore as unworthy of consideration theories that attempt to rationalise the miracle away: that Jesus was walking on the land beside the sea, or walking on a ridge of rock jutting into the sea. They are demeaning both to Mark and the disciples who knew the lake well. It is without doubt intended by Mark to be a messianic revelation of Jesus' closeness to God and his sharing in the power of God, and conclusions are to be made about his identity. The loaves miracle was also a manifestation of his messiahship, and the disciples' failure to comprehend that left them unprepared to understand this message also. Has it any relationship to the kingdom of God, like the other miracles, or is the emphasis, as many commentators insist, really on the identity of Jesus? I believe that it is both a miracle about the kingdom, the guiding providence and care of God for the nucleus of the new kingdom family, and an epiphany of the sharing of Jesus in the power of God. An either/or approach leads to wrong conclusions down the line (eg, J P Meier's rejection of the historicity of the incident because there is no rescue of someone in dire distress, *A Marginal Jew*, Vol II, pp 919-924). Jesus repeats the Exodus miracles of feeding in a deserted place, like the feeding with manna in the desert; and the rescue of the people of God through the sea, by saving the twelve, who represent the future gathering together of God's people, by finding them a path through the waters. The path through the waters in Exodus was of course a manifestation of the power of God, but the people were also rescued. The saving God, whose power Jesus reveals, shepherds his people by feeding them and by guiding them to land, reassuring them that they are surrounded by God's protection and care, so long as they follow Jesus, who reveals the love and power of God. 'For thus says the Lord ... he who formed you, O Israel: Do not fear ... When you pass through the waters, I will be with you' (Isaiah 43:1-2). 'I am the Lord ... who makes a way in the sea, a path in the mighty waters' (Isaiah 43:15-16). Though the disciples were not in peril of death, they certainly felt rescued by Jesus. The message for the disciples is that the guiding hand of God will always be with them, as it was for the Israelites in their journey out of Egypt, and that while they are with Jesus, the Messiah, they will be surrounded by the saving care of God; and that is what the kingdom of God means.

2. REFLECTION

2.1 Mystery

There is enough mystery for us here, to say nothing of the utter astonishment of the disciples. They, like us, are confronted with the mystery of God's presence and power made visible in the extraordinary action of Jesus. This power is initially terrifying, but gradually becomes reassuring, salutary, rescuing them from their distress at sea. For nothing is impossible to God, and the kingdom of God is at hand. When we reflect on Old Testament passages we can begin to see that Jesus is doing something that scripture says can only be done by God, controlling the waters of the deep, and this is the second time the disciples have experienced Jesus' power over wind and sea. It is not just a display of power, but a display of saving power. Putting together the miracle of the loaves and the walking on the water takes us back to the great desert miracles of the exodus from Egypt, where God fed the pilgrim people of Israel with manna in the desert after he had saved them through the waters of the Red Sea, because God was with his people on their journey to the promised land. That saving care and presence is now made visible in the care and compassion of Jesus for the people 'like sheep without a shepherd', and for the twelve, who represent the reconstitution of the tribes of Israel, the kingdom family. We are God's 'pilgrim church on earth' (Eucharistic Prayer III), assured that Jesus guides us on our pilgrim way, though the waters be often stormy, to the fullness of the kingdom.

2.2 Christology

'Who then is this, that even the wind and the sea obey him?' (4:41) The disciples have not yet answered their question; but we need to. At the very least in this passage, Jesus is so close to God that he shares his power over nature, acts and speaks in God's name, becomes his voice and his presence. The disciples are not able to articulate their experience of Jesus, but the reader has information the disciples did not have. We can easily see these twinned miracles as messianic fulfilments of God's promises, now that the time of the kingdom has come. They certainly point to Jesus as Messiah, the 'one who was to come,' and we know there is much more to it than that. This miracle became a source of reflection for the post-resurrection community, which came to see deeper meaning in the words and actions of Jesus than the first disciples at the time, possibly in his 'passing them by' and in his use of the sacred *ego eimi*, 'I am'. The early Church made quick progress in seeing the closeness of Jesus to his Father, and was soon able to apply to Jesus sacred concepts formerly reserved for God himself. Matthew's account of the miracle (14:22-33) can conclude 'Truly you are the Son of God' as the final answer to the question, 'Who then is this ...?'

2.3 Discipleship

Some commentators feel that the disciples' response of astonished bewilderment, is not all negative: it corresponds to that inarticulate wonder of the sporting personality interviewed after some victory: 'unbelievable, fantastic, hasn't sunk in yet' – a general sense of wonder without the words to describe it. Mark, though, thinks that the disciples were worse than just slow on the uptake, they suffered from hardness of heart – and the heart in the Bible is the centre of logical thought as well as of the emotions. It is possible that Mark was thinking in the biblical way that everything is caused directly by God, that it was somehow God who hardened the disciples' hearts, as he is said to have hardened the heart of the pharaoh in Egypt, all as part of the explanation for Jesus' rejection by the majority of his own people. But mostly we have no need to invoke God as the cause of our own slowness on the uptake. Sometimes we fail especially to realise that Christianity is all about a living commitment to the person of Jesus. Doesn't our commitment to Jesus deserve to be based on a little study and reflection and on a heart that is not made of stone, but is open to the promptings of the Spirit? Do you feel that Jesus is with you in the journey through troubled waters, guiding and leading all who believe in him? Listen to him saying to you: 'Take heart, it is I, do not be afraid.'

2.4 Conversion

Conversion means getting our hearts right, which includes getting our thinking right in biblical terms. Put yourself in that boat. You have given up everything to follow Jesus, and you are temporarily (you hope!) separated from him, and the wind is driving you back out to sea, and you have been at it all night, till taking your turn at the oars is torture; you are aching and soaked, and you are getting really cross with each other. Where is Jesus now? Is he waiting for you on the shore where you were supposed to meet, or (unworthy thought) is he fast asleep again, as he was in the storm. Thinking is not too straight at such times. At similar times in your life, when you were down to your emotional uppers, you may have wondered where was Jesus? And then the cry of alarm and the fright at seeing a figure emerge from the gloom and spray right beside the boat walking on the waves. What would you do but be terrified? The familiar voice calls out: 'Don't be afraid, it's Jesus!' And you reach out a hand and help him into the boat, make a space for him in the stern, and he smiles and wipes the water from his eyes, and wrings out his hair, and you realise the wind has died and the boat is going steadily towards the shore. How could he do that? Walk on water? And you remember your unworthy thoughts! He came to help us, to bring us to shore! What kind of thoughts and emotions are going to be in your mind and heart? Trust, calmness, feeling of being looked after, amazement; he is doing God's work that is not going to be thwarted by a stormy night at sea; why do I panic! So come back to earth, and decide that God is always with you, has chosen you in Jesus, and blessed you, is trustworthy, faithful, reliable; loves you enough to trust you to face the challenges of life. That will do for conversion, which means turning to God in humility, trust and love.

3 RESPONSE

Make your personal response by rereading the passage, stopping to pray with phrases or words that strike you.

He made the disciples get into the boat, and go on ahead. Think of the picture of a very small boat with a lone rower in the middle of a vast sea, and the caption: 'Lord, have mercy! My boat is so small, and your sea is so big!' Lord, like the disciples, we often feel overwhelmed when things are going wrong, and you seem far away. We pray for faith, when the winds are blowing and God seems distant. We ask pardon for ever assuming that if we are good and have strong faith, nothing bad will ever happen to us, or our loved ones. You allowed the disciples on the lake to face danger. We pray for the grace to face whatever comes with courage, the disappointments, hurts, setbacks of life. We know that overall we are in your care, now and always, that your plans for us are bigger than this life.

When he saw that they were straining at the oars against an adverse wind, he came towards them … walking on the sea. Lord, we are sorry for ever thinking that our faith is dull! You saved the disciples from a storm at sea, sent them out on a mission with power, fed a crowd with a few loaves, now walk on a rough sea. Whatever about it, it is not boring. We pray for 'wonder and awe in God's presence'. May it keep us young at heart, and help us to understand the mystery of your presence. Jesus, you are doing what only God is supposed to be able to do, trampling on the waves. We believe you are God's messiah and God's Son. As God saved his people from the Egyptians by leading them safely through the sea, so you save your little family, the nucleus of the new Israel. We praise you for your power, and for your saving goodness. You are the one who is always with us, always making intercession for us. 'When you pass through the waters, I will be with you' (Isaiah 43:2).

They all saw him and were terrified, but he said, 'Take heart, it is I (I am?), do not be afraid.' Lord, we long to see your face and fear to look upon it. The disciples were relieved when they heard your voice, but could not believe their eyes. They had already forgotten how you calmed the storm, but now you bestride the deep as only the great God of Israel himself can do. The presence of the divine is scary, and they are properly frightened and do not know what to say. We can say the right words, Lord, after centuries; we call you Lord, only begotten Son of the Father, Saviour and Judge. But we know that we must do more than call you 'Lord' to enter the kingdom of heaven. Give us reverence in your presence, and a great determination to serve you and your people. We pray for the church in the stormy waters of these times. We pray for the leaders of the church and ask you to pour out the Holy Spirit upon them. Help us not to be afraid. Lord, have mercy. Our boat is so small, and your sea is so big.

They were utterly astounded, for they did not understand about the loaves ... Lord, your disciples are criticised for not being very insightful, but they stuck with you, Lord, well, nearly always, and you always gave them more chances in spite of their failures. We know our response is not dependent on how well we can articulate our faith, or how much knowledge we have, but on our hearts, the love and warmth of our commitment to you. We give you true thanks for your care for us, and for all the blessings that come to us through you. We ask for the grace to keep going, and the grace to begin again, and again! We pray for those who have lost direction in life, who are rowing against headwinds, not knowing where they are going or how to get there. We pray that they may come to know your care and compassion for them.

But their hearts were hardened. Lord, preserve us from hardness of heart. Help us to be open to God and to others. Open enough to let God come close to us. Help us to be aware of your saving presence, and to do our best to move forward in hope, and never give up. Help us to find encouragement in your words: 'Take heart, it is I; do not be afraid.'

4. Contemplation

The feeling I want to be left with, to carry around in my mind and heart, is an awareness of the compassionate care of God for each of us. And of encouragement. Though the disciples are blamed at the end of the episode, they are not blamed when they are in the middle of the sea, only encouraged by Jesus. 'Take heart, it is I; do not be afraid.' So I want to hang on to those words of encouragement and repeat them often to myself, especially when the wind is in my face.

The One Bread (Mark 8:13-21)

1. FAMILIARISATION

1.1 Getting to know the text (Mark 8:13-21)

Embarking

8.13   And he left them [Pharisees],
and getting into the boat again,
he went across to the other side.

Going without bread?

14   Now the disciples had forgotten to bring any bread;
and they had only one loaf with them in the boat.

15   And he cautioned them, saying, 'Watch out -
beware of the yeast of the Pharisees,
and the yeast of Herod.'

16   They said to one another,
'It is because we have no bread'

17   And becoming aware of it, Jesus said to them,
'Why are you talking about having no bread?'

Dialogue: challenge to find understanding

    Do you still not perceive or understand?
Are your hearts hardened?

18   Do you have eyes, and fail to see?
Do you have ears, and fail to hear?
And do you not remember?

19   When I broke the five loaves for the five thousand,
how many baskets full of broken pieces
did you collect?'
They said to him, 'Twelve.'

20   'And the seven for the four thousand,
how many baskets full of broken pieces
did you collect?'
And they said to him, 'Seven.'

21   Then he said to them, 'Do you not yet understand?'

1.2 Background

1.2.1 The context: this is the last part of the 'bread section', where the word bread ('loaf', *artos*) is used 16 times between 6:8 and 8:21, and will be used only one more time, at the Last Supper (14:22). Is that a deliberate message from Mark, hinting at a connection? The passage obviously links backwards to both the bread miracles, and reiterates the disciples' failure to understand their meaning, and their hardness of heart (6:52). Jesus is the frustrated teacher whose students can repeat factual information but are unable to raise their minds to the meaning of the facts, so the 'bread section' seems to end with the disappointing: 'Do you not yet understand?' But there is an obvious connection backwards to the healing of a deaf man (7:31-37), and forwards to the healing of the blind man at Bethsaida (the next passage, 8: 22-26), so the disciples' blindness and deafness (v 18) may perhaps be healed. In fact the journey across the sea begun in 8:13 leads to Bethsaida, where the blind man is cured, and on to Caesarea Philippi where Peter at last makes the confession of faith: 'You are the Messiah' (8:29). Even though the accusation of hardness of heart is now distressingly on the lips of Jesus rather than Mark, it is in the form of a question, with the 'not yet' in vv 17 (still) and 21 giving hope that understanding may still come. Jesus' series of questions to the disciples are challenges inviting them to begin to see.

1.2.2 Mark's editing: the background. With so many interconnections backwards and forwards it is evident that the hand of Mark is very much involved in using the material of his tradition to highlight aspects of the mystery which he believes need to be stressed for his readers and his community in dangerous times. His church community, mainly but not exclusively Gentile converts, is faced with persecution, threats of death, needing above all to hold on to its faith in Jesus, who himself faced opposition and death for the sake of his people. A life of hardship, opposition because of their faith, the possibility of arrest, imprisonment and death may have seemed to those Christians a denial of all the promises made to them about life in Christ. The church was only finding its way through the difficulties of reconciling Gentile and Jewish converts called to share the eucharistic gathering together. Therefore Mark stresses the feeding miracle first in a Jewish setting, then in a Gentile setting, hints that Mark was aware of tensions between groups of Christians who need to realise that Jesus feeds all his flock with the one bread. Perhaps we can understand why Mark includes the exorcism on behalf of the Syrophoenician (Gentile) woman's daughter (7:24-30) in the 'bread section'. At first Jesus resists her plea in words that make clear the psychological division between Jew and Gentile: 'It is not fair to take the children's food (lit. bread, *artos*) and throw it to the dogs.' But the woman's persistence and humility settle the issue, she will accept even the crumbs, and he grants her request. So the children's bread is equally for the Gentiles who show faith in Jesus. In the light of all this we must look at the persistent questioning of the disciples, the anxiety about their understanding about the bread. Mark has his Christian community in mind as well as the first disciples. There are messages to which they also are blind, and their eyes need to be opened to the meaning of the bread. And of course the message is for us, who have our own blind spots.

1.2.3 Mark's editing, the details: The discussion about bread happens on the boat going towards Bethsaida (8:22). Jesus left the Pharisees, who were demanding a sign from heaven, and Jesus will have no further dialogue with them. There are two sections of the discussion on the boat, vv 14-17a, and vv 17b-21, each beginning and ending with the same phrasing (technically called inclusion). The first part begins and ends with the disciples having no bread with them; the second part begins and ends with the question: 'Do you not yet understand?' In the first part, the sequence of thought is not at all clear. Look carefully at v 14: the disciples had forgotten to bring bread, then comes a clause given emphasis by unusual word order: 'Now the disciples had forgotten to bring any bread; and they had only one loaf with them in the boat.' The one loaf is never mentioned again, and Jesus in v 15 warns them against the yeast of the Pharisees and the yeast of Herod, which he does not explain, and they do not understand. The saying about leaven was probably preserved in the tradition without a context (Matthew and Luke have a different place for it and interpret it as teaching or hypocrisy), and Mark uses it here to warn about the religious tendencies of the Pharisees and Herod, in an attempt to raise their minds to a symbolic use of the term 'bread'. But the disciples stick to the literal, and return to having no loaves. The emphasis given to the 'one loaf' suggests that it was included by Mark as a symbol, which his readers might understand, that is, Jesus himself is the one bread. As long as Jesus is in the boat with them, they should not worry about having no bread. If we accept that, we may also see a link to the Last Supper, when Jesus gives them the bread which is his body

From v 17b, 'Do you still not (Greek *oupô*, not yet, as in v 21) perceive or understand?', the disciples (and the readers) are challenged by the series of questions, aimed to provoke understanding. V 18 'Do you have eyes, and fail to see? ...' echoes Jeremiah 5:21: 'Hear this, O foolish and senseless people, who have eyes but do not see, who have ears but do not hear?' In Mark 4:11-12, similar words from Isaiah 6:9-10 were directed by Jesus at 'those outside'; now the disciples are asked if they, 'the insiders', are being just as blind to God's revelation. In vv 18b and 19 Jesus appeals to their memories. Remembering is one of the classical ways of coming to faith and maintaining faith. Deuteronomy 8:2-6 asks the Israelites on the verge of entering the promised land to remember all the wonders that God has worked for them, and so to understand that God will always be with them. Jesus asks them to remember the two bread miracles, and they give him the correct factual answers, after which the question remains: 'Do you not yet understand?' Mark has arranged this dialogue for the disciples, but perhaps more especially for his readers. His hope is that Jesus, 'the one bread,' will be revealed to readers in the eucharist, which will gather together all God's people, Jew and Gentile. Paul says in 1 Corinthians 10:17: 'Because there is one bread, we who are many are one body, for we all partake of the one bread.'

2. REFLECTION

2.1 Mystery

The readers' minds are brought from Jesus eating with his disciples, eating with 'tax-collectors and sinners', celebrating with the guests as the bridegroom, breaking bread for the five thousand and for the four thousand, to the Last Supper, to the Christian gathering to celebrate the Eucharist, to the banquet of

God's children in heaven, the fullness of the kingdom. What do all these gatherings have in common? It is God's plan to bring all things together in Christ. 'With all wisdom and insight, [God] has made known to us the mystery of his will, according to his good pleasure that he set forth in Christ, as a plan for the fullness of time, to gather up all things in him, things in heaven and things on earth' (Eph 1:8b-10). Though that full gathering is still far off, little but profound foreshadowings of it are at work in the ministry of Jesus and in the life of the church. That is why it is so important to Jesus that his followers would understand about the bread. When the messianic shepherd feeds the crowd with his word and with bread, it is a sign of how the word of God and the eucharistic bread should draw God's people together and make them of one mind and one heart. Therefore Mark is pained when Gentile and Jewish Christians are unable or reluctant to come together to share 'the one bread' which is Jesus himself. Therefore the pain today of Christians who are unable to share the Eucharist, some lamenting that this is a sign of our disunity, others lamenting that it is a consequence of the fact of our disunity, which must be faced. How we need to keep praying for the guidance of the Holy Spirit.

2.2 Christology

As well as being the shepherd who provides food for the flock, Jesus is himself the food, 'the one bread' that the disciples had with them, though without as yet the awareness of how wonderful the gift is. Soon the disciples will come to a new stage of awareness of Jesus as Messiah, but find that this new insight is only the beginning of a long road to full understanding of the Messiah who will also be the servant who suffers. The one bread will be broken and given at the Last Supper as a preview of the meaning of his death, and Mark desires his readers to understand the meaning of the bread, and so be able to face the possibility that they may have to share in that fate of Jesus for the faith they profess.

2.3 Discipleship

The disciples' problem in the passage is to understand what Jesus means, and it must be admitted that Mark's Jesus is often allusive and mysterious. They are literalistic, unable to rise to

141

the symbolic and mysterious insights that Jesus tries to evoke from them. It is a human failing, our blindness to the transcendent, which can easily become 'hardness of heart', the human incapacity or unwillingness to admit the possibility of truth which we cannot see or count or measure. Jesus is willing to accept that it may be temporary, that illumination may yet come: 'Do you not yet understand?' The next passage will suggest the possibility of going from blindness to sight, and from sight to insight. It is absolutely vital that those whom Jesus is now about to take aside to concentrate on their developing understanding so that they can teach others, should have eyes to see, and ears to hear. It is also consoling for us that they were slow to understand, and helps us to believe that with the help of God we may overcome our own blindness and hardness of heart.

2.4 Conversion

The disciples, of course, are challenged to overcome their blindness and grow in understanding of the messianic identity and mission of Jesus. That journey we will be following through the rest of the gospel story. Mark's contemporaries are challenged to be faithful in their following of a crucified saviour and to accept table fellowship with all who believe in Jesus. We, the modern hearers of the gospel, are challenged to examine the blindness that prevents us from knowing Jesus better and being more faithful in our following. We are challenged to allow our eucharistic worship to create community. It is a task that requires constant vigilance; have we eyes, and do not see?

3. RESPONSE

For a personal response reread the text; spend some time with Jesus' questions as if they were addressed to you.

The disciples had forgotten to bring any bread; and they had only one loaf (artos, *bread) with them in the boat.* Disciples, Lord, including ourselves, often take a long time to get to know you. Like a good teacher you are keen to get them to reach their own answers, rather than give them the answers. Help us, given the answers by the church, to make them our own. We're better at answers of the head that those of the heart. We ask you to help us to open our minds and hearts to your teaching and to your presence among us and in us. We know that you are the 'one bread', and that you want to draw us together and make us a worshipping community sustained by the Bread of Life and the word. Help us to be changed from within by this Bread and to strive to become 'one body, one spirit' in you, through the power of the Holy Spirit.

Why are you talking about having no bread? Do you still not perceive or understand? Lord, it was difficult to raise the minds of the disciples above the literal and the material, to take in that they have all they need with them when they have you, 'the one bread.' We confess it is too often our primary concern also, to have enough to eat and drink. Forgive our concern for our personal needs and acquisitions, all the stuff we surround ourselves with, which we think we couldn't do without. Help us to think of the children who are dying of malnourishment. Help us to know what we really need, and what we can do for those whose needs are real. Help us to nourish the spiritual hunger in ourselves and in this world which bends its knees to material possessions.

Do you have eyes and fail to see? Do you have ears and fail to hear? Help us not to treat casually those great mysteries with which we have become so 'familiar' that we dismiss them lightly. We pray for a greater appreciation of the Eucharist, and for growth in understanding of the mystery that we celebrate. We ask for thankfulness, for the giving heart of the compassionate Jesus to help us to share our gifts with others, for the grace to live the Eucharist when we leave the church. 'Look not on our sins, but on the faith of your church, and graciously grant her peace and unity.'

Do you not remember? Think of your blessings and give thanks. Think of the times when you thought you couldn't make it, and by the grace of God, you got through, and know that he is always faithful. Remembering is what we do at the eucharistic gatherings, in union with you, Lord Jesus, who remain eternally the one offered for us for the forgiveness of sins, and the one offered to us as the life-giving bread which nourishes our spirits and empowers us to 'go and announce the Gospel of the Lord.' Lord, help us to remember, and to relive with you the mystery of our salvation.

4. Contemplation

I want to carry away with me a sense of what I have and above all a sense of what I'm missing, because I am not aware enough of what is happening around me – the beauty of things, the beauty of people, the presence of God. I want to be more alive to things and people. I want to remind myself: 'Do you have eyes and fail to see? Do you have ears and fail to hear?' Lord, help me not to be blind to your presence within me, and within my brothers and sisters.

The Gift of Seeing (Mark 8:22-26)

1. FAMILIARISATION

1.1 *Getting to know the text (Mark 8:22-26)*

8:22   They came to Bethsaida.
        Some people brought a blind man to him
        And begged him to touch him.

Partial sight

23   He took the blind man by the hand
        and led him out of the village;
        and when he had put saliva on his eyes
        and laid his hands on him,
        he asked him, 'Can you see anything?'

24   And the man looked up and said,
        'I can see people, but they look like trees, walking.'

Clear sight

25   Then Jesus laid his hands on his eyes again;
        and he looked intently,
        and his sight was restored
        and he saw everything clearly.

26   Then he sent him away to his home, saying,
        'Do not even go into the village.'

1.2 Background

1.2.1 *'Do you have eyes and fail to see?'* Remember Jesus' question to the disciples (8:18): the miracle of healing blindness is wonderful in its own right, but it is the positioning of the miracle between the emphasis on the failure of the disciples to see and the confession of Peter (8:27-30), that gives it special significance. This is the first miracle of healing blindness in Mark, and it is the only miracle in the Gospels where Jesus fails to complete the cure at the first attempt. The cure is effected in stages: at first the man sees indistinctly – moving figures that must be people but look to him like trees; then Jesus lays his hands on him again and he sees clearly. This too is deliberate by Mark, and he suggests that Jesus expected it by having him ask the man (v 23), 'Can you see anything?' He has never had to ask before, and he doesn't have to ask when he lays his hands on the second time. So the positioning of the miracle makes it clear that Mark intends it to have a symbolic meaning, the gradual healing of the disciples' blindness, which will begin with the confession of Peter in the next passage, and be the major theme of the next big section of the Gospel, the movement from Galilee to Jerusalem, which will end with another healing of blindness, this time instantaneous (10:46-52). So the cure at Bethsaida is fittingly called 'a parable in action' (Mullins p 226).

1.2.2 *Comparison with the cure of the deaf-mute:* The cure of the blind man is structured remarkably like the cure of the deaf-mute (7:31-37). In both, 'they' bring the man to Jesus, beg him to lay hands on him, he takes the man aside in private, uses saliva (thought to have healing properties), touches the ailing parts; afterwards, he tries to keep the cure secret. The differences in the cure of the deaf-mute are that the cure is instantaneous, and there is a reaction from the crowd: 'He has done everything well; he makes even the deaf to hear and the mute to speak' (7:37). The differences are deliberate: the healing by stages, and the lack of reaction are explained by the desire to move quickly to the confession of Peter. Both miracles are seen as fulfilment of prophecy, and so pointers to Jesus' messianic role. 'Then the eyes of the blind shall be opened, and the ears of the deaf unstopped.' (Isaiah 35:5; compare Isaiah 29:18). The words of Jesus to the disciples in 8:18 look backward and forward: 'Do you have eyes and fail to see? Do you have ears, and fail to hear?'

2. REFLECTION

2.1 Mystery

Though in 4:11 the disciples are told: 'To you is given the mystery of the kingdom', the mystery is too deep to be revealed at once, and for the moment it remains partially hidden, if only because of possible political misunderstanding. But the kingdom is destined to come to the light as the eyes and ears of the followers of Jesus become ready to see and hear. We have already seen that miracles are signs of the kingdom in action, and so are prepared to look for their symbolism as well as their literal meaning. The gift of sight to a blind man is an act of compassion, but it is also symbolic of insight, opening the eyes of the soul to see meaning, taking away the blindness that prevents us from seeing God at work in our lives. The kingdom is a kingdom of light. 'But you are a chosen race ..., in order that you may proclaim the mighty acts of him who called you out of darkness into his marvellous light' (1Peter 2:9).

2.2 *Christology*

Jesus is the bringer of the good news of the kingdom, which calls us out of darkness into God's marvellous light. He who brings the light is faced with human blindness, which he strives patiently to overcome, blindness of the disciples, and the repetition of that blindness in every age. It is interesting to see how many ideas that emerge in Mark find a deeper expression in John's gospel: there Jesus is the Word, the embodiment of all that God wishes to reveal to us, he is the light of the world, and the bread of life.

2.3 *Discipleship*

The disciples have been having an exciting but frustrating time; they have witnessed wonders, without being able to articulate their meaning, and consequently been accused of blindness, deafness and hardness of heart. But there is hope in the 'not yet' of Jesus' searching questions. It is in the end the power of God which brings the light; it is revelation, gift, which we cannot discover without God's grace. The dividing line between our blindness, to overcome which we are expected to use our brains and open our eyes, and the moment of faith, where we need God's help, is always difficult to comprehend or to express in words. But the message to all would-be believers is this: use all the gifts we have been given, desire to know the truth, be open to God's grace and grasp the moment. God is more eager that we should see the light than we are to find it. The disciples will receive sight in stages. Maybe that is the normal pilgrim path. Though Paul was dazzled into faith on the road to Damascus, the light is normally absorbed more slowly. 'Truth must dazzle gradually, or every man be blind.'(Emily Dickenson) The stages for the disciples were often painful, for the second half of the gospel is shorter on Jesus' acts of power, and brings a gradual revelation of Jesus the servant Messiah who will suffer and die. Confronting that harsh reality, they will find that 'the spirit indeed is willing but the flesh is weak' (14:38). When news of the resurrection comes, they will know the importance of Jesus' question: 'Do you not remember?' (8:18), and many things he has said will begin to make sense to them, and under the influence of the Spirit, they will find the mystery of the kingdom revealed to them. We hope that our faith will mature, that our eyes and ears will be truly opened to the mystery of the kingdom.

2.4 Conversion

How much light do we wish to have in our lives? Because with the gift of light comes the challenge to let the light shine. So we often settle for just a little light, afraid to search more deeply in case our pattern of life is disturbed. We can be impervious to change. Since the whole tension of the 'bread section' was towards the recognition of the identity of Jesus, so our call to conversion is to a closer commitment to Jesus Messiah, the Son of God. Let the light in, and let the light shine!

3. RESPONSE

Make your personal response by rereading the text, pausing to pray with any verse or phrase that strikes you.

Do you have eyes and fail to see? (borrowed from 8:18). Jesus, you are the one who opens eyes. Thank you for the gift of sight; help us to use it more joyfully. Help us to notice things, take pleasure in their individualities, the infinite variety of human expressions, the loveliness of nature. We praise the Creator by loving his creation. Thank you, Lord, for the gift of insight; we pray for a clearer vision, and for the grace to follow the light of the gospel wherever it may lead us. We pray for the grace to look inwards, to challenge the darkness within, and find the presence of God there. We pray for those who are blind, and those who are faced with the loss of sight, that they may not lose the inner light of faith. We pray for those who are searching for the light of faith, that God's light may lead them kindly on.

Some people brought a blind man to him, and begged him to touch him. We pray with gratitude for those who bring others to Jesus, and for those who brought us to the light. We pray that we may unite with all the anonymous 'theys' who are begging God to enlighten those who are searching for faith, and who strive to bring them to Jesus by the example of their own lives. We pray for the grace to be able to reflect some of the light of Jesus to others.

... when he had ... laid his hands on him, he asked him: 'Do you see anything? I can see people, but they look like trees, walking. Help us to grow in understanding, and never to think that we know it all. Peter will think he sees everything clearly when he confesses that Jesus is the Messiah, but will find he has a long way to go. Haven't we all, Lord? Help us not to presume that we understand the mystery of the kingdom, and help us to handle with care the flickering flame of faith in people around us. You, Lord, are our model and guide; as God's servant you did not break the bruised reed, or quench the dimly burning wick (Isaiah 42:3). Yet we know you long for us to open ourselves completely to your light. Help us to go to the next stage, as the blind man did under your touch, and as Peter did at last.

Then Jesus laid his hands on his eyes again ... his sight was restored and he saw everything clearly. Don't give up on us, Lord, keep laying your hands upon us. Help us on our journey through Mark to see you more clearly, and even if we are slow like the disciples, don't give up on us, as you did not give up on them. Help us to walk in the light, and not to stick to the shadows.

4. CONTEMPLATION

The image to keep in mind is that of Jesus taking the blind man by the hand and leading him out of the village, and laying his hands on him. Allow Jesus to do the same for you, to lead you and lay his hands upon you; he mostly does these things visibly through others, but the hand of Jesus is thereby made visible. The blind man ended by seeing everything clearly. Lord, that we might be able to say that! Perhaps for a text to remember take: 'He took the blind man by the hand and lead him out ...' Or 'Jesus laid his hands on his eyes again ... and he saw everything clearly.'

149

Messiah, Son of Man (Mark 8:27-9:1)

1. FAMILIARISATION

1.1   Getting to know the text (Mark 8:27 – 9:1)

Peter's confession of faith

8:27   Jesus went on with his disciples
to the villages of Caesarea Philippi;
and on the way he asked his disciples:
'Who do people say that I am?'

28   And they answered him: 'John the Baptist;
and others, Elijah; and still others, one of the prophets.'

29   He asked them: 'But who do you say that I am?'
Peter answered him: 'You are the Messiah.'

30   And he sternly ordered them
not to tell anyone about him.

The destiny of the Son of Man

31   Then he began to teach them
that the Son of Man must undergo great suffering,
and be rejected
by the elders, the chief priests, and the scribes;
and be killed;
and after three days rise again.

32   He said all this quite openly.

Peter's thinking is not God's

And Peter took him aside
and began to rebuke him.

33   But turning and looking at his disciples,
he rebuked Peter and said:
'Get behind me, Satan!
For you are setting your mind
not on divine things but on human things.'

The destiny of disciples

34   He called the crowd and his disciples, and said to them:
'If any want to become my followers,

>   let them deny themselves
>   and take up their cross and follow me.

35   For those who want to save their life will lose it,
>   and those who lose their life for my sake,
>   and for the sake of the gospel, will save it.

36   For what will it profit them
>   to gain the whole world and forfeit their life?

37   Indeed, what can they give in return for their life?

38   Those who are ashamed of me and of my words
>   in this adulterous and sinful generation,
>   of them the Son of Man will also be ashamed
>   when he comes in the glory of his Father
>   with the holy angels.'

9:1   And he said to them, 'Truly I tell you,
>   there are some standing here
>   who will not taste death until they see
>   that the kingdom of God has come with power.'

1.2 Background

1.2.1 Context: with this passage we begin a new major section of the Gospel, 8:27 – 10:52 (authors vary as to the precise verses to be included), characterised by Jesus keeping his disciples away from the crowds and instructing them, gradually opening their eyes to the deeper meaning of Messiah and the suffering he was to undergo in Jerusalem. In this section only two healing miracles occur, 9:14-29, the cure of the possessed boy, and the cure of the blind man, 10:46-52. The movements of Jesus are not always consistent (see 1.2.2), but in general there is movement towards Jerusalem, with reference to 'on the way' in 9:33, 34; 10:17 ('setting out on a journey'); 10:46, 52. This 'journey narrative' is not so clearly defined or so long as that of Luke, but has the same purpose, the preparation of the disciples for the traumatic events to happen in Jerusalem. Sometimes 'the way' seems to be more than geographical, a pointer to 'the way of Jesus', as we find in Acts (9:2; 18:25, 26; 19:9, 23 etc). The section ends with the cure of the blind man, Bartimaeus (10:46-52), who follows Jesus 'on the way'. This episode may be seen as an 'inclusion' with the cure of the blind man at Bethsaida (8:22-26), or as another transition passage, this time to the events in Jerusalem.

1.2.2 The geography: The cure of the blind man happened in, or near, Bethsaida, on the eastern side of the inflow of the Jordan to the Sea of Galilee. From there Jesus led his followers north towards 'the villages of Caesarea Philippi,' which was an ancient pagan town called Panias (after the god Pan) near the sources of the Jordan under Mount Hermon, some 25 miles north of Bethsaida. It was given to Herod the Great by Rome and Herod's son, Philip, restored it and called it after the emperor and himself. The villages were presumably small settlements under the control of Caesarea Philippi. The confession of Peter happened 'on the way'. The next episode is the Transfiguration; Jesus led Peter, James and John 'up a high mountain apart' (9:2). The traditional mountain of the transfiguration is Mt Tabor in southern Galilee, but Mt Hermon seems a likelier setting for Mark, though the events afterwards fit better around the shores of the Sea of Galilee. When they came back down the mountain, the cure of the possessed boy occurred, then in 9:30 they passed through Galilee quietly 'for he was teaching his disciples'(9:31), and in 9:33 come to Capernaum, to 'the house'. In 10:1 'He left that place and went to the region of Judea (and) beyond the Jordan' ('and' is lacking in some manuscripts). In 10:10 they are again 'in the house', and in 10:17 he met the rich young man 'as he was setting out on a journey'. In 10:32 the journey seems to be resumed: 'They were on the road, going up to Jerusalem, and Jesus was walking ahead of them.' In 10:46 they come to Jericho, where he healed the blind man, and in 11:1 they are on the outskirts of Jerusalem.

1.2.3 Everything in twos. In line with the two-stage cure of blindness, everything in this passage is in twos: two questions from Jesus; two answers, the people's and the disciples'; two titles for Jesus, Messiah and Son of Man; two destinies revealed, that of Jesus, that of disciples; two ways of thinking, divine and human; two faces of Peter, the confident spokesman for the disciples, the unwitting spokesman for Satan; two facets of the Messiah, the suffering and the glory.

1.2.4 The two answers: Jesus asks: 'Who do people say that I am?' The disciples know from their mingling with the crowds, so they give the various answers: John the Baptist, Elijah, one of the prophets. All these are figures from the past, and fit with the air of expectation in Jewish circles of the time that some of the great figures of their past would reappear to prepare the way for the 'day of the Lord', when all the promises would be fulfilled. The best known of these was Elijah, from Malachi 4:5: 'Lo, I will send you the prophet Elijah before the great and terrible day of the Lord comes.' They are all inadequate answers, preparation figures, but the kingdom of God has come, so Jesus is more than a prophet/precursor. Thus comes the question with the emphatic 'you': 'But who do you say that I am?' Peter answered for the group: 'You are the Messiah (= the Christ).' The word is at last out in the open, and that is good. But the understanding of what kind of Messiah was expected varied in different circles. The popular one, which very probably was that of the disciples, was that the Messiah would be a kingly figure like David, the fulfilment of the promise to David (2 Samuel 7, esp vv 12-16) that there would always be a successor of his on the throne. This figure was called 'Son of David', which we will find on the lips of Bartimaeus, the blind man of Jericho (10:47, 48), and hinted at by the crowds on Jesus' entry into Jerusalem, 'Blessed is the coming kingdom of our ancestor David' (11:10). I'm sure there was some response of praise from Jesus to this declaration, for he seems to have been leading them on towards it, but Mark gives no such response. Instead, there is almost a rebuke: NRSV 'he sternly ordered them not to tell anyone about him' (the same verb *epitimaô*, to disapprove, rebuke, find fault with, is used here by Jesus and again in his rebuke of Peter and in Peter's rebuke of Jesus). A minority of authors even conclude that Jesus refused to accept the title 'Messiah', but that cannot be Mark's intention, because he has given the readers the identification of Jesus in 1:1 as 'Jesus Christ (=Messiah), the Son of God'. So the warning not to tell has to be because of the popular understanding of the title as the one sent by God to rule his people, rescue them from political oppression, and set up the kingdom of justice and peace, the one who could not possibly fail, suffer or die. Jesus has already had to avoid a crowd trying to make him 'king', so he will not allow himself to be publicly called Messiah until he has taught the disciples a different understanding of the role, when there can be no doubt that the role involves suffering.

1.2.5 The Son of Man (8:31): This title comes in abruptly and without explanation, though it has been used already (2:10, 28, with reference to the power to forgive sins and over Sabbath observance). From this time it becomes more important and used frequently, both in reference to the suffering Jesus must undergo, and the glory he will be given by the Father. Here Jesus begins to teach that the Son of Man, ie Jesus, will undergo great suffering, be rejected by the leaders of Judaism (elders, chief priests and scribes), be killed and after three days rise again; and this he said openly. The title Son of Man is used in all three prophecies of the passion (8:31, 9:31, 10:33-34), but it is used again in our passage with reference to his coming in glory, 'when he comes in the glory of his Father with the holy angels' (8:38). The background to this title is Daniel 7:13-14, with influence possibly from the Servant Songs of II Isaiah (especially Isaiah 52:13-53:12) and from the Psalms of the just who are afflicted and cry to God for help (eg Ps 22). Daniel 7 describes a vision in the heavens where God sits enthroned to judge the nations, and a human figure ('one like a son of man', NRSV 'like a human being') comes 'on the clouds of heaven' to the throne of God and has an everlasting kingship conferred on him. The Book of Daniel belongs to the time of the persecution of the Jews during the reign of Antiochus Epiphanes of Syria (165-161 BC), in the time of the Maccabees, and is intended to give the people hope in time of suffering. In Daniel 7:27 the figure on whom sovereignty is conferred is said to be the people of Israel 'the people of the saints of the Most High', so it is originally a representative figure, not an individual. Later however, though the written evidence for it is probably later than Jesus' time, there was speculation in some Jewish circles about the 'Son of Man' as an individual Messianic figure. We can see how the figure fits Jesus' understanding of his role, one who will suffer many things (on behalf of God's People), but who will in the end be vindicated by God and given an eternal kingdom at God's throne. Jesus chose to use this title openly to describe his role; it had messianic overtones without any of the nationalistic baggage of the title 'Messiah'. We will see later, when he is directly challenged by the High Priest: 'Are you the Messiah?'(14:61), Jesus will for the first time say openly: 'I am,' though he goes on to use language that echoes the vision in Daniel 7.

1.2.6 First Passion Prophecy: From being on a high, the disciples heard these words about suffering, rejection and death as a total shock to their system, absolutely at variance with their concept of Messiah. Is Jesus saying the whole mission will end in failure? The words about suffering registered, but whatever Jesus said about rising from the dead meant nothing to them. The 'must' has meaning which they probably did not grasp: 'the Son of Man must undergo great suffering'. The little impersonal Greek verb *deî*, it is necessary, it must be, is a biblical way of saying, it is part of God's plan. In 9:12 (no exact parallel in Mt or Lk) Mark expands a little: 'How then is it written about the Son of Man, that he is to go through many sufferings and be treated with contempt?' 'It is written' is shorthand for 'it is foretold in the scriptures.' Most authors point to texts like Isaiah 53, the suffering servant (not given a messianic meaning by Jews), the psalms of the just man afflicted by others but to be vindicated by God, like Psalm 22, and the generally poor reception of the prophets sent by God, many of whom were killed, as sources of such belief. Three other things to note about the passion prophecy: (1) So far we have met the Pharisees as opponents of Jesus, but they are not mentioned in the list of rejecters in v 31, 'the elders, the chief priests, and the scribes'. The elders represent the leading laymen who were probably members of the Sanhedrin, the chief priests include the current High Priest, ex-High Priests and members of their families, collectively the Sadducees. The scribes were experts on the law and interpreters of the tradition, and could be either Pharisees or Sadducees, but the way the list is repeated by all the evangelists bears witness to the conviction that the Pharisees, though accused of plotting Jesus' death in Mark 3:6, had no great part in his eventual condemnation and death. (2) It is generally accepted that the earliest language about the resurrection, evidenced in Paul and Acts, is that God raised up Jesus from the dead, also normally 'on the third day'. This is the wording in Matthew's 3 prophecies, and in the first two of Luke; 'and on the third day be raised' (Mt 16:21). But Mark, usually seen as the earliest Gospel, has consistently 'and after three days rise again.' This wording usually represents a time when it was accepted that Jesus was the divine Son, and so could rise by his own power. 'After three days' is to be interpreted by 'inclusive reckoning', part of a day counting as a day. Perhaps sometimes the other evangelists use tradition that is earlier than that of Mark. (3) Did Jesus predict his passion? Certainly. Did he predict it in such detail? Probably not. The predictions are made more explicit in the light of what happened; the disciples were especially unprepared for the resurrection, and references to it were probably more enigmatic than the present text suggests. Resurrection was a relatively recent doctrine for Jews; the Sadducees did not believe in it at all, and those who did thought only of a general resurrection when the end of the world would come.

1.2.7 Peter's human thinking: Peter was no doubt intensely proud of his act of faith in Jesus Messiah, and out of very loyalty feels compelled to take Jesus aside and 'rebuke him' for even thinking that such things could happen to God's Messiah. We feel the passion of Jesus' rebuke, which is addressed to Peter but before all the disciples, for no doubt they thought the same: 'Get behind me, Satan!' What an accusation for a chosen disciple, that he was aiding the work of Satan, whose kingdom is in opposition to the kingdom of God. We see that the human Jesus knows the strength of the temptation to avoid the way of suffering. 'For you are setting your mind not on divine things but on human things,' (NRSV) translates the Greek, 'For you do not think (comprehend?) the things of God but the things of human beings.' The agony in the garden shows how hard is the transition from human ways of planning to God's mysterious way. For the disciples it is going to be very difficult; how can the Messiah who has shown such power over Satan, over sickness, even death, and over the powers of nature, himself be rejected and killed? The next words of Jesus make it even harder to comprehend.

1.2.8 Sharing the destiny of the Son of Man: Jesus' words from v 34 are addressed to 'the crowd with his disciples'. Mark does not ask where the crowd came from on this private journey; he wishes to stress that Jesus' words apply to the chosen disciples and to anyone else who wishes to be his follower. So all of us are standing there before him as he speaks. The elements he speaks of are well known, even if we do not like to dwell on them. To deny ourselves, take up the cross, each our own, and follow wherever it takes us, be ready to lose our lives for his sake and for the sake of the gospel, never to be ashamed of Jesus or of his words. Only thus will we gain true life, nothing is of real value if we lose that. That is 'thinking in God's way'. So we save our 'life', our true self, the core of our being, and find eternal life, by being ready to give our mortal life for the sake of Jesus. The disciples were faced with the real possibility of martyrdom, and the members of Mark's community faced the same reality, if they wished to stay faithful to Jesus. V 38, 'Those who are ashamed of me and of my words in this sinful and adulterous generation,' addresses the real concern of Mark for his community, the possibility that some would prove to be weak, ashamed of Jesus and of his words. The terrible consequence: 'of them the Son of Man will also be ashamed when he comes in the glory of the Father with the holy angels.' Most of us face less dire prospects than persecution and death: for some missionaries and some who live in areas of racial or religious conflict being killed is a real possibility, but most of us face the temptation 'to be ashamed of (Jesus) or of (his) words' in a lesser but very real way, letting go of our faith, never thinking to deepen our childhood understanding of Jesus and his teaching, going with the trend towards indifference, gaining not the whole world but other things we put high above the following of Jesus. Just what would we be prepared to give up for the sake of Jesus or for the sake of the gospel?

1.2.9 The Son of Man in glory: we can see from 8:38 and 9:1 that Jesus believes his mission will not end in failure but in his vindication by God, and that those who share in the way of the cross will also share in his glory. The title Son of Man is used in the passion prophecies, but it is also used in the sayings about his 'coming in glory' as in 8:38. The 'when' of that coming we will look at with reference to chapter 13 (Session 19), but Jesus and the early Christians were absolutely sure that it would come. The juxtaposition of 'the coming of the kingdom of God with power' (9:1) with the 'coming in glory' of the Son of Man shows that they are related. The text of 9:1 is difficult to translate as well as being difficult to interpret. Whatever it means, Jesus obviously thought it would happen within the lifetime of at least some of his audience (the proposal that the reference is to the transfiguration which happened 'six days later,' 9:2, is too soon for 'will not taste death until they see'!). The RSV and JB translate 'before they see the kingdom of God come with power' (ie they will see it actually coming); the NRSV translates 'until they see that the kingdom of God has come in power'(they will know that it has already come and is active). It does not refer to the final stage of the kingdom, but to some evidence that it is already working with power among the people. Such evidence would be the resurrection, the coming of the Holy Spirit, the consequent life and energy they feel within them, the fantastic growth of the church.

2. REFLECTION

2.1 Mystery

'The Son of Man must undergo great suffering, and be rejected … and be killed, and ... rise again.' Reflect on the mystery of the kingdom that 'must' come through the suffering of Jesus. It is foretold in scripture and will bring about the release of divine power when he is raised up by the Father. 'Some standing here will not taste death until they see that the kingdom of God has come with power.' What sort of power is it? Not the power of compulsion: the Messiah will not be given power to force people to accept his mission. Mark does not explain how it works, and it may only be approached by 'thinking the things of God', instead of in a human way. Human thinking would never have conceived this plan. Yet we know that God loves the Son, and wishes all to accept the blessings of the kingdom, and that Jesus makes God's love visible by his compassion and healing. So we have to reflect on what divine love will do to save his people. Love does not work by violence, retaliation, revenge, compulsion. It works by attraction, invitation, self-giving, and it ceases to be love when it resorts to the methods of earthly leaders who impose their will on others. The mystery is that God asks his Son to bring about the coming of the kingdom only by love, and love makes him very vulnerable. Human thinking says 'It cannot be done; people will trample over him and get rid of him.' Human thinking does not get us beyond the moment of rejection and destruction, the moment of death. Has love got power over death? Could we live by love and never use force to get our way? Are we able to see our plans come to apparent nothing rather than cease to act with love alone? How human I feel and far from trusting only in the power of love!

2.2 Christology

Identify with Peter as he hears the question: 'Who do you say that I am?' I am Peter, mightily pleased with myself. I know this one! Not a figure from the past, but one very much of the present. I bring out, 'You are the Messiah'. He doesn't say no, but says: 'Do not tell anyone that about me.' Then he calls himself by another name, Son of Man, that doesn't mean much to us, and says un-messiah like things, that he has to suffer and be rejected and die and somehow be alive again. It doesn't make sense and I tell him so. Well, he calls me 'Devil', and says I can only think like a human being, and God's ways of seeing things are wasted on me. And he says to us all: 'If you are in this with me, not only will I have to suffer, but you as well; forget yourselves and be ready to die for me or for my message. That is the only way you'll have real life.' And then he said something even more strange: 'If any of you is ashamed of me or my words, then the Son of Man will be ashamed of you when he comes in the glory of his Father with all the angels.' What am I to make of that? First this Son of Man is killed, then he is coming in glory, and calling God his Father. And I thought I knew who he was. I, Peter, need to do a lot of thinking, and listening. Maybe something will happen that will help us to make up our minds. God help him, and us, if he has to face that.

2.3 Discipleship

'If any want to become my followers, let them deny themselves and take up their cross and follow me.' It is not going to be easy for Jesus, nor for his disciples, nor for Mark's community, nor for us. Yet we cannot doubt God's love for his Son, or Jesus' love for his followers. So this must be what they call 'tough love'. Love obviously does not prevent God asking hard things from those he loves, including his Son. God does not intend to 'spoil' his children, even if they are going to fail sometimes; failure too is something we must face. Thereby we may learn to grow and be stronger. Peter's failure to grasp what Jesus is saying won't be the last time. It is not the end, but the beginning of wisdom, to know that we must not rely on ourselves, but on him. So look at Jesus' sayings to 'the crowd with his disciples' and admit this is tough, calling for more courage than we have. 'Deny yourself ... take up your cross ... lose your life for my sake and for the sake of the gospel ... do not be ashamed of me and of my words.' Where am I in the light of these hard sayings? Even if it is only like Peter – nowhere yet, but I'll stick with him – that is a good beginning.

2.4 *Conversion*

I learn from Peter that it is possible to be right (about Jesus being Messiah), but to find it hard to believe that the truth may be more than I now understand, and that true statements can be not the whole truth. So it is important to reflect on the words: 'The way you think is not God's way, but a human way.' Conversion – turning towards God – means having a new mind-set, that let's me think in God's way. I need to deepen my understanding of God and Jesus and his words of revelation. How can I do that except by keeping my eyes firmly fixed on him, learning from him by being 'with him'? And not become a miserable old grump in the process.

3. RESPONSE

To make a personal response reread the text, pausing to pray with any verse or phrase that strikes you.

Who do you say I am? Respond to the question in your own words. Who is Jesus for you in the light of his destiny revealed here? Find words to describe him, like courageous, determined, challenging, and react to them. Ask him before you finish, 'Lord, who do you say I am?' You would be surprised how highly he thinks of you!

The Son of Man must undergo great suffering ... Jesus, Son of Man means that you are mortal, subject to death like we are, vulnerable, shrinking from suffering, your emotions are open to disappointment, hurt, rejection. Yet you are going to choose to face death, to identify fully with the worst that can happen to us. You see glory ahead but it still takes courage. (Spend some time with him, in gratitude for his choice to do this for us.)

Peter took him aside and began to rebuke him. Lord God, many of us want to tell you how to run the world. We want you to use your power to sort out all the things we think are wrong. Deep down, we believe it is foolish to think that love alone will bring about the kingdom. How foolish to expect us to use only love! Yet we know that prayer is about trying to put our thinking in line with yours, not trying to persuade you to think like us. We pray for the help of the Holy Spirit. God, forgive us for knowing better than you do! Forgive us for all the misuse of power in the world, in the Church, in our families, in our own lives.

Take up your cross and follow me. Perhaps we need to reflect on some questions, and try to give honest answers. What things in your present life would you call 'your cross'? What things do you fear will become your cross in the future? Does doing hard things out of love make them less of a cross? What do you think would amount to 'being ashamed of Jesus and of his words'? Is there anything you do now that you fear may be tending that way? What do you think Jesus is challenging you to do at this time? Remember he wants you to be fully alive. A wise man said: 'Don't pray, "Lord, I'm sorry I'm so lazy." Pray, "Lord, help me to be alive, to be active and use my talents".'

For what will it profit them to gain the whole world and forfeit their life? Some more questions for reflection. If your life is dull and uninspiring, what would make it brighter? Winning the lottery? Or does it have to come from within? What is 'success', thinking in the human way? What is 'success', thinking in God's way? How much 'stuff' do we need in our lives? When does it start to take over our lives? We need to ask the Lord for help to sort out our priorities.

... until they see that the kingdom of God has come with power. 'See' means 'to experience'. Would you like to spend a while telling the Lord all the great things you have experienced that make you rejoice that the reign of God, God's saving love, is at work among us? In yourself? In your family? In your own life? In your parish? In the church? A big thank you to Father, Son and Holy Spirit would be good!

4. CONTEMPLATION

What we might like to keep alive within us is a sense of the rightness of walking life's journey with Jesus, for he has walked it for us, in life and death. He surely walks the journey with us still, offering us help in our weakness. There is nothing we can give in return for our life in him. Our human lives are in God's hands, even if we lose them. Remember the text, 'For those who want to save their life will lose it; and those who lose their life for my sake, and for the sake of the gospel, will save it.'

Transfiguration (Mark 9:2-13)

2. FAMILIARISATION

1.1 Getting to know the text (Mark 9:2-13)

Preview of Jesus in glory

9:2   Six days later, Jesus took with him
Peter and James and John,
and led them up a high mountain apart, by themselves.
And he was transfigured before them,

3   and his clothes became dazzling white,
such as no one on earth could bleach them.

4   And there appeared to them Elijah with Moses,
who were talking with Jesus.

Listen to him

5   Then Peter said to Jesus, 'Rabbi,
it is good for us to be here;
let us make three dwellings,
one for you, one for Moses, and one for Elijah.'

6.   He did not know what to say,
for they were terrified.

7   Then a cloud overshadowed them,
and from the cloud there came a voice,
'This is my Son, the Beloved;
listen to him.'

8   Suddenly, when they looked around,
they saw no one with them any more,
but only Jesus.

Command to silence

9   As they were coming down the mountain,
he ordered them to tell no one
about what they had seen,
until after the Son of Man had risen from the dead.

10   So they kept the matter to themselves,
questioning what this rising from the dead could mean.

Elijah to come first?

11   Then they asked him, 'Why do the scribes say
that Elijah must come first?'

12   He said to them, 'Elijah is indeed coming first
to restore all things.
How then is it written about the Son of Man,
that he is to go through many sufferings
and be treated with contempt?

13   But I tell you that Elijah has come,
and they did to him whatever they pleased,
as it is written about him.'

1.2 Background

1.2.1 Mark's editing: By his unusually precise time reference, 'and after six days' (NRSV 'six days later'), Mark seems to anchor the transfiguration to the previous text. Some see it as fulfilling the statement in 9:1 that 'some of those standing here' would see the kingdom come in power before they died, namely, Peter, James and John seeing the glory of Jesus and beginning to understand his role in the coming of the kingdom. This cannot be pressed, for the impression in 9:1 is that the promised coming will be after the death of many, but not all, of those listening to Jesus, and a fulfilment only six days later just does not fit. More likely, by placing it on 'a high mountain' Mark is echoing the scene of Moses ascending Mount Sinai in Exodus 24:15-18, where the cloud that veils the glory of God covers the top of the mountain for six days, and on the seventh day Moses is called up to enter the cloud in the presence of God. Six days is a regular biblical period of preparation for an experience of God, so it is wiser to translate the Greek of 9:2 literally, 'and after six days', suggesting that they saw the glory of Jesus on the seventh day. Jesus 'was transfigured before them' (lit. his form was changed, *metemorphôthê*): Mark does not elaborate about the change in Jesus personal appearance as Matthew and Luke do, but the best suggestion is that what they saw was an anticipation of the resurrection body of Jesus. Think of Paul's attempts to explain what a resurrection body would be in 1 Corinthians 15:35-44 (without suggesting that Mark was influenced by that passage). Paul speaks of a change of form in terms of body: a seed is sown and dies, but what is produced is not like the seed, but a new kind of 'body'. 'So it is with the resurrection of the dead. What is sown is perishable, what is raised is imperishable. It is sown in dishonour, it is raised in glory. It is sown a physical body [a body animated by a human *psychê*, (soul)], it is raised a spiritual body (animated by the divine Spirit of God)' (1 Cor 15:42-44). So the risen body is imperishable, glorious, Spirit-filled. Paul says the risen Jesus will share this transfiguration with us: 'He will transform the body of our humiliation that it may be conformed to the body of his glory' (Phil. 3:21). Mark mentions how unearthly white Jesus' garments were, with reference to the whiteness of the garments of heavenly beings (Daniel 7:9, God's robe is white as snow; Revelation 6:11, 7:13f, the white robes of the martyrs; Mark 16:5, the young man at the tomb, dressed in a white robe). Yet Mark edits the account to show it was all for the sake of the disciples: Jesus was transfigured 'before them', Elijah with Moses appeared 'to them', the cloud overshadowed 'them', the voice from the cloud points out the Son to them in the third person: 'This is my Son, the Beloved, listen (ye) to him'; in v. 8 they saw no one but only Jesus 'with themselves'. The conclusion is that the three disciples were confirmed in faith for the coming suffering and death of Jesus with the knowledge that his ultimate destiny would be glory. The heavenly voice tells them to listen to Jesus' message about the necessity of suffering and death before glory.

1.2.2 What kind of narrative is it? Because it is unique, there is no other story for comparison. Some think it is really a post-resurrection story, but though there are some similarities with the resurrection appearances, there are more differences, and this approach is unhelpful. It is probably best described as a 'christophany' (*Christos, phainô*, I show, reveal), a revelation of Jesus' identity as the Christ (Messiah) (like a 'theophany'). Mark describes something that was present and visible; Elijah and Moses spoke with him, Peter wanted to make tents for them, so it wasn't just some inner vision. 'Elijah with Moses' appear (Matthew and Luke will say 'Moses and Elijah'), probably as the two who saw the glory of God on Sinai, and perhaps because they were the undying ones who were taken to heaven (Elijah taken to heaven in a chariot of fire, 2 Kings 2:11; Moses' tomb was never found, so a tradition grew up that he did not die and was taken to heaven), but principally because they were associated with 'the day of the Lord' in Malachi 4:4-5, 'Remember the teaching of my servant Moses, the statutes and ordinances that I commanded him at Horeb (Sinai) for all Israel. Lo, I will send you the prophet Elijah before the great and terrible day of the Lord comes.' Speculation about the Messianic times included the coming of Elijah and the appearance of a 'prophet like Moses', based on the promise of Deuteronomy 18:15, 'The Lord your God will raise up a prophet like me from among your own people; you shall heed such a prophet.' In John 1:19-21 priests and Levites are sent to ask John the Baptist: 'Who are you?' and he said: 'I am not the Messiah'. And they asked him: 'What then? Are you Elijah?' He said: 'I am not.' 'Are you the prophet (ie like Moses)? He answered: 'No.' Because the speculation was centred on Elijah, Mark puts Elijah first.

1.2.3 Reaction of the disciples (vv 5-6): The three are frightened, and Peter in confusion says: 'It is good for us to be here,' but again cannot stop when he's ahead. So he offers to build tents for Jesus and Moses and Elijah – presumably expecting the event to last. We shouldn't search for too much meaning, for Mark says he did not know what to say. Mark is possibly hard on Peter because he puts Jesus on the same level as Moses and Elijah.

1.2.4 The voice from the cloud (v 7): Reminding us of the visions on Sinai and the cloud that accompanied the Israelites on the journey through the desert, a cloud overshadows them (probably all of them), and a voice out of the cloud is addressed to the disciples, an impressive confirmation of Jesus' identity and affirmation of his destiny as outlined in the previous section. Jesus is God's Son, the Beloved (as the readers have known since the baptism of Jesus), therefore glory is his ultimate destiny; they are to listen to him when he says that the path to glory is through suffering and death.

1.2.5 The command to silence (vv 9-10): As they descend the mountain, Jesus orders them to tell no one about what they have seen until the Son of Man has risen from the dead. They obeyed his injunction, but have no clear understanding yet of what Jesus' rising from the dead might mean. If the purpose of the experience of Jesus' glory was to strengthen their faith for the coming passion, it is strange to think that they were unable to talk to the other disciples about it, though we can readily understand what kind of excitement and dangerous assumptions might come from breaking the news more widely. We can only guess, but the wording is close enough to that in 8:30 after the confession of Peter ('he sternly ordered them to tell no one about him'; 'he ordered them to tell no one about what they had seen') to make me wonder whether in both cases it means not to tell anyone outside the immediate circle of disciples. Questioning about 'what this rising from the dead could mean' suggests that they understood resurrection as a communal rising from the dead on the day of judgement, and do not comprehend how it could apply to Jesus right after his death.

1.2.6 The dialogue about Elijah (vv 11-13): The sequence of ideas in these few verses is difficult to follow. But they show that the disciples are trying to puzzle things out, and explain why Elijah is important. The realisation that Jesus is the fulfilment of all God's plans makes them wonder why Elijah has not come first, for that is what the experts on the scriptures have led them to believe. Jesus replies, indeed, Elijah is to come and put everything in order, but then (if he has put everything in order) how come the scriptures say that the Son of Man is to suffer and be spurned? For Elijah has indeed come (it is clear that Mark intends us to think of John the Baptist, though he does not actually name him) 'and they did to him whatever they pleased' – he too suffered and was killed. Elijah in his new identity has suffered as he did in the past. There he spoke out about the king marrying the pagan Jezebel, and for that he was hounded and had to flee; John the Baptist spoke out about the marriage of Herod Antipas to his brother's wife, and for that he was executed. This is what the history of God's dealings with his people leads us to expect ('it is written'): those he sends with his messages are rejected and have to suffer. The disciples were no doubt wondering why Jesus whom they saw in glory needed to suffer to reach that glory, but Jesus reasserts that the way of suffering will be his way to glory. They cannot stay on the mountain; they must come down and follow the path of suffering.

2. Reflection

2.1 Mystery

What a striking though mysterious revelation of God's plan to bring about his kingdom. What a tremendous privilege for Peter and James and John to behold Jesus in this heavenly way, so changed and dressed in splendour, conversing with those greats from their history, Elijah and Moses. Seemingly Peter has no difficulty recognising Moses and Elijah, he just does not know what to make of it, so hopes it will continue. Then he is enveloped in the heavenly cloud and hears the voice of God acclaiming Jesus as his Son and calling on them to listen to him. Peter recalls the strange things Jesus had said a few days before, and how he had dared to correct him. He can feel the words from heaven burning into his unbelieving heart. Now he knows that he must listen to all that Jesus says, put complete faith in him and wait for it to become clearer. (In John 6:68 he will say, 'Lord, to whom can we go? You have the words of eternal life.') Elijah was supposed to come first to prepare God's people, but as they go down the mountain, they learn that he has already come, and received a bad reception: so that must have been the Baptist. Someone doing God's work, then, can suffer, seem to be a failure, but can, for all that, be doing what God wants and be making something clear about God's plan. Something is then clearer about Jesus. Jesus said he must die, but he will also come 'in the glory of his Father' (8:38), and they saw that glory on the mountain. Peter can see that he is being called to believe that it is possible for God's Son to suffer before he comes to glory, though every human bone of him wants to say no. It is surely true that God's way of thinking and human ways of thinking are very different. Suddenly on the mountain the heavenly appearance of Jesus and the heavenly witnesses are gone, and they are back with Jesus as they have known him. Maybe, Peter says to himself, if I hang on to that picture of his altered appearance and shining clothes and the words from heaven, I'll be able to follow him even to death.

2.2 Christology

It is all there. Jesus is seen in glory, a preview of the resurrection, and God says from the cloud: 'This is my Son, the Beloved.

Listen to him.' And it is clear that God means, listen to him when he says he must suffer and die and then rise again. The presence of Moses and Elijah show that Jesus is the completion point of God's plan, that all God's plans will find fulfilment in Jesus. Elijah saw the glory of God on Sinai, but he had a hard time, was hounded out of the Land by Jezebel, reduced to despondency before God rescued him. And according to Jesus he has come again in John the Baptist and been treated cruelly by Herod Antipas at the request of another heartless woman. The great Moses had to flee from Egypt, found it hard to get his people to accept him, was subject to their grumbles and complaints, and in the end did not enter the Promised Land. So many prophets and messengers of God have been treated badly that there seems to be a pattern – 'it is written' (vv 12,13). In spite of the glory, v 12 returns to the theme of rejection: 'It is written about the Son of Man that he has to go through many sufferings and be treated with contempt.' Jesus is to conform to the pattern, the rejected messenger of God. But nobody is honoured among the people as Moses is, and the prophets too. So Jesus will be rejected but in the end vindicated and glorified. Mark does not attempt to explain why this pattern is part of God's plan, he proclaims it and asks for faith.

2.3 Discipleship

When God says: 'Listen to him,' he means also listen when Jesus says that disciples must be ready to share in his suffering and death if they wish to find true life. Peter and the other two have got strong confirmation of Jesus' words and his challenge to them. Puzzles remain, especially about 'rising from the dead', for they are not to speak of their experience 'until after the Son of Man had risen from the dead' (v 9). Peter, in spite of his confusion and fear, did say the striking thing: 'It is good for us to be here' (v 5). He just needs to broaden it: it is good for disciples to be wherever Jesus is, and in whatever situation, whether suffering or glory. It is the call to disciples, to pilgrim followers of Jesus at all times, to walk in faith along the way of Jesus, knowing that Jesus is with them, and that the end of the journey is in God's hands. The temptation is to build tents on the mountain in times of joy and hope to remain there, but the journey must continue. There is work to do. The kingdom must grow. The good news must be spread. Difficulties must be faced. Suffering cannot be avoided. It is to be accepted in union with him, given meaning thereby. But never may a disciple forget that the power and the glory of the kingdom may be experienced in and with Jesus, in the power of the Spirit.

2.3 *Conversion*

We now know that the challenge to the disciple of Jesus is to begin to think in God's way, not in the human way with its own narrow, and self-preserving, view of things. Here's the mystery. Jesus is full of compassion for those who suffer, he heals and brings hope to them. He sends out disciples to cure the sick. It seems to be part of the kingdom of God which he embodies to offer good news, to promise real life, to enable people to stand up and walk with heads held high. Yet he must suffer himself, and refuses to be diverted from the path, and calls disciples to share that path. And if disciples try to dodge it, to save themselves from hurt and suffering, then they will lose their true life. We hear the words: 'Listen to him.' He is speaking the words which bring life. To Mark's readers the message is: stand strong, do not be afraid, do not be ashamed of him or of his words. Suffering accepted out of love is worthwhile, as every parent or lover knows. Jesus loves life, but he has not come to bring us escapism, easy shortcuts to maturity or wholeness. Unselfishness, taking up the cross, showing concern and compassion for others, belief in the good news, dedication to following Jesus on his kind of path, these are the things we are to put first. These things bring deep meaning to our lives.

3. RESPONSE

For your personal response reread the text, pausing to pray with any verse or phrase that strikes you.

Jesus ... led them up a high mountain apart, by themselves. Lord, we can see your glory in others that we love, but the vision fades if we do not allow you to lead us apart to see your face. Help us to be with you for a while, to know that you enjoy our presence, and help us to tell you what you mean to us.

He was transfigured before them. It was a gracious gift to the disciples, to us therefore. Spend time before the picture of splendour; pray in adoration, thanksgiving. Remember some moments that transformed your life: conversion, experience of loving and being loved, strength from togetherness with family, friends, moments of insight. Remembering makes them present. Remember this then, that Jesus was seen in glory on the mountain. It will sustain you. So look long on the scene: see Jesus, Elijah, Moses, three disciples veiling their eyes. 'Lord, it is good for us to be here.'

Elijah with Moses, who were talking with Jesus. If Jesus appeared with Patrick, Brigid and Colmcille (or George or Andrew or David) you would know that your history was being affirmed, that you were built into the story of God's plan of salvation. So think what it meant to Peter, James and John: all the great ones in their history were leading to Jesus. Never neglect the roots from which Christianity sprang. Give thanks that we are, in Jesus, all children of Abraham, and promise never to be guilty of prejudice or meanness towards God's chosen people. Give thanks for the great people who have gone before us, on whose shoulders we stand. And follow their way. 'Stand at the crossroads, and look, and ask for the ancient paths, where the good way lies; and walk in it, and find rest for your souls' (Jeremiah 6:16).

This is my Son, the Beloved; listen to him. The Father's voice points us to Jesus. He is the image of the Father, makes the Father's love visible to us. Pray for a listening ear; the word of God in the gospels is Jesus speaking to us. What do you feel Jesus is saying to you through this text? Renew your resolve to continue to nourish your life with the word of God.

Suddenly ... they saw no one with them any more, but only Jesus. It was just the 'ordinary' Jesus now! But he was there! Isn't that something for which to be thankful! We do not often have an experience of the glory of Jesus, but we know he is there in the ordinary ups and downs of life. Make an act of faith in Jesus' presence with us: in his word, in the sacraments, in ourselves, in our brothers and sisters, in the needy people we encounter, in our parish community.

4. CONTEMPLATION

The object is to keep this presence of the Lord alive in our hearts. Pilgrims travel with an awareness of where they are going and who is going with them. Share his presence with others where you can, by being someone who is conscious of living in the presence of the Lord. We have moments of insight, but work out our salvation in the 'ordinary', when we come down from the mountain. Choose a text to live with: 'They saw no one with them any more, but only Jesus.' Or 'He was transfigured before them.' Or 'Rabbi, it is good for us to be here.'

Third Passion Prophecy
(Mark 10:32-45)

1. FAMILIARISATION

1.1 Getting to know the text (Mark 10:32-45)

The third prophecy

10:32 They were on the road, going up to Jerusalem,
and Jesus was walking ahead of them;
they were amazed, and those who followed were afraid.
He took the twelve aside again
and began to tell them what was to happen to him,

33 saying: 'See, we are going up to Jerusalem,
and the Son of Man will be handed over
to the chief priests and the scribes,
and they will condemn him to death;
then they will hand him over to the Gentiles;

34 they will mock him, and spit upon him,
and flog him, and kill him;
and after three days he will rise again.'

The ambition of James and John

35 James and John, the sons of Zebedee,
came forward to him and said to him:
'Teacher, we want you to do for us
whatever we ask of you.'

36 And he said to them:
'What is it you want me to do for you?'

37 And they said to him:'Grant us to sit,
one at your right hand and one at your left,
in your glory.'

38 But Jesus said to them:
'You do not know what you are asking.
Are you able to drink the cup that I drink,
or be baptised with the baptism
that I am baptised with?'

39   They replied: 'We are able.'
Then Jesus said to them:
'The cup that I drink, you will drink;
and with the baptism with which I am baptised,
you will be baptised;

40   but to sit at my right hand or at my left
is not mine to grant,
but it is for those for whom it has been prepared.'

The lesson about service

41   When the ten heard this,
they began to be angry with James and John.

42   So Jesus called them and said to them:
'You know that among the Gentiles
those whom they recognise as their rulers
lord it over them,
and their great ones are tyrants over them.

43   But it is not so among you;
but whoever wishes to become great among you
must be your servant,

44   and whoever wishes to be first among you
must be slave of all.

45   For the Son of Man came not to be served,
but to serve,
and to give his life a ransom for many.'

1.2 Background

1.2.1 Setting: There are three major prophecies of the passion; we have looked at the first (Session 14). The second is 9:31, and we have now come to the third one. Each of the three follows the same pattern, the prophecy, followed by some new evidence of misunderstanding by the disciples, which allows for a follow-up teaching by Jesus on the implications of the pathway on which they have set out. After the second the disciples were found arguing about which of them would be the greatest, presumably among Jesus' followers on earth (9:34), so Jesus taught them that whoever wants to be first 'must be last and servant of all' (9:35), and presented to them a child – one with no social standing – as an example to them. Similarly our present passage has three units, the prophecy, 10:32-34, the misunderstanding by some disciples, vv 35-40, and Jesus' teaching about service, vv. 41-45, one of the most important teachings of the gospel. The introduction (v.32) sees Jesus and more than one set of followers on the road to Jerusalem, the first mention of the destination, and Jesus determinedly walking ahead of them on his chosen path. There is a feeling of apprehension among those who followed. The first group were amazed, the second group were afraid. The order seems to be Jesus, the immediate group of disciples including the twelve, who are 'amazed', then a larger group of followers, probably pilgrims favourable to Jesus travelling to Jerusalem for the feast of Passover.

1.2.2 The third passion prophecy: directed only to the twelve, it is given in much more detail than the previous two, while retaining some of the same features. Jerusalem is to be the place of his death, and he is to be 'handed over' to the chief priests and the scribes (no mention of Pharisees). They will condemn him and in turn hand him over to the Gentiles, the Romans, who will 'mock him and spit upon him and flog him and kill him' (all of which happened in Mark's account, chapter 15, but not exactly in that order; the flogging came first, 15:15). There is no mention of crucifixion, but that was known to be the usual Roman penalty for upstart colonials, and was always preceded by flogging to weaken the victim. After all that horror, we almost lose sight of the climax, 'and after three days he will rise again,' and indeed the disciples seem to have done just that. So detailed is the prophecy that many writers think it is 'a prophecy after the event' put on the lips of Jesus. There is no difficulty in admitting that the prophecy as it stands is coloured by the events, but neither is there difficulty in accepting that Jesus was going deliberately to confront the religious authorities in Jerusalem, and was aware that they would try to get rid of him, and the only way they could have him executed was by convincing the Romans that he was a danger to their rule. The mode of execution by the Romans was all too easy to predict. Note that there is no reaction by the disciples to all this dreadful news, but Mark uses the following episode to show that they still did not take in the implications of what Jesus was saying.

1.2.3 The ambition of James and John: Originally it may not have immediately followed the passion prophecy, but even so, the audacity of the request by the sons of Zebedee is striking, especially when placed in its present position. They ask that Jesus will grant whatsoever they request. What is it? That they will sit at Jesus' right and left hands in his glory! Ignoring all the suffering to come first, and the reward promised 'in this age' (10:30), they jump to 'the age to come' and get in their 'we asked first' bid for the top places in the time of glory. Peter has already shown his failure to grasp the first prophecy, now the other two members of the inner circle try to outdo him in refusal to comprehend. Jesus explains that before any question of places beside him in glory, there is the question of following him through his suffering. This suffering he describes metaphorically as 'drinking the cup' and receiving 'a baptism'. The cup is a well known biblical symbol for the cup of the Lord's blessing (Psalm 116:13, 'I will lift up the cup of salvation and call on the name of the Lord'; Pss 16:5, 23:5), but more often the cup of the Lord's anger with sinners (Psalm 75:8, 'For in the hand of the Lord there is a cup with foaming wine, well mixed; ...and all the wicked of the earth shall drain it down to the dregs'; cf Jeremiah 25:15-29); and in Isaiah 51:17-23 it is an image for the suffering of God's people. The primary meaning of 'baptism' is immersion; so John the Baptist says of the coming one: 'He will baptise you with the Holy Spirit', which means 'plunge you into Holy Spirit'. The cup and baptism are used here as graphic images for Jesus' suffering and death. Are James and John able to share in those? Nothing daunted, they say yes, with startling incomprehension, we feel, of what lies ahead. Even Jesus will beg the Father to 'remove this cup' from him (14:36). But Jesus, I think with compassion, says that indeed they will share in his cup and his baptism. Even so, places at his right or left in glory he cannot offer them; that offer is 'for those for whom it has been prepared', ie for whom God has prepared it.

1.2.4 Teaching about service (vv 41-45): Here we are at the heart of the gospel, at the core of the 'mystery of the kingdom of God,' which Jesus promised to reveal to the disciples (4:11). 'The ten', who must include Peter, are angry with James and John. So Jesus calls them together and uses the analogy of Gentile rulers (it would be difficult for them not to think about Roman emperors or governors in the provinces, though they may have thought the Herod family were not really Jews) who lord it over their people and will not tolerate any slight on their dignity. It must not be so among the followers of Jesus. 'Whoever wishes to become great among you must be your servant (*diakonos*), and whoever wishes to be first among you must be the slave (*doulos*) of all' (vv 43-44). *Diakonos* eventually became a recognised 'order' (deacon) in the church, but this is not intended here. The root meaning is one who serves at table, and then one who serves others unselfishly. *Doulos* may sometimes be used as a synonym for 'servant', but Jesus probably wishes to give it its full impact as 'slave'. A slave works for one master, but the follower of Jesus has to be the slave of everyone, to whom no payment is due. Service done for the sake of the kingdom and for God's people is the true mark of greatness. Jesus leads by example: 'For the Son of Man came not to be served but to serve (the verb *diakonein*), and to give his life a ransom for many.'

1.2.5 '*A ransom for many*,' *v 45:* This is the most profound statement of the reason for Jesus' suffering and death, but it is not without controversy. Commentators are divided as to whether these are words of Jesus or represent developed theology of the early church, and whether they refer to Isaiah 52:13-53:12, the last and greatest of the Songs of the Suffering Servant. I cannot here go into all the intricacies, and refer you for more detail to the commentaries, especially those of Michael Mullins and J. R. Donahue/D. J. Harrington, (see bibliography). Matthew (20:28) follows Mark, but Luke in the parallel passage (though in a different setting) has only 'I am among you as one who serves' (22:27), and many think that Luke is likely to be closer to the original words of Jesus. The word 'ransom' (Greek *lutron*) is not used anywhere else in the gospels except by Mark and Matthew at this place, though similar language is used frequently by St Paul, and a very similar phrase in 1 Timothy 2:6: 'Christ Jesus, who gave himself a ransom (*antilutron*) for all.' In secular usage *lutron* was a payment to secure the release of a captive or slave; in the Old Testament (LXX) *lutron* is used for the 'redemption' of a life, eg of the first born male, and the verb *lutroô* is used metaphorically for God's redemption of his people. The word 'redemption' is derived from the Latin *redimere* (*re* and *emere*, to buy again) and literally means 'buying back', but in biblical usage about redemption of people by God there is no exchange of payment: God does all that is necessary to set his people free, receives back his people who belong to him. Jesus restores the people to their proper relationship with God, and there is no question of a payment (eg his blood, life) made to anyone, not to God, and certainly not to Satan. Jesus freely gives his life to redeem 'many', the biblical way of saying everyone. This is his biggest service offered for his people. He lays down his life voluntarily, as the only way to complete his God-given mission in the face of rejection and opposition, and as the way which makes God's love for his people most visible. At the Last Supper the idea is repeated: 'This is my blood of the covenant, which is poured out for many' (14:24). The background to that thinking was in the air: in the books of Maccabees the deaths of martyrs are seen as atoning for the sins of Israel. The apocryphal 4 Maccabees 17:20-22 says of the martyrs: 'These then who have been consecrated for the sake of God are honoured ... and the homeland purified, they having become as it were a ransom for the sin of our nation. And through the blood of these devout ones and their death as an atoning sacrifice divine providence preserved Israel that previously had been mistreated.' But pretty certainly the immediate background was the Servant Songs of Second Isaiah, especially the great Song, 52:13-53:12, which should be read in full. I can only quote some verses, eg 53:10-12, 'Yet it was the will of the Lord to crush him with pain. When you make his life an offering for sin, he shall see his offspring, and shall prolong his days. Through him the will of the Lord shall prosper ... The righteous one, my servant, shall make many righteous, and he shall bear their iniquities.' The verbal echoes linking Mark 10:45 with the servant of Isaiah are not exact, and the translation of parts of the Song is uncertain, with the Greek version sometimes at variance with the Hebrew, but there is no doubt that Isaiah 53 is clearly about a servant of God who voluntarily gives up his life 'for many', ie on their behalf, not instead of them, that they may find forgiveness of sins. This idea is embedded in the whole Gospel right from the baptism of Jesus, and it is typical of Mark to hint at it gradually and then reveal it in one swoop. Jesus acting the way he did, and speaking as he did, and knowing his scriptures, would have been less wise and radical than we think he was, not to have reflected deeply on the Servant Songs, and seen therein the divine plan, 'it is written', for his mission. So I agree totally with R. T. France (Commentary p 420f): 'It would be hard to construct a more adequate short summary … than the clause 'to give his life a ransom for many' (France quotes the Greek text), quite apart from the obvious verbal echoes (with Isaiah 53). It is as if Jesus said: 'The Son of Man came to fulfil the task of the *'ebed* Yahweh (the servant of God).' Similarly, Donahue/Harrington (Commentary p 315): 'Rather than being a foreign body attached to the end of Mark 10:41-45, the 'ransom' saying provides the key to the whole passage and to Mark's gospel as a whole.'

2. REFLECTION

2.1 Mystery

'The mystery of the kingdom of God' (4:11) is now much clarified for the disciples and for us, if they or we are able to make it part of our thinking. It is vital to understand the close connection between the mystery of the kingdom and the mystery of the identity and mission of Jesus. It is through the mission of Jesus, which includes his self-giving service, that the kingdom is established, begins to grow on earth, will find its powerful impetus in his death and resurrection, and finally come to its fulfilment in the age to come. Jesus has come to be what he asks his disciples to be, servant (*diakonos*), even slave (*doulos*, one totally under the power of others), at the service of 'many' (everyone). The kingdom comes by the power of God, but the power of God working through Jesus, at terrible cost to him. The kingdom of God must overcome the power of Satan and all its outreach into the lives of human beings, which makes them hard of heart, unreceptive to God's initiative, and mysteriously it can only be done not by using human methods of overcoming opposition (thinking in the human way), but by surrendering to the opposition, accepting its worst, absorbing it with forgiveness and compassion (thinking in God's way). And if satanic power and the cruelty of human power cannot thwart God's plan by doing their worst, but actually accomplish it, then God's plans come to brilliant fruition. Jesus by not fearing death and accepting it overcomes it; God's power raises him to new and indestructible life.

'Failure' becomes the new success, because it is only failure in human thinking; in God's thinking it is success, because it uses only the 'weapons' of love and self-sacrifice. Therefore if the kingdom is to begin to grow on earth, there must be formed, in the strength of this new way of thinking, a community of those who serve in humility and love, who are willing to be last and not first, who accept the role of serving others and helping them to live in Jesus' way.

2.2 *Christology*

We have new names for Jesus then. He has been reluctant to accept titles like Messiah until the meaning that God gives to the title is understood, the Servant Messiah who will accomplish his mission by service and sacrifice, so becoming a 'ransom for many'. There are all kinds of good ways to serve, but the greatest service is to give your life in the service of others for the sake of the kingdom of God. This is what will bring him to glory with God. By giving his suffering the religious symbolism of 'the cup' and 'a baptism' he gives it positive meaning. The cup of God's wrath for sinners becomes the cup of God's saving compassion for sinners, a real cup of blessing. Whether or not Mark intended to link this scene with the Last Supper, it seems difficult not to think of the 'cup words' of 14:24, 'This is my blood of the covenant, which is poured out for many.' Compare the christological hymn in Philippians 2:6-11.

2.3 *Discipleship*

We can probably say that Mark's continued emphasis on the incomprehension of the disciples, who never seem to learn, allowed him to repeat and deepen the teaching of Jesus, not least for the benefit of the members of his persecuted church, hoping that they would come to understand their call to share in the way of Jesus. The way of service to the point of death is easier to expound than to live, even for us who have the benefit of hindsight and years of celebration of the passion, death and resurrection of Jesus. Probably without the fruits of that death and resurrection, the coming of the Spirit, our poor attempts would be even feebler. So we need not be too hard on James and John, or the ten, for they have not got that experience yet. And yet the very length of our experience and our familiarity with the concepts perhaps cause us to lose the impact of the words of Jesus, and prompt us to compromise. We need to use our time of prayer to rediscover the force and the implications of his words. Don't we get the impression that Mark's emphasis on the incomprehension of the disciples was written for our times, and for the church in our times, when in spite of the call of John Paul II at the turn of the century to put out into deep water (Luke 5:4), so often we are satisfied to paddle in the shallows of Jesus' words without plunging into the deep, allowing them to influence hardly at all our desire for status and power and the approval of our peers? Imitating Jesus' example of service and humility 'reminds believers of their Lord, enabling unbelievers too to glimpse Christ himself as the central meaning of the church's life and faith' (Fr Rodney Schofield in *The Pastoral Review*, March/April 2011, p 46).

2.4 Conversion

This is where we return to Jesus' words to Peter after the first prophecy of the passion: 'The way you think is not God's way but the human way' (8:33). The disciples have not made much progress since then, except that now I think they accept that Jesus is going to die in Jerusalem at the end of this journey, and at some time in the future that they cannot really grasp he will appear in glory. They are going with him to Jerusalem, however reluctantly, and perhaps they hope that God will save Jesus from suffering and then allow the disciples to share in the glory to come. James and John say they are able to face the cup and the baptism that Jesus will accept, but their eyes are still on the glory. All too soon they will be put to the test. We pray not to be put to the test ('Lead us not into temptation'), but we face the daily call to be faithful to the way of service in our relationships with our families and our community.

3. RESPONSE

Make your personal response by rereading the text, pausing to pray with any verse or phrase that strikes you.

Jesus was walking ahead of them ... and those who followed were afraid. Jesus goes ahead of us in all situations which cause us pain or frighten us. We give thanks to him who came to share the harsh reality of our lives, and ask his help to face our problems with courage, knowing he is with us. Do not worry that you are human and feel afraid sometimes. He also showed trepidation before his suffering in the garden of Gethsemane. Only machines are never afraid. Ask him for courage to face our fears and do what we have to do.

The Son of Man will be handed over (lit. given over) to the chief priests and the scribes ...and they will hand him over to the Gentiles (v 33) ... The Son of Man came ... to give his life as a ransom for many (v 45). Lord Jesus, you are to be handed over, powerless in the hands of others. You do so freely for us. Lord, your free loving choice gives meaning to your sufferings. This is the 'must' of your mission, and the part that is pleasing to God. We wish to stand with you in this being given over, learning from your acceptance, because we hate to feel powerless. We praise and thank you for the love which makes so great a difference. We ask for the grace to be able to do hard things with love.

They will mock him, and spit upon him, and flog him, and kill him. Our hearts say, if he has to die, let him die with dignity. How could they do this to him? All that is worst in the human condition seems to surface when a helpless victim is placed in the hands of those who feel superior. It is happening today at the hands of dictators, at the hands of our great democracies (though they do not condone it, they say), torture and humiliation. It happens in child abuse, the abuse of power over the helpless. 'Whatever you do to one of these, you do to me.' Jesus will die, willingly, lovingly, for those who humiliate him and torture him. Our compassion for him perhaps does not need to be put into words, but to be felt – to be felt in such a way that it nourishes our compassion for all who suffer, those whose feeling of worth is taken from them. Can we go the further step as he does, compassion also for the perpetrators of torture and abuse? Pray for those who suffer, that they may find their true selves again in Jesus, and the power of his death and resurrection. Pray for the perpetrators if you are able.

Teacher, we want you to do for us whatever we ask of you! Seen like that, we understand manipulative prayer, selfish prayer, 'my will be done, not yours' prayer. It is more difficult to imitate Jesus in Gethsemane: 'Not what I want, but what you want' (14:36). Is there anything you need to say to Jesus about your own prayer, selfish or unselfish; about how you feel when your prayers are not answered as you would like? What do you feel are your real needs that you should pray for at this time?

Are you able to drink the cup that I drink, or be baptised with the baptism that I am baptised with? Lord, you allow us to partake of your cup in the Eucharist, 'my blood of the covenant, which is poured out for many' (14:24). We unite all that we are suffering and all that frightens us to your offering of yourself; through you, may it become fruitful rather than just destructive. Make it a cup of blessing. Lord, thank you for drinking the cup for us; help those who are drinking their cup now, and help us to drink our cup when the time comes.

Whoever wishes to become great among you must be your servant, and whoever wishes to be first among you must be the slave of all. Of course I don't want to be first, but I sure hope I'm ahead of Mr X or Ms Y. It is hard to avoid comparisons, and treat everyone as a sister or brother. Lord, help us to understand that you are not against leadership, and that you certainly want us to use the gifts God has given us. But we pray that we will use God's gifts as Jesus would have us, not bullying but inviting, not domineering over anyone, but in unselfish service. When someone or some situation needs us, we pray to respond to it with patience and good humour. We pray for those in leadership roles in the Church: it is not an easy place to be, and those in leadership have inherited, along with their gifts and charisms, structures and modes of behaviour which are very difficult to break out of. We pray for the spirit of John XXIII, the opening of windows, the willingness to take some risks, reaching out in love, putting forth into the deep water.

4. CONTEMPLATION

There is much to hold in our minds and hearts and think about quietly. Firstly, there is the tremendous goodness of Jesus, the distance he is prepared to go for us in love. Then there is the human weakness of the disciples, our own human weakness. But we also know the heroism that the disciples were able to show later on, and the great goodness that Jesus is able to foster in human weakness. So we are realistic but hopeful. In him we can do all things. Choose a text to keep in your thoughts as you go about your daily routines. 'The Son of Man has come not to be served but to serve, and to give his life a ransom for many'.

Entry into Jerusalem (Mark 11:1-11)

1. FAMILIARISATION

1.1 Getting to know the text (Mark 11:1-11)

Preparations

11:1   When they were approaching Jerusalem,
at Bethphage and Bethany, near the Mount of Olives,
he sent two of his disciples

2   and said to them,
'Go into the village ahead of you,
and immediately as you enter it,
you will find there a colt that has never been ridden;
untie it and bring it.

3   If anyone says to you: "Why are you doing this?'
just say this: 'The Lord needs it
and will send it back here immediately.'"

4   They went away and found a colt
tied near a door, outside in the street.
As they were untying it,

5   some of the bystanders said to them,
'What are you doing, untying the colt?'

6   They told them what Jesus had said;
and they allowed them to take it.

Messianic procession

7   Then they brought the colt to Jesus
and threw their cloaks on it;
and he sat on it.

8   Many people spread their cloaks on the road,
and others spread leafy branches
that they had cut in the fields.

9   Then those who went ahead
and those who followed were shouting, 'Hosanna!
Blessed is the one who comes in the name of the Lord!

10   Blessed is the coming kingdom of our ancestor David!
Hosanna in the highest heaven!'

Jesus contemplates the temple

11   Then he entered Jerusalem
         and went into the temple;
         and when he had looked around at everything,
         as it was already late,
         he went out to Bethany with the twelve.

1.2 Background

1.2.1 *Approaching:* It is a stiff day's walk, uphill, from Jericho to Jerusalem. When you approach the top of the ridge there are villages and then the Mount of Olives, and just over the summit you see Jerusalem spread before you on the opposite side of the Kidron valley. The Mount of Olives may be mentioned because of its association in the prophet Zechariah with 'the day of the Lord' and the coming of the kingdom. 'See, a day is coming for the Lord ... on that day his feet shall stand on the Mount of Olives, which lies before Jerusalem on the east ... and the Lord will become king over all the earth' (Zech 14:1-9). Pilgrims crossed the valley and went up through the walls by the east-facing Golden Gate into the temple. Jesus will make the village of Bethany, just to the east of the summit, his 'camping site' in the time leading up to the feast of Passover. Over the hill to-wards the foot of the valley of the Kidron is the Garden of Gethsemane where he will spend his last night of liberty.

1.2.2 *Plans for a special entry:* We soon realise that Jesus has plans for his entry into the city. It is difficult to know whether Mark wants us to think of Jesus having prophetic vision in the commands he gives to his disciples about finding a tethered donkey, or that there is a prearranged plan. Mark treats this as Jesus' first visit to Jerusalem, but we know that Jewish males were expected to visit Jerusalem for the Pilgrim feasts every year, and we know from St John that Jesus had contacts in Bethany, and presumably in the city also. So he sends two disci-ples to a nearby village to bring him a (donkey) foal, which they are able to take away using what looks like a prearranged 'pass-word', 'The Lord has need of it.' Lord (*kurios*) was soon to be-come Christian usage for Jesus, but we cannot with certainty say that 'The Lord' refers to Jesus, though that is how the NRSV translation takes it – Jesus needs it and will send it back again.

But Mark could intend to say, 'God has need of it,' meaning the foal which has never been ridden before is required for religious purposes, 'and he (the owner) will immediately send it here' (some manuscripts have 'again', omitted by NRSV). The Bible often requires for religious purposes animals that have not been yoked or ridden (see Numbers 19:2, Deut 21:3). The donkey has no riding cloth, and the two disciples spread their own cloaks on its back so that Jesus could ride into the city. People became enthusiastic and spread their cloaks on the road as a sort of red carpet, and others cut branches or undergrowth from the fields around and spread them in his path. Mark has no mention of palms, and the branches are not waved by hand. So Jesus is escorted into the city with some (modest) solemnity and a crowd chanting religious greetings.

1.2.3 What is the meaning of this procession? It is obvious from the detail of Mark's description of what happened that Jesus intended to make a public statement about his mission. Coming to Jerusalem knowing the likelihood of being arrested, he could have walked quietly into the city among the other pilgrims without being noticed. But he intended to be noticed. What we have is a kind of 'parable in action', which amounts to a claim to be the Messiah, without any specific words of interpretation from Jesus. Though Mark does not explicitly quote the prophet Zechariah 9:9 (as Matthew does), Jesus seems to be re-enacting that prediction: 'Rejoice greatly, O daughter Zion! Shout aloud, O daughter Jerusalem! Lo, your king comes to you, triumphant and victorious he is, humble and riding on a donkey, on a colt, the foal of a donkey.' The crowd seem to see the riding on the new colt as fulfilling Zechariah, and they begin to chant with enthusiasm, partially quoting Psalm 118:25-26, and adding their own paraphrase (vv 9-10). This was one of the Pilgrimage Psalms that were chanted by pilgrims coming to visit the temple, and the words, 'Blessed is the one who comes in the name of the Lord' were probably used by a priest in the temple welcoming pilgrims as they arrived, with no reference of course to a messianic coming. But the crowd see it as particularly apt to apply to Jesus, the 'Son of David', as he was greeted by Bartimaeus in Jericho (10:47, 48). The greeting is prefaced by the cry of 'Hosanna' which is the Hebrew prayer, 'Save us now,' (the first part of Psalm 118:25, 'Save us we beseech you, O Lord'), but became with usage a cry of joy and blessing. V.10 begins with a paraphrase of 'Blessed is the one who comes ...' referring not to the king but the kingdom; 'Blessed is the coming kingdom of our ancestor (lit. 'father') David!' Jesus does not accept or reject the acclamation, and there is no immediate reaction yet from the Jewish authorities if they heard it. We may infer that the enthusiasm of the crowd had died down before Jesus entered the temple quietly by himself, 'looked around at everything', then left and retired for the night with the Twelve to Bethany.

1.2.4 Palm/Passion Sunday: On Palm Sunday, at the beginning of Holy Week, Catholics bless 'palms' and read the story of the Entry into Jerusalem from Matthew, Mark, or Luke (Years A, B, C respectively). We acclaim Jesus as king and commit ourselves to following him, and in case we too get the wrong idea about his kingship, we later read the passion narrative from the same Gospel. So Jesus is proclaimed as a king through suffering. Though in Mark it is the kingdom that is hailed, not the king, Matthew in the parallel passage has 'Hosanna to the Son of David' (21:9) and Luke has 'Blessed is the king who comes in the name of the Lord' (19:38). Only John mentions palms carried by the crowd (12:13); Mark and Matthew speak of branches spread on the road, and Luke does not mention them at all.

2. REFLECTION

2.1 Mystery

At this stage of the gospel the mystery of the kingdom begins to be publicly revealed, but slowly and enigmatically, as so often in Mark. The crowd, a mixture of Jesus' disciples and pilgrims from Galilee and Jericho (including Bartimaeus who hailed Jesus as 'Son of David' and 'followed him on the way' 10:52), acclaim Jesus with the pilgrim greeting: 'Blessed is he who comes in the name of the Lord,' and add to it: 'Blessed is the coming kingdom of our ancestor David.' In Mark, when there is no reaction of acceptance or rejection by Jesus, it usually means that there is some truth in the acclamation, but that it is not the full truth. The crowd's, even the disciples' hopes of what the coming kingdom will be like are going to be disappointed. It will not be the nationalist political kingdom of David, but the kingdom of a suffering Messiah, who will be seen to be powerless against his opponents. Yet Jesus has deliberately staged this entry into Jerusalem, heavy with symbolism, to make a statement about his messiahship, which will not go unnoticed by the Jewish authorities or by the Romans, who make no fine distinctions between kingship with a political meaning and kingship with a religious meaning. We bow in faith before the mystery of the kingdom which comes in the very suffering and apparent defeat of the one who claims to be Messiah.

2.2 Christology

Jesus for the first time openly puts forward his claim to be Messiah, even if the crowd's enthusiastic response is not in line with his intended meaning. He approaches 'humble and riding on a donkey' (Zech 9:9), a 'parable in action' revealing God's plans for his peaceful Messiah who will not use any other than peaceful means to counter opposition, even when the opposition becomes deadly. The words of Psalm 118:26 were not at the time messianic, but used to greet a pilgrim coming to Jerusalem; the crowd thought them particularly appropriate for Jesus' coming, and there is little doubt that Mark thought the same. In other words Mark has given them a meaning loaded with later Christian understanding of the importance of Jesus' visit to Jerusalem, and the profound significance of the mission entrusted to Jesus by the Father. So those words have become a Christian prayer, part of the Sanctus in the Eucharist: 'Blessed is he who comes in the name of the Lord. Hosanna in the highest.' In Latin, they have become well known through Karl Jenkins' Benedictus. Jesus is always with us as the One who comes in the name of the Father, the Beloved Son who brings us the blessings of the kingdom of God, the One through whom we are invited to give praise to God our Father.

2.3 Discipleship

The disciples with the crowd who acclaim Jesus are almost entirely Galileans, few if any belonging to Jerusalem. So once and for all forget the old easy verdict on fickle humanity, that the crowd who saluted Jesus on his entry to the city cried for his blood a few days later. The crowd, who cried 'Crucify him' before Pilate, belonged to a different group, probably all from Judah and Jerusalem, and their primary concern, as we will see, was to get Barabbas released. The disciples and the crowd who welcomed Jesus to Jerusalem were sincere in their acclamation, though later shocked at his fate and at their own human weakness in time of crisis. That gives us our entry as disciples, sincerely praising Jesus, welcoming him as our king, conscious always of our human weakness and praying for the strength to resist the temptation to abandon our faith in times of crisis.

2.4 Conversion

The whole episode makes us conscious of the need to celebrate faith with others, conscious of frailty, and of forgiveness. We make a positive choice to commit ourselves again, as we do on Palm Sunday, to the faithful following of Jesus, the king and servant of God, Son of David, Son of Man, Son of God. At the same time we make a realistic assessment of our human weakness, and resolve to pray for God's help in times of crisis. We also know our need for help if we are to imitate Jesus' willingness to serve.

3. RESPONSE

To make a personal response, reread the text pausing to pray with any verse or phrase that strikes you.

You will find tied there a colt that has never been ridden; untie it and bring it. Imagine yourself walking beside the donkey on which Jesus is riding towards the city. What is in your mind? What is in your heart? Speak to him. Tell him what a privilege you find it to be a disciple at this time. Commit yourself to continuing and perhaps growing as a disciple. Know that he understands our will to serve and the weaknesses that often get in the way of it.

Humble and riding on a donkey. Respond to the text of Zechariah 9:9, which Mark does not quote but which is dramatised in the episode. 'Rejoice greatly, O daughter Zion! Shout aloud, O daughter Jerusalem! Lo, your king comes to you, triumphant and victorious he is, humble and riding on a donkey, on a colt, the foal of a donkey.' He is 'humble and riding on a donkey', not like riding in a winner at the Curragh or Cheltenham! Dignity, no pomposity, no triumphalism. Pray for the gifts we need in the church today: leadership, strength of purpose, courage, but with humility and a willingness to serve.

Hosanna. Blessed is the one who comes in the name of the Lord. Welcome Jesus, the one who comes from the Father, sent out of love, but also the one to be 'handed over' before many days are out. Pray in gratitude to Jesus and to God our Father for this beginning of the week of salvation. Blessed are we that he comes. 'God so loved the world that he gave his only Son ...' (John 3:16). Lord, our feelings are a mixture of joy at your coming, and sorrow at what you have foretold about your treatment in Jerusalem. We are glad that your identity begins to be publicly recognised, but know the danger that comes with it. We admire your courage in facing the danger with faith in your Father's plan and in his care. Help us to renew our trust that, no matter what we have to face, God's support will always sustain us.

Blessed is the coming kingdom of our ancestor David! Lord, it is for our good that the kingdom comes, for it is the fulfilment of God's loving plan for his people, and we pray that the kingdom may come and may grow, like the seed in good soil. We know that it's coming is going to be a costly victory, and we thank you for loving your people enough to shoulder all burdens for us. Help us, as workers for the kingdom, to be willing to go the extra mile, and to complain less about the burdens we carry. Bless those who carry very real burdens of sickness or pain or bereavement, who carry hurts inflicted by those who should have cared for them, and bless all who go on year after year patiently caring for those who are dependent on them. Help them to know that whatever they do for those in need they do for you.

4. CONTEMPLATION

Bring with you, perhaps, the sense of celebration in the midst of sadness. Though Jesus is on his way to suffering and death, there is still a place to celebrate all that is truly blessed in his coming and his passion, death and resurrection. No matter how much we have to bear at times in our lives, the knowledge of his presence and his saving death and new life give us hope and help us to say 'Hosanna in the highest.' Carry with you the words, 'Blessed is he who comes in the name of the Lord.'

Cleansing the Temple
(Mark 11:15-19, 27-33)

1. FAMILIARISATION

1.1 Getting to know the text (Mark 11:15-19, 27-33)

Cleansing the temple

11:15   Then they came to Jerusalem.
         And he entered the temple
         and began to drive out those who were selling
         and those who were buying in the temple,
         and he overturned the tables of the money-changers
         and the seats of those who sold doves;

16   and he would not allow anyone
         to carry anything through the temple.

17   He was teaching and saying: 'Is it not written,
         "My house shall be called a house of prayer
         for all the nations"?
         But you have made it a den of robbers.'

The authorities bide their time

18   And when the chief priests and the scribes heard it,
         they kept looking for a way to kill him;
         for they were afraid of him, because the whole crowd
         was spellbound by his teaching.

19   And when evening came,
         Jesus and his disciples went out of the city.

The leaders confront Jesus

27   Again they came to Jerusalem.
         As he was walking in the temple,
         the chief priests, the scribes, and the elders came to him

28   and said: 'By what authority
         are you doing these things?
         Who gave you this authority to do them?'

29   Jesus said to them, 'I will ask you one question;
         answer me, and I will tell you
         by what authority I do these things.

30   Did the baptism of John come from heaven,
        or was it of human origin? Answer me.'

31   They argued with one another:
        'If we say: 'From heaven,' he will say:
        'Why then did you not believe him?'

32   But shall we say: 'Of human origin' –
        they were afraid of the crowd,
        for all regarded John as truly a prophet.

33   So they answered Jesus: 'We do not know.'
        And Jesus said to them: 'Neither will I tell you
        by what authority I am doing these things.'

1.2 Background

1.2.1 The chosen text: Apologies for taking liberties with the text by omitting the story of the fig tree (11:12-14, 20-25), in which Mark has 'sandwiched' the cleansing of the temple. It is a difficult story to interpret, and Mark obviously thinks it sheds light on the temple incident. I want to include the Jewish leaders' challenge to Jesus after the temple-cleansing.

1.2.2 A word on the fig tree: On the way back from Bethany to Jerusalem, Jesus looks for fruit on a fig tree (out of season), and curses it when he finds none. When they pass it on the following morning they find it withered, and Jesus draws a lesson for the disciples on faith. Most commentators interpret it as a parabolic action; the fig tree with no fruit is a symbol of the Jewish authorities (some include the temple itself), who do not produce fruit as God expects from their stewardship, and whose tenure is therefore coming to an end.

1.2.3 The temple: the temple area enclosed by Herod the Great in his refurbishment of the temple is huge, and the site of the Holy of Holies and the Holy Place is now occupied by the Muslim shrine, the Dome of the Rock. The Holy of Holies could only be entered by the High Priest on the Day of Atonement, the Holy Place by the priests who carried out the sacred rites and sacrifices. Jesus himself had no access to them, not being of the priestly families. They were surrounded by a number of courts, the Court of the Jews (open to males), the Court of the Women, and the very much larger Court of the Gentiles (who under pain of death could not enter any of the inner courts). Everything in this episode happens in this Court of the Gentiles. To accommodate pilgrims and worshippers, money-changing and arrangements for buying and selling the necessities for sacrifice and offerings took place here. Money which had engravings of kings and rulers or graven images was not acceptable in the temple, so pilgrims had to change their 'foreign' money into Jewish money to pay for their sacrifices, to pay the temple tax (the half-shekel), or to make offerings to the treasury. The selling and buying (v 15) was about animals for sacrifice. Mark only mentions doves (v 15) for sale in the actual Court of the Gentiles (the offering of the poor). Only John 2:14 mentions cattle and sheep in the temple area.

1.2.4 The cleansing: Jesus acts on his own, and we can only admire his moral authority in single-handedly driving out the buyers and sellers, overturning the tables of the money-changers and the seats of the dove-sellers, over a very large area. Only Mark adds that he refused to allow anyone to carry things through the sacred area (forbidden by Jewish tradition). The question is, does he object to the doing of these things at all, or to the doing of them in the wrong place? We do not really have any evidence to go beyond the latter, that they showed great disrespect for the sacredness of the temple. This then becomes an indictment of the manner in which the temple affairs are being conducted, and so a direct challenge to the temple authorities, in particular to the priestly families who controlled the sacrifices.

1.2.5 Scriptural interpretation: Jesus in Mark (similarly in Mathew and Luke) justifies his action by two Old Testament quotations, Isaiah 56:7 and Jeremiah 7:11. Isaiah 56 (Third Isaiah, post exilic) speaks of bringing foreigners who worship God and keep his covenant into their due place in the temple worship: 'for my house shall be called a house of prayer for all peoples.' Only Mark includes the words, 'for all the nations', conscious of the gentile converts in his community. Gentiles had only this outer court in which to pray if they wished. The second quotation comes from a famous sermon of Jeremiah in the temple, in which he accused his listeners of having a false sense of security that the temple would always keep them safe – safe to continue in their sins. Those who ignored God's covenant and expected the temple to keep them safe were acting like bandits, who commit crimes and retire to a safe haven. They should not believe that the temple would always protect them. Jesus seems to be focusing on the disrespect of the temple, rather than an accusation that the sellers and money-changers were cheating their customers, and there is no hint that the temple would be destroyed until chapter 13 (See Session 19). The authorities reject his right to act like this, but it seems that his message was approved by many: 'the whole crowd was spellbound by his teaching' (v 18). Reforms in biblical times always included reform of the temple, under Hezekiah, Josiah and the Maccabees, and prophets from the exile looked forward to an ideal, reformed temple. Zechariah 14:20-21, speaking of the holiness of the temple and the care that will be given to the sacred rites, finishes with (v 21), 'And there shall no longer be traders in the house of the Lord of hosts on that day.' Malachi 3:4 says, 'Then the offering of Judah and Jerusalem will be pleasing to the Lord as in the days of old ...' So Jesus stands in line with a strong prophetic tradition.

1.2.6 Confrontation with the authorities: Initially (v 18) the chief priests and the scribes bided their time; 'they kept looking for a way to kill him,' but were afraid to act when the crowd were on his side and enthralled by his teaching. By the next day they have decided on their tactics, to discredit Jesus as a teacher and hope that he will say something that will turn the crowd against him and/or provide them with evidence they can use to denounce him to the Roman authorities. There follows a series of examples of this attempt to discredit Jesus: firstly, the challenge by the chief priests, scribes and elders to his authority (11:27-33), then by Pharisees and Herodians, on the question of paying taxes to Caesar (12:13-17); thirdly, a challenge from Sadducees about the resurrection (12:18-27); fourthly, the question from a scribe (who ends up agreeing with Jesus) about which is the most important commandment (12:28-34); finally, Jesus takes the initiative by asking whether 'Son of David' is an adequate title for the Messiah if David himself (the supposed author) calls him 'Lord' in Psalm 110 (12:35-37). In all this Jesus, conscious that they wish him to incriminate himself so that they can arrest him, shows consummate teaching skill and is able to hint at his identity without ever putting it into words that they can use against him. His moment of revelation of his identity will come only after they have arrested him (14:61-62).

1.2.7 'Who gave you this authority?' The challenge (11:27-28) comes from 'the chief priests, the scribes and the elders' (those whom he prophesied would reject him in 8:31). They demand an answer to the questions, 'By what authority are you doing these things? Who gave you this authority to do them?' Jesus asks a prior question before he can give his answer (v.30): 'Did the baptism of John come from heaven, or was it of human origin?' R. T. France notes (Comm. p 454): 'the counterquestion was a recognised move in both Hellenistic and rabbinic debate … and they do not question it.' The questioners had hoped that Jesus would overstep his credibility in the eyes of the people by claiming authority 'from heaven'. Jesus and the crowd were seemingly aware (though Mark has not told his readers so) that the Jerusalem authorities had not accepted that John the Baptist had authority from God ('from heaven'), though the general population had accepted this, and so he placed them in a dilemma. Are they capable of recognising authority from God? They deliberate: if they say no, the crowd will be angry; if they say yes, then their leadership is in question, because they had not recognised John's mission from heaven. Jesus would also be able to say that John pointed to one who was to come after him, the stronger one, who will baptise with the Spirit (1:7-8). So they say, 'We do not know.' Jesus' answer to their initial question is implicit in the answer he (and the crowd) expected to his question, that John's baptism came 'from heaven', but he refuses to put it into words.

2. REFLECTION

2.1 Mystery

There is now a dramatic sense that things are coming to a climax. Jesus is implicitly claiming to stand in line with the prophets of the time of fulfilment, Zechariah, Malachi etc. In the coming kingdom of God worship of God must come from a sincere and purified heart. The initial call to repent and believe in the good news (1:15) becomes urgent. The Messiah has come to his temple as the purifier, and those in leadership who shepherd God's people, who fail to perceive what God is doing, will become like the fruitless fig tree and lose their leadership. There are strong hints that the kingdom will involve Gentiles, admitted to what will become a 'house of prayer for all nations'. 'The kingdom of God is at hand.'

2.2 Christology

By what right does Jesus challenge the High Priest and his supporters over the conduct of affairs in the temple? Jesus' actions have to speak, for he will not yet put it into words. He is resigned to his death, but he will not deliver himself up to the authorities as a martyr, and uses his teaching skills to avoid the traps they set for him, while always dealing in the truth. Some of his most profound teachings come in the confrontations with the different groups: rendering to God what is God's, to Caesar what is Caesar's, the resurrection, the primacy of love. So he asks their opinion of John the Baptist: was his baptism from heaven? If John was sent by God, and John was preparing the way of the Lord, and looking to a greater one, then they would begin to see where Jesus' authority must come from also. Jesus is therefore implicitly claiming to perform these prophetic actions, riding into Jerusalem on the donkey, cleansing the temple, as actions of the one 'who comes in the name of the Lord', by the authority of God.

2.3 Discipleship

The disciples are presumably staying close to Jesus, but their reactions are not commented upon by Mark. They see Jesus' courage and the integrity that refuses to compromise, and knowing all he has foretold, they must be worried about his safety. The admission of Gentiles to the kingdom is hinted at, and we should be grateful. But a big message for all disciples of Jesus is the lesson that sincere and respected religious leaders are able to totally miss the moment of God's grace, while believing that they are doing good and serving the Lord. How often has that been, is that being, repeated in history? There are disciples of Jesus here who are going to let him down because of their weakness, and religious leaders who are going to try to destroy him because of their power. A salutary warning to each of us. But it seems to be better to be weak and know your need for healing and forgiveness, than to be powerful and not be aware of that need. Ah, to be open enough to the Spirit to be aware of what God is asking of us, and to have the courage to do it!

2.4 Conversion

Learning to think in God's way rather than our human way is difficult and ongoing. As we approach the mystery of salvation, we know that we need to have a deeper faith in Jesus than the all too frequent 'human thinking' about him as a good man who teaches us to love one another, who has been overladen with theological doctrines and mystification that is long outdated. Was John's baptism from heaven or from men? A strong temptation today is to dismiss doctrines and teaching that we do not like as 'man-made' and select our own menu which suits us. Conversion is making a serious effort to discover what comes from God, and resolving to do what God is asking of us. Religious leaders are also called to make sure that they truly understand what comes from God and is eternally binding on the human conscience, and what is in fact 'man-made' and may well be dispensed with, despite being 'what we have always done'. And of course all of us are called to make God's house 'a house of prayer' and to make sure that we bring to the worship of God reverence and humility.

3. RESPONSE

For your personal response, reread the text, pausing to pray with any verse or phrase that strikes you.

He entered the temple and began to drive out those who were selling ... We welcome the cleansing Messiah to his temple; 'The Lord whom you are seeking will suddenly come to his temple ... and will purify the sons of Levi ...' (Malachi 3:1,3). We thank God for the fulfilment of his promises; pray for the grace to open our minds and hearts to the need for redemption and purification. Lord, purify and heal your children that we may become your people, remade in the image of Christ. We have been made temples of the Holy Spirit: we pray that we may be more worthy of that sacred presence, that the temple of our bodies may be freed from sin.

My house shall be called a house of prayer ... We pray for reverence in God's house, in his sacred presence. 'To fear the Lord (reverence) is the beginning of wisdom' (Ecclesiasticus 1:14). We ask pardon for any time we have made it difficult for others to pray by our lack of reverence. 'The fear of the Lord delights the heart and gives gladness and joy and long life' (Eccl.1:12).

... for all the nations. We pray that the Lord will gather all the nations to himself, and pray in thanksgiving that we the Gentiles have been grafted on to the people of God. Pray for the missionaries who are trying to bring the good news to those who are hungry for it. Pray for Jesus' own people, the Jews, still God's chosen people, that God's plans for them may be fulfilled, and that they may forgive Christians for centuries of anti-semitism.

The whole crowd was spell bound by his teaching. Reflect on the courage and strength of character that Jesus showed in the temple. He knows there will be repercussions, but speaks the truth without fear. Praise him. Pray for courage in living our Christianity. Is it possible to follow Jesus without respecting his words, listening to them with gladness, studying them and praying about them? Resolve to listen gladly to our great teacher. He is God's Word to us, everything that God wants to say to us. Remember the voice from the cloud: 'This is my Son, the Beloved. Listen to him,' (9:7). Have you ever felt your heart burn within you as you listened to his word (Luke 24:32)?

Who gave you this authority ...? John the Baptist's authority came 'from heaven'; much more so that of Jesus. 'Whoever has seen me has seen the Father' (John 14:9). Jesus, mirror-image of the Father, sent by his love, guide us and lead us so that the reign of God may grow in our hearts, and that we may be so alive with your life that we may witness to the kingdom at work among us.

4. CONTEMPLATION

Continue your prayer in the consciousness of your own weakness made strong by his strength, and ask the Spirit again to give you his gift of awe and wonder in God's presence. 'My house shall be called a house of prayer.' Jesus demanded respect for the temple, because it was the place of the divine presence in their midst. That is exactly what Jesus is; the human dwelling place of the divine, among us, and in us. And therefore in him, we become temples: places where the divine wishes to dwell. 'O Christian, be aware of your nobility' (St Leo the Great).

The Son of Man in Glory
(Mark 13:1-4, 14, 19, 23-33, 37)

1. FAMILIARISATION

1.1 Getting to know the text (Mark 13:1-4, 14, 19, 23-33, 37)

Jesus foretells the destruction of the temple

13:1   As he came out of the temple,
one of his disciples said to him, 'Look, teacher,
what large stones and what large buildings!'

2   Then Jesus asked him,
'Do you see these great buildings?
Not one stone shall be left here upon another;
all will be thrown down.'

3   When he was sitting on the Mount of Olives
opposite the temple,
Peter, James, John and Andrew asked him privately,

4   'Tell us, when will this be,
and what will be the sign
that all these things are about to be accomplished?'

The requested sign: 'about to be accomplished'

14   But when you see the desolating sacrilege
set up where it ought not to be
(let the reader understand),
then those in Judea must flee to the mountains ...

19   For in those days there will be suffering,
such as has not been seen
from the beginning of the creation that God created
until now, no, and never will be ...

23   But be alert; I have already told you everything.

Temple's end, in this generation; new presence of God

24   But in those days, after that suffering,
the sun will be darkened,
and the moon will not give its light,

25   and the stars will be falling from heaven,
and the powers in the heavens will be shaken.

26   Then they will see the 'Son of Man coming in clouds'
      with great power and glory.
27   Then he will send out the angels,
      and gather his elect from the four winds,
      from the ends of the earth to the ends of heaven.
28   From the fig tree learn its lesson:
      as soon as its branch becomes tender
      and puts forth its leaves,
      you know that summer is near.
29   So also, when you see these things taking place,
      you know that it [NRSV 'he'] is near, at the very gates.
30   Truly, I tell you, this generation will not pass away
      until all these things have taken place.
31   Heaven and earth will pass away,
      but my words will not pass away.

The coming in judgement, known only to the Father
32   But about that day or hour no one knows,
      neither the angels in heaven, nor the Son,
      but only the Father.
33   Beware, keep alert; for you do not know
      when the time will come …
37   … And what I say to you, I say to all:
      Keep awake.'

1.2 Background

    1.2.1 Mark's 'Little Apocalypse'? Chapter 13 is too long for us to look at as a whole. It is frequently called Mark's 'Little Apocalypse' (like the Book of Daniel or the Book of Revelation – 'apocalypse' is simple the Greek word for 'revelation'). In a true apocalypse, the writer records a vision given him by God, mostly in fantastic language, then has the vision explained to him by an angel. This kind of writing is used especially in time of suffering or persecution of God's people, to give them hope and reassurance that God has a plan for their good through and beyond the present suffering. Trouble is, this has to be explained to them in language that their oppressors will not understand, so it is full of symbolism, poetic language and imagery. Unfortunately, we are not used to this kind of language, and often misunderstand it, or take it too literally. It turns up in our liturgy, especially around the beginning of Advent. Because chapter 13 speaks of the triumph of the Son of Man, in a gospel with no resurrection appearances, it is worth looking at.

1.2.2 *Is it really an apocalypse?* It shares characteristics with other apocalypses, but much of it is not apocalyptic at all; indeed, often it warns against reading too much into human events or calamities like 'wars and rumours of wars' (13:7). It is really more like a 'farewell discourse', frequent enough in the Old Testament, and seen in Acts 20:18-35, (Paul's farewell to the people of Ephesus) or Jesus' farewell discourse, John 14-17, giving encouragement to his followers to face the trials ahead of them. This perspective is actually more helpful to disciples, both then and now, for it tells us of Jesus' promise that we will never be alone in facing hard decisions and situations. It begins with a prophecy about the destruction of the temple (v 2), and then the four disciples who were the first to be called ask him a double question: when will it happen, and what sign might be looked for to warn of its coming (v 4)? At this point Matthew adds: 'What will be the sign of your coming and of the end of the age' (24:3), but that should not influence our interpretation of Mark. We cannot be really sure of the date of Mark's writing, but I feel that Martin Hengel (*Studies in the Gospel of Mark*, p 22) is right in putting it in 69 AD, ie nearing the end of the Jewish rebellion against the Romans (65-70), but before the siege of Jerusalem and the destruction of the temple. Mark never speaks explicitly of the actual end of the temple or the destruction of Jerusalem. Mark's readers had certainly lived through a time of great upheavals and danger for those living in the Holy Land or in the regions nearby, or even for Jews or Christians living in Rome. During the period between the beginning of the church and the destruction of Jerusalem there were earthquakes, the emperor Caligula insisted on putting a statue of himself in the temple area (rebellion only averted by his assassination in 41 AD), Christians were blamed by Nero for the fire of Rome in 64 AD and subjected to savage persecution; false messiahs arose in Judea and gathered followers, riots and repression occurred frequently – more than enough to cause people to be afraid, to hope that Jesus would return again soon in judgement to end this world and establish the kingdom finally. Mark chapter 13 is an attempt to allay fears and false hopes, to strengthen the people for all the hardships to be endured, and to try to make sense of them without false expectations of an immediate return to earth by Jesus in glory to sort everything out. Once the rebellion started, it was fought with such ferocity by the Jews that the full resources of Rome were sooner or later going to crush and destroy Jerusalem, and people had begun to mix up in their minds the end of the temple, the second coming of Jesus (called in Matthew by the technical word *parousia*; which Mark never uses), and the end of the world. So you will find that in Mark Jesus plays down speculation about the end in 13:5-13 (not quoted above): 'Beware that no one leads you astray...the end is still to come ... the good news must first be proclaimed to all nations.' Only in 13:14-31 does he answer the disciples' questions, fist the sign (vv 14-23), and then the event itself (vv 24-31), but now in difficult apocalyptic language, suggesting that Mark is writing before it happened. Therefore authors differ about the meaning of vv 24-31 (the Greek of v 29b is ambiguous). Only in the last part, vv 32-37 may we with certainty say that Mark is speaking about the last judgement, the 'end of the world'.

1.2.3 The Son of Man in triumph: What we wish to concentrate on for our prayers is the assurance that all the sufferings to come for Jesus and the disciples will end in the triumph of Jesus over suffering, that he will be enthroned as the Son of Man at the right hand of God, be able therefore to strengthen and safeguard his flock in the midst of suffering and persecution, and assure those who face death about the reality of resurrection (13:13). My explanation is more dependent on the commentary of R. T. France than any other; see alternative views in other commentaries listed.

The critical verses for us to examine are 13:24-28, especially v 26, 'Then they will see the Son of Man coming in clouds with great power and glory' an obvious reference to Daniel chapter 7. Mark 13:30 specifies who will see: 'Truly I tell you, this generation will not pass away until all these things have taken place.' The majority opinion among scholars is that this coming of the Son of Man refers to the *parousia*, his final coming in judgement. That leaves us with two awkward problems: (1) 'this generation' certainly did not see the *parousia*; (2) Jesus' words in v. 32 certainly refer to the *parousia*: 'But about that day or hour no one knows, neither the angels in heaven, not the Son, but only the Father.' There are various arguments for getting out of the quandary, none of them convincing, among them the opinion that Jesus himself thought that his second coming would be 'in this generation', and that he was just wrong (why then v 32, 'no one knows, neither the angels ...nor the Son'?). The alternative is to see the coming of the Son of Man in v 26 as a 'coming' to the throne of God in heaven. For the background of the saying is Daniel 7:13-14: 'I saw one like a son of man coming with the clouds of heaven. And he came to the Ancient One (God), and was presented before him. To him was given dominion ...' (see Session 14, 1.2.5). This 'coming' is a coming to God's throne, not to earth; and it refers to enthronement, not to general judgement. The effects of that enthronement 'will be seen' with the end of the temple; Jesus enthroned will take the place of the temple, be from that time on the place of God's dwelling among his people ('the temple not made with hands' 14:58). With the end of the temple, the priestly leadership (Sadducees) will have no function; there will be no more animal sacrifice. So the threat to the leadership of the tenants of the vineyard will be fulfilled (parable of the tenants, 12:1-12). What people feared would be 'the end of the world' will be only 'the end of the world as they know it', the plan of God for Israel fulfilled. Therefore v 27: 'Then he will send out the angels, and gather his elect from the four winds, from the ends of the earth to the ends of heaven,' is not the final gathering of the elect at the *parousia*, but the expected messianic gathering of the scattered children of God, the twelve tribes of Israel, from all the places where they were exiled. The Son of Man extends his gathering of God's people to the whole world, not the final gathering for judgement, but the reconstitution of the Covenant People. Before the *parousia*, 'the good news must first be proclaimed to all nations' (v 10).

1.2.4 The requested sign (13:14-19): Let us now return to look at the selected verses in order. In v 14 Jesus speaks of 'the desolating sacrilege set up where it ought not to be'. This is the sign of the beginning of the terrible things that are to happen. But though it will be a time of terrible suffering, it speaks of some desecration of the temple rather than its destruction, and there is still time to flee. The language used to describe the sacrilege (which will be 'the sign that all these things are about to be accomplished', v 4) is taken from Daniel's description, in cryptic language (Daniel 9:27; 11:31; 12:11), of King Antiochus Epiphanes' desecration of the temple in 167 BC, when he stopped the temple sacrifices and built an altar to Zeus, the chief god of the Greeks, over the altar in the temple. What exactly 'the desolating sacrilege' will be on this occasion we cannot say: Mark suggests his readers will know, '(let the reader understand)', but it set in train the events that led to the siege of Jerusalem and the destruction of the temple and its environs in September 70. The Greek of Mark makes a neuter noun, an 'it', the sacrilege, take a masculine participle, a 'he', standing where 'he' ought not to be, so perhaps it was a male statue (v 14).

1.2.5 The end of the temple and the new presence of God (13:24-31): Verses 24-25 use apocalyptic language which echoes especially Isaiah 13:10 (a graphic depiction of God's anger being unleashed on the world, specifically on Babylon), and Isaiah 34:4 (similar graphic language directed particularly at Edom). The end of these regimes is depicted in cosmic terms, the sun darkened, the moon giving no light, stars falling from heaven, the powers in the heavens (probably the stars) shaken. Many authors say this is language about the end of the world, and interpret verses 26-27 which follow as the final coming of the Son of Man. But the language of Isaiah reflected in Mark 13:24-25 is not about the end of the world, but about the end of the regimes in Babylon and Edom, and the world continues, but reshaped, more in keeping with God's intentions. So what is suggested by these verses in Mark is the end of the Jewish leadership and its sacrificial system, the end of the temple as the place of God's presence, and its replacement with the enthroned Son of Man. Not the end of the world but the new order of things, where the risen Lord is seen to reconstitute the true Israel by calling together his chosen ones from all the nations (see 1.2.3 above). On the assumption that we made above that Mark is writing during the Jewish war but before the fall of Jerusalem his use of biblical cosmic language to describe it is understandable, since he did not know exactly how events would turn out. If we look back to v 3, where Jesus has left the temple and gone to the Mount of Olives to look

back, having foretold the destruction of the temple, we are reminded of the vision of Ezekiel chapters 10 and 11, where the
glory of the Lord leaves the temple, and rests on the Mount of
Olives as it departs, a prelude to the destruction of the temple of
Solomon by the Babylonians. The hidden irony is that Jesus is
the glory of the Lord, leaving the temple and resting on the
Mount of Olives. In v 28 the fig tree is offered as a symbol: when
it begins to bud, it is a sign that summer is near. In v 29 this is allied to 'these things' as the sign of what is to come. But the translation of v 29 is important for interpretation. It is usually translated,
'when you see these things taking place, you know that *he* is
near,' which is taken to be the *parousia*, the final coming of Jesus
in judgement. But the Greek is totally neutral (*hoti eggus estin*): it
may equally be translated, 'you know that IT is near', ie the destruction of the temple which the disciples had asked about in v
4 (see the alternative reading of v 29 offered in NRSV footnote).
And this is of course supported by v 30, which has the solemn
introduction: 'Truly, I tell you, this generation will not pass
away until all these things have taken place.' 'This generation'
will see the fall of Jerusalem, but not the *parousia*. This interpretation is confirmed by Mark 8:38-9:1, and 14:62, the two other
texts about the Son of Man in glory, which also refer to the vision of Daniel 7, and to its effects being 'seen' in this generation.

1.2.6 The final coming in judgement, vv 32-37: 'But about that day
or that hour no one knows …' For the first time Jesus speaks
about the singular 'that day or that hour'. Up to this he has spoken of 'in those days' (vv 19, 24), referring to the times of suffering
and the sign that was requested about the destruction of the temple, all of which will happen in 'this generation'. But nobody
knows about 'that day or that hour', not the angels and not even
the Son, but only the Father. So now we are speaking of the *parousia*, the end time, the last day, when the Son will return in judgement. But it cannot be predicted; the only thing we can do is to
stay awake and be ready. It will be totally the Father's decision,
and the human Jesus acknowledges his ignorance of the time. He
exhorts all his followers to stand in readiness. And again Jesus
widens out to a larger audience than the four disciples who questioned him in vv 3-4, for all generations will be involved in the
task of being prepared and ready for the final coming. 'And what

I say to you I say to all: Keep awake' (v.37).

1.2.7 Secondary causes: remember that the biblical language attributes everything to God's causality and tends to ignore secondary causes. Therefore tone down your picture of a wrathful God destroying his own people, or any image of Jesus enjoying the prospect of the holiest place in Israel being destroyed. Secondary causes are at work here. The evangelists believe that in rejecting Jesus and, as we will see later, choosing Barabbas, whom Mark will describe as 'in prison with the rebels who had committed murder during the insurrection' (15:7), the Jewish leadership would in effect be choosing the way of rebellion against Rome, and thus inevitably setting their course for the destruction of the temple and the loss of their own leadership of the people. God's permissive will allows his people to make their own choices. His 'wrath' is our human way of conveying the great rift that grows between God and his people because of their wrong choices, and the consequences of those choices. Repentance always bridges that rift. Remember that all the first Christians were Jews, and in Acts 6:7 we read that even 'a great many of the priests became obedient to the faith.'

2. REFLECTION

2.1 Mystery

God's plans mysteriously come to fruition even as they appear to be frustrated by human choices. We have come to the end of Jesus' preaching mission in the temple, and from now on dramatic events will rapidly lead to his humiliating death. But there is no mention of that death in this chapter, only about the vindication of Jesus by the Father and the completion of the Father's plans for his kingdom. Jesus has failed to win over the Jewish leadership and leaves the temple for the last time. In predicting the end of the temple he is also predicting the end of the Jewish cultic worship of God (not the worship of their hearts), and with it the end of the Jewish leadership of his chief opponents, the chief priests. This will be a 'world-shattering' experience for the Jewish people, and will lead to the setting up of a newly constituted people of God, the twelve tribes extending to all nations. The power of the Son of Man in glory will be at work among his people unifying them and enabling them to carry on the mission to the whole world, until an unknown day when he will come again in judgement.

2.2 Christology

Jesus is confident that the Father will vindicate him and raise him up. The main emphasis, if the explanation given in the background notes is correct, is on the enthronement of Jesus before the throne of God in heaven, in fulfilment of the vision of Daniel 7, an enthronement in heaven, which will influence events on earth. The Son of Man in glory will be an inspiration and hope for his people on earth who like himself will have to face opposition, and know that they will only be able to use his 'weapons' of witness to the truth, love and endurance. When the temple is gone, the risen Lord will be the new presence of the living God among his people. Others like Paul and John will work out the theology of how Jesus in glory will be present to his people, but Mark as usual proclaims the reality without explanation. Some of Paul's letters may already be known to Mark's readers, and they will learn like him to treasure the inner life 'in Christ' and the presence of the Holy Spirit. The latter is hinted at by Mark in 13:11 (not quoted in our text): 'When they bring you to trial and hand you over, do not worry beforehand about what you are to say; but say whatever is given you at that time, for it is not you who speak, but the Holy Spirit.' In this way the emphasis given by Mark to the idea of the enthronement of Jesus 'being seen' by this generation will be fulfilled; people will experience the presence of the living God in Jesus risen from the dead. With reference to the coming of the Messiah in judgement on the 'day of the Lord', Mark emphasises the reality of Jesus' humanity: the Son does not know when that will take place, but only the Father.

2.3 Discipleship

In one sense Jesus has no comfort for his disciples even in this farewell address: there will be many hardships to come, suffering and betrayal, imprisonment and even death. False leaders will arise, either claiming to be messiah or claiming to have been sent by the messiah, and many will be lead astray. Jesus has forewarned them already that those who wish to be his disciples will have to take up the cross and follow him, and he warns them again: 'Be alert; I have already told you everything' (v 23). On the other hand what he tells them is most encouraging and supportive. We suspect the even though each prophecy of the passion ends in the words, 'and after three days rise again', the disciples were so taken aback by his words about suffering and death that the idea of resurrection, as applied to an individual this side of the general resurrection, made no impact on their consciousness. They say as much in 9:10: 'Questioning what this rising from the dead could mean.' We can only hope that sitting with Jesus during these solemn pronouncements on the Mount of Olives, at least these four disciples began to see that Jesus was certain that his Father would vindicate him and raise him to that eternal kingship promised to the Son of Man in Daniel, and that he would sustain them in the dangerous times ahead. Their part is to be alert, have faith, endure. And looking further ahead, in view of the uncertainty of the final coming, the advise again is to 'beware, keep alert, keep awake.' Verse 37 extends the advice to all disciples, including ourselves, keep awake, be ready, be patient, have faith and hope.

2.4 Conversion

It is a great sadness, that though the crowd even in Jerusalem had been receptive to Jesus, the leadership of the Jews by and large hardened their hearts and refused to listen to him. Luke 19:41 tells us that Jesus wept over Jerusalem, for its missed opportunities. The door will always be open to them, and Paul assures us that God does not abandon his covenant people. The followers of Jesus will only 'endure to the end' if their devotion to Jesus is great and their faith strong. So for each of us. Our weaknesses are known to us. We know how we do best as 'fair weather disciples', and pray not to be put to the test. But we know that Jesus has gone through great hardships for us, and that the Son of Man in glory will claim us if we remain faithful, in spite of falls. Complacency and indifference are the problems. So we are warned to be awake, not to take God's compassion for granted, not to expect that we will be spared from all suffering. We know that our Lord is enthroned in glory and that his power may be experienced here below by struggling disciples.

3. RESPONSE

Make your personal response by rereading the text, pausing to pray with any verse or phrase that strikes you.

Not one stone shall be left upon another ... Herod's great blocks of stone thrown down. God's own house. We pray for a sense of reality. Jesus loves beauty, and human creativity, and art that honours the glory of God. But things are passing, impermanent, no matter how beautiful or sacred. It is the face of God that we seek. You have made us for yourself, O Lord. Things change; the church will remain, but not necessarily here or in me. 'O thou who changest not, abide with me.'

Tell us, when will this be, and what will be the sign. We have a great need to know the future, but faith tells us we are in God's hands, come what may. Be content (rejoice even!) to be in God's hands; make an act of trust in his providence for yourself and for your loved ones, even in times of disappointment, sickness or the prospect of death. Fruitful death, bearing within it the seed of new life.

For in those days there will be suffering ... Lord, personal suffering or the suffering of the world can be overwhelming. It frightens us, challenges our faith. I know, Jesus says, it frightened me too: 'Father, remove this cup from me' (14:36). But in embracing humanity, I embrace suffering too. When you suffer, remember that I embrace your suffering. Through it, I see life. Lord, help us to embrace the Father's will, for our human thinking is so limited by our horizons, and help us to believe that God has a life-filled destiny for all who suffer.

The sun shall be darkened, and the moon will not give its light ... The world of the Jewish leaders was to be shattered. We have dream-shattering experiences also. The power of darkness can take hold of our human souls. Pray for those in darkness. Pray that the light of Christ may penetrate the darkness within us. There was darkness around the cross. The absence of light. But that darkness was a sign of God's power. Light of Christ, illumine our darkness. 'Christ my light and only way, Christ my lantern night and day.'

Then they will see the Son of Man coming in clouds with great power and glory. The light that destroys the darkness. We say in different language, 'He ascended into heaven and sits at the right hand of the Father.' Give praise to Christ sharing in his risen humanity in the glory of God. Sit in his presence with joy in your heart. Then think that he also is enthroned for us: our humanity, our suffering humanity, that he embraced, shares in the glory of the Father. Think of 'they will see' as 'his power and glory will be seen,' and think of 'will be seen' as 'will be experienced'. And earnestly desire to experience that new and glorious life that he wants to share with us, suffering humanity whom he embraces. Lord, help us to be truly alive, fill us with your life.

This generation will not pass away until all these things have taken place. We were not part of that first generation, when the power of the Lord in glory enlivened a generation to witness fearlessly to the risen Lord with such world-changing results. Lord, empower our generation also. Let us experience your power. We pray that we may be so alive with your life that our generation may not fail to know that God is at work among us.

My words will not pass away. Rejoice that his word remains alive and life-giving for us. Remember the voice from heaven, 'Listen to him.' Resolve to continue trying to hear the word and live by it.

But about that day or hour no one knows. That day for us will be the day of the second coming of Jesus or the day of our death. Pray for the grace to take his advice: 'Beware, keep alert, for you know not when the time will come … Keep awake.' Lord, help me to stop planning to do things tomorrow: I have only today.

4. CONTEMPLATION

Take the words that have meant most to you and hold on to them, or to the image of the Son of Man at the right hand of the Father, 'Christ, the mediator between God and humanity, judge of the world and Lord of all, has passed beyond our sight, not to abandon us, but to be our hope.' (Preface of the feast of the Ascension). Choose a text to keep in your heart: 'He will send out the angels to gather his elect from the four winds,' or 'Heaven and earth will pass away, but my words will not pass away.'

The Last Supper (Mark 14:10-31)

1. FAMILIARISATION

1.1 Getting to know the text (Mark 14:10-31)

Judas decides to hand Jesus over

14:10 Then Judas Iscariot, who was one of the twelve,
went to the chief priests
in order to betray him to them.

11 When they heard it, they were greatly pleased,
and promised to give him money.
So he began to look for an opportunity to betray him.

Preparation for the Passover meal

12 On the first day of Unleavened Bread,
when the Passover lamb is sacrificed,
his disciples said to him,
'Where do you want us to go
and make the preparations for you to eat the Passover?'

13 So he sent two of his disciples, saying to them,
'Go into the city,
and a man carrying a jar of water will meet you;
follow him,

14 and wherever he enters, say to the owner of the house,
"The Teacher asks, Where is my guest room
where I may eat the Passover with my disciples?"

15 He will show you a large room upstairs,
furnished and ready. Make preparations for us there.'

16 So the disciples set out and went to the city,
and found everything as he had told them;
and they prepared the Passover meal.

'One of you will betray me.'

17 When it was evening, he came with the twelve.

18 And when they had taken their places and were eating,
Jesus said: 'Truly I tell you,
one of you will betray me,
one who is eating with me.'

19   They began to be distressed
and to say to him one after another,
'Surely, not I?'

20   He said to them, 'It is one of the twelve,
one who is dipping bread into the bowl with me.

21   For the Son of Man goes as it is written of him,
but woe to that one
by whom the Son of Man is betrayed!
It would have been better for that one
not to have been born.'

Institution of the Eucharist

22   While they were eating,
he took a loaf of bread,
and after blessing it (having said the blessing)
he broke it, gave it to them, and said,
'Take; this is my body.'

23   Then he took a cup,
and after giving thanks he gave it to them,
and all of them drank from it.

24   He said to them,
'This is my blood of the covenant,
which is poured out for many.

25   Truly I tell you,
I will never again drink of the fruit of the vine
until that day when I drink it new
in the kingdom of God.'

26   When they had sung the hymn,
they went out to the Mount of Olives.

The sheep will be scattered

27   And Jesus said to them,
'You will all become deserters; for it is written,
"I will strike the shepherd,
and the sheep will be scattered."

28   But after I am raised up,
I will go before you to Galilee.'

29   Peter said to him,
'Even though all become deserters, I will not.'

30   Jesus said to him, 'Truly I tell you,

this day, this very night, before the cock crows twice,
you will deny me three times.'
31   But he said vehemently,
'Even though I must die with you,
I will not deny you.'
And all of them said the same.

1.2 Background

1.2.1 The Passover: I have omitted 14:1-9, which begins: 'It was two days before the Passover and the feast of Unleavened Bread', and continues with the chief priests and scribes looking for a way to arrest Jesus 'by stealth', for they were afraid of a riot among the crowd if they arrested him openly at the feast. So the following events have a Passover setting. The Last Supper to celebrate the liberation from Egypt was held after sunset as the official 'day' of Passover began (day reckoned as sunset to sunset), traditionally understood as Thursday night, and the paschal lambs for the feast were ritually slain in the temple by the priests on the 'previous' day, during the afternoon of Thursday. After the meal Jesus went to the garden of Gethsemane, where he was arrested, and by early on the morning of Friday, still on the feast day, he was crucified, according to Mark, Matthew and Luke. According to John, Jesus celebrated the meal with his disciples on the evening before Passover, and died on the eve of the feast at the time when the lambs were being slaughtered, rather than on the feast itself. The details of the chronology of these few days are complex and there is no agreement among the commentators. What is important is that Jesus gave a new meaning to the Passover meal and died at Passover time, giving new meaning to the feast.

1.2.2 Mark's arrangement: Mark's 'sandwich' technique can be seen in the selection of verses above: the celebration of the Last Supper is preceded by the decision of Judas to hand over Jesus secretly to the chief priests, then we have the preparations for the meal, and the beginning of the meal at which Jesus startles the disciples by announcing that one of them is going to betray him. Then comes the central part, the institution of the Eucharist, which is followed by Jesus' prediction that the twelve will all be scattered and become deserters, which they all deny, most strenuously Peter. So before and after the meal, which signifies the deep bonds of table fellowship between Jesus and his disciples, we find betrayal, forebodings of desertion and denial by disciples.

1.2.3 Judas: Mark has no interest in telling us what motivated Judas, or in what happened to him afterwards. The chief priests are delighted when he comes to them with the offer of handing Jesus over to them, and promise him money. They need someone to guide them, or more likely their temple police, to the place where Jesus spends the night, no easy task among an estimated crowd of 180,000 swelling the city's population 6 times over at Passover time. So Judas began to look for an opportunity to betray him (v 11): literally: 'He was seeking how he might hand him over at an opportune time.' Mark does not use the ordinary verb to betray, *prodidômi*, and only Luke 6:16 uses the noun *prodotês* for betrayer. Otherwise it is always *paradidômi*, hand over, the verb used for the handing over of John the Baptist and Jesus, even by the Father and by Jesus of himself. 'At an opportune time' translates Mark's word *eukairôs*, a compound adverb from *kairos*, the time of divine choice announced at 1:15, 'the time (*kairos*) is fulfilled, and the kingdom of God has come near.' Mark is saying that the human agent, acting of his own free choice, is nevertheless finding the divinely appointed time of salvation. Judas' handing over will also be the free acceptance of the Father's will by Jesus, lovingly handing himself over 'to give his life as a ransom for many' (10:45).

1.2.4 Preparation for the Passover: The preparations take place 'on the first day of Unleavened Bread, when the Passover lamb is sacrificed' (v 12). Jesus, as he did in 11:2ff on his entry to Jerusalem, gives precise instructions to two disciples to go into the city, where they will see a man carrying a pitcher of water (very unusual for a man); they are to follow him to a house, and they are to say to the owner, 'The Teacher asks, where is my guest room ...?' and they will be shown a large upstairs room, where they are to prepare the paschal meal. Jesus obviously had contacts in Jerusalem, which suggests he had been to the city before, and perhaps had used this room previously: 'my guest room' he calls it. Either Mark is stressing Jesus' prophetic vision, or he is hinting at a prearranged plan. Overall, Mark is showing that Jesus is still in control, up until the end of the meal. After the meal, on their way to the garden, everything turns gloomy, and Jesus allows his vulnerability to be seen.

1.2.5 *The betrayal of friendship:* Mark seems to say that only the twelve were with Jesus at the Supper. They reclined on mats, or perhaps couches. When they began to eat, Jesus shocked the twelve by declaring solemnly that one of them would hand him over, 'one who is eating with me'. When they protest, he repeats, 'One of the twelve, one who is dipping bread into the bowl with me.' Betrayal of friendship is always hard to bear, but the greatest betrayal in the culture of Jesus' time was this betrayal of table friendship, which Jesus has shared with the twelve since Galilee, and which he had highlighted in the multiplications of the loaves. Two quotations from the Psalms show this hurt: 'Even my bosom friend in whom I trusted, who ate of my bread, has lifted his heel against me' (Ps 41:9), and 'It is not enemies who taunt me – I could bear that ... but it is you, my equal, my familiar friend, with whom I kept pleasant company' (Ps 55:12-14). Jesus does not identify Judas, and there is no indication that Judas left the meal early: indeed, that might have frustrated his purpose, for he needed to be sure where Jesus was going to spend the night. Jesus does not identify Judas to the others, and may even be seeking his conversion by the dire warning of v 21, 'better for that one not to have been born.'

1.2.6 *Institution of the Eucharist:* Mark intends us to see this as a Passover meal, but he takes for granted that the details of such a meal are known and he does not even mention the paschal lamb, nor the recounting of the story of Israel's deliverance from Egypt. Because his account is so focused, it is more difficult to fit the words of Jesus over the bread and the cup into the pattern of the Passover meal than with Luke (see my *Praying with St Luke*, pp 135-6, 2.1.2). His emphasis is on the interpretative words and their relationship to Calvary. He goes fairly straight to the word 'bread' (artos), its first use since 'the bread section', 6:32-8:21 (see Sessions 10 and 12) – other intervening uses of the word 'bread' in NRSV are not found in the Greek, eg Unleavened Bread is Greek *azuma*. 'Taking bread (NRSV a loaf of bread), having said the blessing, he broke it and gave it to them and said, 'Take; this is my body.' The NRSV 'after blessing it' is not

215

likely, since Jews bless not the food, but God who gives the food, and 'having said the blessing' is parallel with 'having given thanks' when he took the cup. He took the cup of wine, gave it to them, and they all drank. Then come the momentous words: 'This is my blood of the covenant, which is poured out for many.' 'Poured out for many' brings our attention to what is going to happen on Calvary, interpreting his death as a self-giving sacrifice 'for many' (everyone). We are brought back to 10:45, 'The Son of Man came not to be served but to serve, and to give his life as a ransom for many', and through that to the great Servant Song of Isaiah, '… he poured out himself to death … he bore the sins of many, and made intercession for the transgressors' (Is 53:12). His death is not a meaningless tragedy, but foreseen and planned by God for our salvation. So Mark emphasises the total self-giving of Jesus, a voluntary offering of himself as God's servant for the forgiveness of the sins of 'many', countless multitudes who will accept it. That giving is anticipated in his giving of himself to the twelve: they eat the bread, 'my body', and drink the cup, 'my blood of the covenant', and so become sharers in his life, a life to be given up in service for others. As sharers in his sacrificial giving of himself, they are called to be ready to give themselves in service to others and for others. His blood is 'the blood of the covenant', which takes our minds back to the covenant-ratification ceremony in Exodus 24:3-8, where Moses asks the people of Israel whether they will accept the words of the covenant, to be God's people and accept the Lord as their God, and they say yes. Moses sprinkled half of the blood of sacrificed oxen on the altar (representing God) and the other half on the people, symbolising their sharing of life, with the words, 'See, the blood of the covenant that the Lord has made with you.' So Jesus' words, 'my blood of the covenant' tell us that a new covenant is being made between God and all believers in Jesus, represented by the twelve, a covenant written on their hearts, as Jeremiah prophesied (31:31-34), because they receive the blood (life) of Jesus within them, not externally, as at Sinai. Some later manuscripts insert the word 'new' before covenant to make the reference to Jeremiah explicit, but in Mark the newness is obvious and does not need to be stated. It is saddening, but hope filled, that the new covenant in the blood of

Jesus is made with frail disciples, who will variously let him down. It shows that the covenant with disciples then and now is a fragile relationship that needs to be renewed often and requires much divine forgiveness.

1.2.7 Looking forward with confidence: Jesus does not only lead our minds forward to his death, but forward to the banquet of God in heaven. 'Truly I tell you', he solemnly begins, 'I will never again drink of the fruit of the vine until I drink it new in the kingdom of God' (v 25). This is his last meal on earth; the next time he drinks wine will be in the presence of the Father in the kingdom (his last kingdom of God pronouncement). Jesus is full of confidence that God will vindicate him and bring about his kingdom, in spite of, indeed through his terrible suffering and death.

1.2.8 Scattered sheep, and the hope of regathering: 'With hymns (chanting of the Hallel Psalms, 115-118) on their lips they went out to the Mount of Olives' (v 26). The disciples are well intentioned but weak, and Jesus is suddenly filled with feelings of abandonment. 'You will all become deserters' (the Greek verb is 'you will be scandalised in me'). They are not yet sure which of them will be the betrayer, and now all of them are to let him down. Jesus quotes Zechariah 13:7, 'I will strike the shepherd, and the sheep will be scattered' (the result of the striking). The original is, 'Strike the shepherd, that the sheep may be scattered' (the purpose of the striking). They will all be found wanting when the shepherd is struck. Immediately Mark puts in a note of hope that they will be forgiven and called together by the shepherd: 'But after I am raised up, I will go before you to Galilee' (v 28). This is a tremendously important verse in Mark in view of the absence of recorded meetings between the twelve and the risen Jesus, with the abrupt ending of Mark at 16:8. Jesus again speaks of his resurrection, and 'will go before them' (as a shepherd leads his sheep) to Galilee, so promising reconciliation. The note of hope triggers Peter's indignation at the thought of becoming a deserter, and his protests lead to Jesus' prophecy of his three fold denial before the cock crows twice. The scene ends sadly with Peter and the others protesting their readiness to die with him.

2. Reflection

2.1 Mystery

We have come a long way since Jesus told his disciples in 4:11: 'To you has been given the mystery of the kingdom of God.' At that time they had little idea what it was about, and they have not had an easy journey to deeper knowledge. Now they have all the ingredients. To attempt to enumerate them is difficult. The mystery is closely associated with the person of Jesus, with his death and resurrection, and the new covenant community, which his death and the sharing in the one bread and the one cup will create; the enthronement as Lord of all nations of the Son of Man, the keystone on whom the new community is based, and the focal point of God's presence with his people; the mission to all the nations, and the future hope of the fullness of the kingdom in the presence of God at the messianic banquet. As you see from that rather clumsy attempt to summarise all that is involved, the kingdom is a very rich concept, and it takes a lived experience of it to bring some sense. It is pretty close to what we have always called the Paschal Mystery, which we are called to live.

2.2 Christology

In fulfilment of the Isaian prophecies about the Servant of God, Jesus is the Son of Man who came not to be served but to serve and to give his life as a ransom for many. So he takes bread, breaks it, and gives it to be eaten, symbolising his body broken and given 'for many'. He takes the cup, and all share in it, and he says it is his blood of the covenant poured out for many. His greatest service is to be the self-giving sacrifice of his life for sinners. He is firm in his assertion that he will be raised up, and will drink the new wine in the kingdom of God. When he is raised up, he will lead his scattered sheep back to Galilee, where there will be a great reconciliation. The nucleus of the kingdom community on earth will be established, and the challenge will be to spread the news to all nations.

2.3 Discipleship

I suppose it is the fragility of the disciples that is most apparent. When Jesus is giving himself to his disciples to celebrate and consolidate his relationship with them, when he as father of the family brings them to his table to give the feast and the table-sharing new meaning, they are complacent about their own capacity for loyalty and courage, and we who know the outcome of the story are conscious of their weakness. So our Eucharist is a time to remember (as the Jews remember their deliverance from Egypt, we remember also our deliverance through the death and resurrection of Jesus), a time to unite with the self-sacrifice of Jesus ('Let the same mind be in you that was in Jesus Christ', Phil 2:5), a time to renew our commitment to him and our covenant with God, a time to be strengthened and nourished for that task by his body and blood, a time to unite with him in intercession for sinful suffering humanity, and a time to look forward in confidence to the fullness of the kingdom of God.

2.4 Conversion

Conversion is turning away from sin and selfishness, and turning towards God. The emphasis here should be on the turning towards. The challenge is to get into the heart of the mystery, to allow the power of the death and resurrection of Jesus to make us truly alive, and able to be self-giving as he was. To do that we have the Eucharist, and we need not only to do this in his memory, but to learn more and more how to be like him who is unselfish and gives everything in the service of God and of God's people. Knowing that we will often fail, we take heart from the promise of Jesus to gather his scattered disciples again in Galilee, and we can guess from the resurrection appearances in the other gospels that his first words are going to be: 'Peace be with you.'

3. RESPONSE

To make your personal response, reread the text, pausing to pray with any verse or phrase that strikes you. I suggest you concentrate on the two sections at the meal and on the last section as they go towards the Mount of Olives

One of you will betray me, one who is eating with me ... one of the twelve, who is dipping (bread) into the bowl with me. ... Surely not I? Of course you or I could not be Judas! Well, not if we are still holding on, however weakly. But how often we come perilously near to it! We cannot hand him over to death, except in his brothers and sisters! We might run down the list of modern betrayals and see how we do: apathy, indifference, non-involvement, individualism, complacency, superiority, selfishness, meanness – all things that can turn our hearts to stone. It is good to ask for pardon, and to resolve to be more than a nominal disciple. Lord, deepen our understanding, strengthen our resolve.

Take; this is my body. Give thanks for the gift of Jesus' body, given for us, given to us. Lord, we are privileged to be called to close union of hearts and minds with you by sharing this bread. Your giving is total. Help us to be givers, saying to you, this is my body, to be used in your service. Lord, help us to grow more like you, to have your mind in us.

This is my blood of the covenant ... Lord, you have bound us to God our Father in a new relationship of the heart, healed, forgiven, enriched. 'This is the covenant that I will make with the house of Israel ... I will put my law within them, and I will write it on their hearts' (Jeremiah 31:33). Thank you for believing that my heart is able to respond. I wish to be faithful. Help me to remember that the covenant binds me to my brothers and sisters as well as to God. Do I mean it if I sing: 'Bind us together, Lord, bind us together with cords that cannot be broken'?

... *which is poured out for many.* We give thanks for Jesus the servant. Ask yourself how you are doing in the service of others. We know what it cost you, Lord. The Father's will is written on our hearts through the new covenant. Help us to be ready to do his will.

You will all become deserters ... 'Even though I must die with you, I will not deny you.' The scriptures build up the awfulness of Peter's denials deliberately, giving out a message of hope to sinners. So thank you, Peter! You give me hope. I feel no special bravery within me, and in your shoes I'd have deserted too. Lord, thank you for being able to use broken instruments to further your kingdom.

After I am raised up, I will go before you to Galilee. This is hopeful, Jesus will be vindicated and offer reconciliation to the disciples who deserted. God of new beginnings, we thank you. Renew us, and make us alive with your new life.

4. CONTEMPLATION

I want to carry away with me and keep in my heart two things:
the awareness of my own frailty, lest I get above myself, and the
permanent gift of Jesus' sacramental presence in us and around
us. So I will try to remember two texts: Peters' words: 'Even
though all become deserters, I will not.' And Jesus' words, 'This
in my blood of the covenant, which is poured out for many.'

Agony and Arrest (Mark 14:32-52)

1. FAMILIARISATION

1.1 *Getting to know the text (Mark 14:32-52)*

Jesus' prayer in distress

14:32   They went to a place called Gethsemane;
         and he said to his disciples, 'Sit here while I pray.'

33   He took with him Peter and James and John,
         and began to be distressed and agitated.

34   And he said to them,
         'I am deeply grieved, even to death;
         remain here, and keep awake.'

35   And going a little farther,
         he threw himself on the ground and prayed that,
         if it were possible, the hour might pass from him.

36   He said, 'Abba, Father, for you all things are possible;
         remove this cup from me;
         yet, not what I want, but what you want.'

Keep awake and pray

37   He came and found them sleeping;
         and he said to Peter, 'Simon, are you asleep?
         Could you not keep awake one hour?

38   Keep awake and pray
         that you may not come into the time of trial;
         the spirit indeed is willing,
         but the flesh is weak.'

39   And again he went away and prayed,
         saying the same words.

40   And once more he came and found them sleeping,
         for their eyes were very heavy;
         and they did not know what to say to him.

The hour has come

41   He came a third time and said to them,
         'Are you still sleeping and taking your rest?
         Enough! The hour has come;
         the Son of Man is betrayed into the hands of sinners.

42   Get up, let us be going.
      See, my betrayer is at hand.'

Jesus is handed over

43   Immediately, while he was still speaking,
      Judas, one of the twelve, arrived;
      and with him there was a crowd with swords and clubs,
      from the chief priests, the scribes and the elders.
44   Now the betrayer had given them a sign, saying,
      'The one I will kiss is the man;
      arrest him and lead him away under guard.'
45   So when he came, he went up to him at once
      and said: 'Rabbi!' and kissed him.
46   Then they laid hands on him and arrested him.

'Let the scriptures be fulfilled'

47   But one of those who stood near drew his sword
      and struck the slave of the high priest,
      cutting off his ear.
48   Then Jesus said to them,
      'Have you come out with swords and clubs
      to arrest me as though I were a bandit?
49   Day after day I was with you in the temple teaching,
      and you did not arrest me.
      But let the scriptures be fulfilled.'
50   All of them deserted him and fled.

Flight

51   A certain young man was following him,
      wearing nothing but a linen cloth.
      They caught hold of him,
52   but be left the linen cloth and ran off naked.

1.2 Background

1.2.1 Gethsemane: The 'garden of Gethsemane ('oil-press') is today remembered on the lower slopes of the Mount of Olives, where there is an olive grove with ancient olive trees. Jesus goes here to spend his last night, although that realisation has not registered with the disciples. There two things happen: he prays in an agony of mind, and he is arrested by people, guided by Judas, sent by the 'chief priests and scribes and elders'. We can only imagine how Jesus had to steel himself to go and remain there where Judas would know how to find him; he went from being prostrated with anguish to a state of composed acceptance through prayer to his Father. The three inner group disciples he took with him fell asleep, though he warned them to 'watch and pray' because of the coming testing, and when he was arrested, all the disciples left him and fled. Apart from Peter, who will deny him, the disciples do not appear again in the narrative. There is hope for them at the finding of the empty tomb: 'Go tell his disciples and Peter that he is going ahead of you to Galilee; there you will see him, just as he told you' (16:7).

1.2.2 Jesus' weakness and vulnerability: Some people so stress the humanity of Jesus that they never hear the Father's words: 'You are my Son, the Beloved.' Others are so used to thinking of Jesus as God's Son, that they lose sight of his humanity. In his agony we are absolutely sure that he is human, and no disciples would have invented this story about their beloved teacher, or indeed about their own behaviour either. Jesus asked the main body of disciples to wait while he prayed, and drew aside a little with Peter, James and John. 'He began to be distressed and agitated', saying to them: 'I am deeply grieved, even to death.' He seemed to need their company and support; 'remain here and keep awake.' Hitherto determined to follow the path laid out for him by God, now he slumps to the ground in a state of collapse, praying that 'the hour' might pass from him, if possible. For once we hear the content of his prayer: 'Abba, Father, for you all things are possible; remove this cup from me; yet, not what I want, but what you want.' The Aramaic/Hebrew 'Abba' is the affectionate but reverent address of a child to a father, and is recorded here for the only time in the gospels (though Paul, Rom 8:15, Gal 4:6, shows that the Christians continued to be impressed with this remembered evidence of Jesus' intimate relationship with the Father, even in the crisis of Gethsemane). We remember him asking James and John (10:38): 'Are you able to drink the cup that I drink?' At the Supper (14:24), he shared the cup with the disciples, saying: 'This is my blood of the covenant, which is poured out for many.' Now he is earnestly begging the Father to remove it from him. We are impressed by the honesty and humanity of this moment, and the manner in which Jesus has embraced the agony of suffering humanity and shared its horror. All who hear that dreaded sentence, the final diagnosis that nothing more can be done to prevent death, know that Jesus is with them. And his prayer includes the readiness to do God's will, if there is no other way. After the prayer, he comes to the three and finds them sleeping. He addresses Peter in the singular (not with his new name denoting strength.): 'Simon, are you asleep? Could you not watch one hour?' Then switching to the plural: 'Keep awake and pray, that you may not come into the time of trial; the spirit indeed is willing, but the flesh is weak' (vv 37-38). The pattern is repeated three times; twice more he retires to pray, using the same words (the third time it is implicit), twice more he returns to find them sleeping. When he comes back the third time he is composed. The message of Mark is that this type of 'testing', a crisis of life or death, must be faced with honesty and deep prayer to find the strength to go on. Jesus did that, the disciples were unable to take his advice, so they are unprepared for the moment that is upon them.

There are some difficulties of interpretation in the last two verses (41-42), depending partly on punctuation. The Jerusalem Bible (used in the Lectionary) has: 'You can sleep on now and take your rest. It is all over.' But immediately after he has to tell them, 'Get up! Let us go!' NRSV is probably correct to take it as a question, 'Are you still sleeping and taking your rest? Enough!' The Greek word *apechei*, translated 'enough', or 'it is all over' is a commercial word which means something like 'paid with thanks', and Mullins' translation (p 398) is as good as any, 'The deal is done,' indicating that the die is cast and the crisis time has come. 'The hour has come; the Son of man is betrayed (handed over) into the hands of sinners. Get up! Let us be going. See, my betrayer (the one who hands me over) is at hand.' The Father had given no words in reply to Jesus' prayer. His answer is the arrival of Judas. Jesus is accepting, prepared beforehand for the arrival of the arresting party.

1.2.3 The arrest: There is no break in the narrative between the agony and the arrest. Judas arrives –'one of the twelve' – leading 'a crowd with swords and clubs'. Probably Mark does not want to give them dignity, but they would have been an official group of temple guards, responsible to the Sanhedrin, as he says, 'from the chief priests, the scribes and the elders', and there was with them 'the slave of the high priest', which could be translated 'the servant', the high priest's man to report back to him. Mark's focus is on Judas, who 'hands him over': the agreed sign is an act of respect and friendship, a kiss, with which a disciple would greet his teacher. Mark lets the actions speak for themselves without comment: Judas went straight up to Jesus, greeted him as 'Rabbi', kissed him, and they laid hands on him and arrested him. We remember Jesus' words at the Last Supper (14:20): 'It is one of the twelve, one who is dipping into the bowl with me.' Jesus is deprived of his liberty, but his handing over is also the action of the Father and the voluntary act of Jesus, to fulfil the plan of salvation.

1.2.4 Reactions to the arrest: In a futile attempt to resist, a by-stander (identified by Matthew and Luke as one who was with Jesus, and named by John as Peter) drew a sword and cut off the ear of the high priest's servant. The other three evangelists record that Jesus forbade further resistance, Mark's answer is given to the arresting party (really through them to the chief priests): they have come to arrest him in the night with a show of force as if he were a bandit (the word *lêstês* is used also for a revolutionary, describing the two who were crucified with him, 15:27). Yet, Jesus says, he taught day after day in the temple and they did not arrest him. The next part is especially for his followers: 'But let the scriptures be fulfilled.' The disciples know then that he will not resist and 'all of them deserted him and fled.' The prophecy is fulfilled (14:27), 'You will all become deserters'. Only Peter will appear again, following from a distance, and then only to deny him. Mark stresses the abandonment of Jesus during his passion, by those who were called 'to be with him'.

1.2.5 The young man who tried to follow (vv 51-52): the incident of the young man who tried to follow is strange and recorded only by Mark. He followed too closely, and the guards tried to grab him, but he fled leaving his linen garment in their hands. Some suggest that it was the young Mark himself, but there is no way of knowing whether that is so. Others suggest symbolic explanations: the young man was wearing a *sindôn*, the same Greek word used for the shroud in which Jesus was wrapped for burial (15:46), and another young man appeared at the empty tomb, 'dressed in a white robe'. So perhaps the incident is symbolic of the resurrection. In all honesty, there may be little more in the incident than Mark giving a nod to his readers about someone known to them who could corroborate the events.

2. REFLECTION

2.1 Mystery

The realisation of God's plan is not easy, even for someone with the courage and determination of Jesus. It seems to end up with one man against the world and the power of Satan, with only the weapons of faith, love and endurance. To give some meaning to human suffering Jesus has to embrace it; to take away the tyranny of death he has to endure it. The thought of it shatters him, but he manages with repeated prayer to go from 'remove this cup from me' to 'let the scriptures be fulfilled'. The Father gives the only answer possible: events march on and the one who hands him over arrives in the garden. The Father loves the Son and yet allows him to be handed over to his enemies. The only consolation offered is that it is foretold in the scriptures. Where in the scriptures is not specified: Mark seems to be pointing us towards the whole complex of human opposition to God's plans in the lives of the prophets, the Songs of the Servant of God, the psalms of lament where the just put their trust in God in spite of oppression and injustice, the sufferings of Israel in Egypt, in the Exile, in the persecution of Antiochus Epiphanes of Syria. They are all somehow embodied in the suffering of the Son of Man.

2.2 Christology

We have never had any reason to doubt Jesus' total dedication to the mission his Father gave him; now we realise how much it cost him. And in his prayer we see the intimacy between Jesus and the Father; whom he addresses as Abba, the diminutive of *ab*, father. This must have been so striking to his disciples that it was remembered in the original form even in Greek speaking areas. Mark is not afraid to let Jesus' human weakness be seen, his need for prolonged and earnest prayer for the strength to do the Father's will, and even his need for human companionship in his distress, from disciples whose own human weakness he well understands. After his threefold prayer he is again in control of his emotions, and ready to allow the human agencies to take their course in his handing over. 'Let the scriptures be fulfilled.'

2.3 Discipleship

We are not given a very inspiring picture of the leading disciples, Peter, James and John, who had shared the moments of power with Jesus. His raw need frightens them; they are not used to seeing this vulnerability in Jesus, and are unable to stay awake when he begs them to. As the night goes on, Jesus is more worried about them, for he can see that they are unable to take his urgent advice to 'pray that they may not come into the time of trial'. Jesus feared not just that they would run away but that they would lose all faith in him, and hoped that his predictions of all that was to come would lead them back to him for reconciliation. When the arresting party arrives and Jesus allows himself to be seized, they can only think of self-preservation and run away. Their weakness is the weakness of many in Mark's community in time of persecution, and Mark is stressing for them and for us the remedy: earnest prayer not to be put to the test.

2.4 Conversion

The behaviour of the disciples challenges us, especially if we think we would have done better! The challenges are not new, but the same old ones, that we grow weary of attending to. Watch and pray, you know not the time when crisis will come, when death may come. Strange how the Lord's Prayer is in the background: we are allowed like Jesus to speak directly to God, Our Father; all things are possible for God –we acknowledge his power and might, we are in his hands; 'Not what I want, but what you want' – 'your kingdom come, your will be done'. Then the requests, subject to his will. Especially the request for strength in time of crisis – 'lead us not into temptation,' we say, but it means, 'do not put us to the test' followed by 'deliver us from evil, or the evil one'. This is Jesus praying and teaching us how to pray. The thing is, he did it, with deep honesty, out of his real need, and he kept at it. The disciples did not do it. The challenge to us is there. Remember that once the disciples received the Holy Spirit at Pentecost, they changed, and how! The flesh is still weak, though the spirit is willing. As Jesus spoke those words, they simply meant that human nature is weak. 'Spirit' came to mean not just our human spirit, but our spiritual selves renewed by the Holy Spirit living is us. With the gifts of the Spirit we can be strong, if we are prayerful. But even the gifts of the Holy Spirit may lie unused and neglected.

3. RESPONSE

Make a personal response by rereading the text, pausing to pray with any verse or phrase that strikes you.

He ... began to be deeply distressed and agitated ... Lord, like the disciples we are dismayed and bewildered by your distress in the garden. We 'understand' better than they that there is meaning to this suffering, that it is in weakness that you will triumph. But it is still shocking. It helps to think that you are sharing the untold sufferings of humanity, sharing with every man or woman facing frightening ordeals: victims of violence, abuse, injustice, cruelty, victims of accidents, incurable illness, mental distress. We pray for them, that they will begin to see that God has not abandoned them, any more than he abandoned his Son. Pray for acceptance that we are in God's hands, even when our prayers are not answered.

Abba, Father ... remove this cup from me; yet, not what I want, but what you want. Three things about Jesus' prayer to pray about: 1) He goes straight to his Father with confidence. That is what he wants us to do; go to the Father in his name. Pray for trust in God our Father, that he will answer all our prayers, even when he cannot give us what we want. 2) Total honesty: Jesus knows well the plan of God; now he tells the Father that he does not want to go through with it, remove this cup. The Father knows that what he needs now is not for the cup to be removed, but the strength to drink it, and by the time of his third prayer Jesus has received that strength. So pray to learn: God will help you to find resources within you that you did not know you had. 3) Always pray with the condition that the Father's will is the right thing, and the best thing for you. If he handed over his Son for you, how can he not be with you in whatever bad situation you find yourself?

Could you not keep awake one hour? Pray for perseverance in prayer. Even when it is difficult, distracted and hard work, keep on going, keep on starting again. Not always will the Lord pour sweetness and light on us, lest we think we are great at this and it is all our own work. Pray for the knowledge that just keeping on doing it is good.

The spirit indeed is willing, but the flesh is weak. Pray for a real grasp of the truth of Jesus' words. Of course we are weak. It is better to accept it than to be unaware of it. But pray not to make it an excuse for not trying. If our spirit is willing, the Holy Spirit will be given to us to strengthen us.

The one I will kiss is the man; arrest him … The sign of love becomes a sign of betrayal! One of the twelve, called 'to be with him', dipping his hand in the dish with him, eating his bread. How could you, Judas? Yet we know how. Betrayals are commonplace, marriage vows broken, children abused, loved ones subjected to violence, cut dead with the razor tongue. 'Whatever you do to one of these, you do to me.' Pray for forgiveness for our own betrayals, and for the battered spirits of the abused, the bullied and the neglected. Pray especially for those who have suffered at the hands of those who were supposed to show them the love of Jesus. It is hard for them to trust again.

Then they laid hands on him and arrested him. Lord, you put yourself in our hands when you took our flesh, and armed yourself only with the weapons of love and sacrifice. So we dare to mistreat you, and mistreat all who arm themselves only with those weapons. Human beings mishandle you, try to prevent your speaking God's truth and fulfilling God's design, cruelty tries to destroy love, force to put an end to your freedom. We thank you, Lord for the love and the self-sacrifice, for accepting the end to your freedom, the bonds, the blows, the nails.

4. Contemplation

Things to remember and keep in our hearts: the willingness of Jesus to drink the cup that repelled him, for love of sinful humanity; the Beloved Father, Abba, sometimes 'must' (that mysterious biblical 'must'!) watch his children facing heart-breaking suffering without stopping it; and the salutary lesson of the weakness of disciples who do not learn how to pray. Texts to keep repeating: 'Abba, Father, for you all things are possible … yet, not what I want, but what you want'; and 'Pray that you may not come into the time of trial.'

Jesus before the Sanhedrin
(Mark 14:53-72)

1. FAMILIARISATION

1.1 *Getting to know the text (Mark 14:53-72)*

Setting the scene

14:53   They took Jesus to the high priest;
         and all the chief priests, the elders and the scribes
         were assembled.

54   Peter had followed him at a distance,
         right into the courtyard of the high priest;
         and he was sitting with the guards,
         warming himself at the fire.

False testimony

55   Now the chief priests and the whole council
         were looking for testimony against Jesus
         to put him to death; but they found none.

56   For many gave false testimony against him,
         and their testimony did not agree.

57   Some stood up
         and gave false testimony against him, saying:

58   'We heard him say,
         'I will destroy this temple that is made with hands,
         and in three days I will build another,
         not made with hands.'

59   But even on this point their testimony did not agree.

Jesus declares his identity

60   Then the high priest stood up before them
         and asked Jesus, 'Have you no answer?
         What is it that they testify against you?'

61   But he was silent and did not answer.
         Again the high priest asked him,
         'Are you the Messiah, the Son of the Blessed One?'

62   Jesus said, "I am:

and you will see the Son of Man
seated at the right hand of the Power,'
and 'coming with the clouds of heaven."

63   Then the high priest tore his clothes and said,
'Why do we still need witnesses?

64   You have heard his blasphemy!
What is your decision?'
All of them condemned him as deserving death.

65   Some began to spit on him, to blindfold him,
and to strike him, saying to him, 'Prophesy!'
The guards also took him over and beat him.

Peter's denials

66   While Peter was below in the courtyard,
one of the servant-girls of the high priest came by.

67   When she saw Peter warming himself,
she stared at him and said,
'You also were with Jesus, the man from Nazareth.'

68   But he denied it, saying, 'I do not know
or understand what you are talking about.'
And he went out into the forecourt.
Then the cock crowed.

69   And the servant-girl, on seeing him,
began again to say to the bystanders,
'This man is one of them.'

70   But again he denied it.
Then after a little while
the bystanders again said to Peter,
'Certainly you are one of them;
for you are a Galilean.'

71   But he began to curse, and he swore an oath,
'I do not know this man you are talking about.'

72   At that moment the cock crowed for the second time.
Then Peter remembered that Jesus had said to him,
'Before the cock crows twice,
you will deny me three times.'
And he broke down and wept.

1.2 Background

1.2.1 Courage and cowardice: The scene begins with an introductory statement: they took Jesus to the high priest (not named), and there gathered 'all the chief priests, the elders and the scribes'. Mark seems to suggest that the whole Sanhedrin was assembled, or more likely all who could be gathered together in the night. Then he frames the attempt to make a case against Jesus between two scenes involving Peter. In v 54 Peter follows Jesus at a distance and gets into the courtyard of the high priest, where he sits with some guards warming themselves at a fire. Then Mark goes back to Jesus inside while they try to make a case against him, and Jesus makes his first really open declaration of his identity. In v 66 Mark turns again to Peter, who is challenged as a follower of Jesus but strongly denies even knowing him. So the courage and forthrightness of Jesus before his accusers, the foremost in the land, is contrasted with the cowardice of Peter before a servant girl and some bystanders.

1.2.2 Was it a trial? At first sight it looks like a formal trial with witnesses and a verdict, but on looking deeper it may well have been an informal interrogation to try to assemble a case to bring to Pilate. We know the law about Jewish trials at a later period: by that law a night trial would have been illegal, it would have had to be held in a proper courtroom, not in the high priest's house, a verdict could not have been reached until a day later, and the Sanhedrin had no authority to condemn anyone to death – that was reserved to the Roman governor. The trouble is, we are not sure that these rules applied in the time of Jesus. In addition, comparison with the other gospel accounts raises difficulties. Matthew follows Mark's pattern of a night 'trial' before the high priest (he names Caiaphas), and both Mark (15:1) and Matthew speak of a hurried consultation in the morning before they bring Jesus to Pilate. Luke however has no night trial, and uses the content of Mark/Matthew for a morning meeting of the Sanhedrin, which is shorter and has no verdict. John has a night interrogation before Annas, the deposed high priest and father-in-law of Caiaphas, and no morning trial. A possible rationalisation of the traditions is that there was a night interrogation, followed by a fuller meeting of the Sanhedrin in the morning, probably to settle on the case against Jesus that they would bring to the Roman governor. Mark is clear that they wanted Jesus put to death, and that the case to be given to the Romans had to be 'political', not the religious reasons that were the priority of the Sanhedrin.

1.2.3 False testimony: Vv 55-59 describe the attempt to find witnesses against Jesus who would agree in their testimony. For legality, at least two witnesses had to agree. Mark dismisses this testimony as false because they could not agree. The chief accusation (v 58) is that Jesus threatened to destroy the temple and raise another in three days, but Mark says they could not agree on this either. We know that in Mark (13:2) Jesus prophesied that the temple would be totally destroyed, but he did not threaten to do it himself. But though Mark describes the evidence as false, from the words he uses we suspect that he wishes the reader to see some mysterious truth in the 'false' statement. The temple to be destroyed is 'made with hands' and the one to be built in three days is 'not made with hands'. 'Made with hands' is used in biblical texts for idols, things of human construction that lead people away from God; 'not made with hands' means of divine construction. Of course it is outrage to the Jewish leaders to suggest that the temple could be compared to pagan idols, and Jesus will be taunted on the cross for his perceived threats against the temple (Mark 15:29). The question remains, what does Mark intend by 'another [temple] not made with hands'? Suggestions are the risen body of Jesus, or the community of the church ('three days' being taken as 'within a short time'). It is interesting to compare John 2:19-21. When Jesus is challenged to give a sign to support his authority for cleansing the temple, he replies: 'Destroy this temple and in three days I will raise it up.' The evangelist explains: 'But he was speaking of the temple of his body', that is, in both parts of the statement, and admits that it was only after the resurrection that his followers remembered this statement and understood it. So perhaps Mark is hinting at the deeper truth that after the temple, the place of the divine presence, is destroyed, that presence of the divine among them will then be in the person of the risen Jesus, 'the temple not made with hands.'

1.2.4 Jesus' testimony: The high priest decides to try to make Jesus incriminate himself. He asks Jesus the direct question, 'Are you the Messiah, the Son of the Blessed One?' The reader, who has listened to Jesus demanding silence about such claims, is as-

tounded at the directness of Jesus reply: 'I am.' It seems proba-
ble that the high priest was asking one question, not two: in
other words, he meant 'the Son of the Blessed One' as equivalent
to Messiah. But Jesus goes on to make a higher claim than being
Messiah: "And 'you will see the Son of Man seated at the right
hand of the Power' and 'coming with the clouds of heaven."
NRSV puts inverted commas around the two parts of Jesus'
words that recall texts from scripture. Psalm 110:1 pictures God
saying to the newly crowned king: 'Sit at my right hand, until I
make your enemies your footstool.' This implies that the
Messiah as son of David is given earthly power. But when it is
combined with the reference to Daniel 7:13: 'I saw one like a son
of man coming with the clouds of heaven' to the throne of God
in the heavens and receiving an eternal kingship, then the picture is of Jesus sitting at God's right hand, not on earth, but in
heaven sharing in his heavenly power. This is the high moment
of Mark's christology, when he takes up the titles he used at the
very beginning: 'The good news of Jesus Messiah, the Son of
God' (1:1), and combines the three titles Messiah, Son of God
and Son of Man, revealing Jesus as more than just Messiah, one
who will share in God's power in heaven because he is God's
Son in a different way to the kings of Judah. Now when all his
followers have fled and he is a prisoner in front of the
Sanhedrin, knowing that he is to die, Jesus makes open claims to
be Messiah and more than that, because now there can be no
doubt that the Messiah is also the Servant of God who will 'give
his life as a ransom for many' (10:45). The other striking thing is
that he says that his real dignity will be made manifest soon:
Mark changes the 'I saw' of Daniel 7:13 to 'you will see', referring to Jesus' hearers. Matthew 26:64 strengthens the proximity
of the manifestation by adding 'from now on you will see', and
Luke 22:69 similarly adds 'from now on'. So he must be referring to Jesus' resurrection and exaltation to the presence of the
Father, the effects of which will be 'seen' on earth.

The high priest then declares they have no need of witnesses,
for Jesus has condemned himself out of his own mouth, making
claims that no human being should dare to claim. In protest he
tears his garments, denounces the blasphemy, and asks the
members of the assembly: 'You have heard the blasphemy!

What is your decision?' All agreed that he deserved death. This seems to be the charge that they will bring to Pilate, rather than a verdict, since they do not have power to enforce it. The charge of being Messiah will be politicised to claiming to be 'king of the Jews', a charge that Pilate will have to take seriously. Pilate asks Jesus in all four gospels: 'Are you the king of the Jews?'

1.2.5 Peter's denials: simultaneously with Jesus' dignified and courageous testimony, Peter challenged in the courtyard out- side loses both dignity and courage. As Jesus asserts his identity, Peter denies his identity as disciple. When first challenged by the servant girl, he says he does not understand what she means, then he denies that he is a follower of Jesus, then the third time he swears he does not even know him. At the cock- crow he remembers the prophecy of Jesus, and bursts into tears - the sign of repentance. So Mark holds up to his readers in time of persecution an example of how to face the crisis with courage, even in the face of death, and how not to face it, with fear and denial. But Peter's failures, his reconciliation with Jesus, his courageous leadership of the early church and his martyrdom all exemplify, to those who have failed in the face of persecution and have perhaps betrayed other Christians, the possibility of forgiveness and a new beginning of courageous witness to the risen Jesus.

2. REFLECTION

2.1 Mystery

The working out of God's plan of salvation is indeed mysteri- ous. It will come about through Jesus' weakness and self-surren- der. And it will happen soon, so that must mean from the time of his resurrection onwards. Since Mark has gone to some pains to word his reference to the temple accusation carefully, so that though false in its attribution of the destruction of the temple to Jesus, nevertheless there is to be a new way in which God will be present among his people and in which he may be worshipped, a 'temple not made with hands'. Soon the people of God will offer worship to God the Father through the risen Lord. The people, in the unity of the Spirit, through him, with him, and in him, will offer to the Father all honour and glory.

2.2 *Christology*

The truly amazing thing is that the greatest revelation of Jesus' identity is made when Jesus is in custody, abandoned by his disciples, subject to bullying and abuse, the Servant who suffers for the sake of others. Ironically, the high priest says something about him that is undeniably true. '… the Messiah, the Son of the Blessed One.' Jesus' 'I am' asserts that he is indeed the Messiah, and he develops his claim in the light of the prophetic vision in Daniel 7 and Psalm 110. He will be seated at the right hand of God, as the long-desired Son of David, not on earth as David was, but in heaven, as the Son of Man called to God's throne and given eternal sovereignty. As he is then accused of blasphemy, seen as deserving death, and abused by his captors, we are reminded of the Psalm which Jesus quoted in the parable of the Tenants (Mark 12:10-11, quoting Psalm 118:22-23): 'The stone that the builders rejected has become the cornerstone; this was the Lord's doing, and it is amazing in our eyes.' The revelation was made to those who rejected Jesus, but at least one member of the Sanhedrin came to believe in Jesus, for in 15:43 we meet Joseph of Arimathea, 'a respected member of the council, who was also himself waiting expectantly for the kingdom of God', who asked for the body of Jesus from Pilate and buried it in a tomb.

2.3 *Discipleship*

Peter is presented by Mark in contrast to Jesus as an example of the disciple who has failed to 'pray not to be put to the test' and so lacks the courage to stand up for Jesus in his time of suffering. While Jesus is giving testimony before his captors, Peter panics before a mere servant girl who claims that he is 'with Jesus, the man from Galilee.' Even the first crow of the cock did not make him recall how he had professed his readiness to die with Jesus if necessary (14:31), and he had denied Jesus twice more before the cock crowed a second time and he remembered the words of Jesus, 'Truly I tell you, this day, this very night, before the cock crows twice, you will deny me three times' (14:30). Just as Jesus was being mocked as a prophet, blindfolded and struck and ordered to prophesy, ironically his prophecy about Peter's denial was being fulfilled. As we said above (1.2.5), Mark proposes

237

Jesus as a model of how to be true and strong before a persecutor, and Peter as a model of how not to face the accuser. For most of us the challenge is to show courage before the derision of our peers, to live up to our beliefs before the indifference and apathy of modern society.

2.4 Conversion

Our text begins with Peter following Jesus 'at a distance' (v.54), and ends with the last action of Peter recorded in the Gospel (presuming it ends at 16:8): 'And he broke down and wept' (v 72). So Peter is presented as one who follows at a safe distance, but loses all courage when challenged, but one who repents and does not despair of forgiveness. He will eventually justify the name that Jesus gave him, the Rock. Do his failure and his tears help us to see that non-involvement may be the beginning of loss of faith? The positive side of being weak and sinful is the self-knowledge it can bring, so that we learn not to rely on our own strength but on God's grace, and we learn to pray 'not to be put to the test.'. We are called, not to try to stay at a safe distance, but to bear witness to our faith in Jesus, by what we say and do.

3. RESPONSE

For your personal response reread the text, pausing to pray with any verse or phrase that strikes you.

Peter had followed him at a distance ... Consider what fears and obstacles prevent you from seeking a closer relationship with Jesus. What might it mean for you to have deeper involvement with Jesus or with fellow parishioners? Give thanks for the times or the areas where you have been able to have deeper in-volvement. Ask pardon for the times you stood back and re-fused to be involved.

Many gave false witness against him ... Lord, we find it hard to forget bad experiences that still hurt. Help us to find forgiveness in our hearts, not to hold on to old hurts; it just makes us relive the pain. You know how it feels, and identify with everyone who has been wrongly accused or condemned. 'When he was abused, he did not return abuse; when he suffered, he did not threaten; but he entrusted himself to the one who judges justly' (1 Peter 2:23).

Are you the Messiah, the Son of the Blessed One? ... I am ... We say when professing our faith in church: 'This is our faith; this is the faith of the church. We are proud to profess it in Christ Jesus our Lord.' Jesus seizes this moment to speak, the only time in the Gospel when he speaks out so clearly about his identity in a public place. Now it is clear that he is Servant-Messiah, the Son of God who emptied himself for our sakes. Be proud to acknowledge him as Son of God and Saviour. His revelation fell on hostile ears, as it still does so often. Pray that ears may be opened everywhere. Unite with the angels and saints and Christians everywhere in professing your faith in our Messiah, the Son of God.

And 'you will see the Son of Man seated at the right hand of the Power' and 'coming with the clouds of heaven.' Pray that more people will lose hostility and accept Jesus as God's Son. In our generation too we see the contrast between those who consider Jesus a mere man and Christian belief. How do we experience, 'see', the effects of his resurrection and exaltation? Are we able to say with Paul, 'It is no longer I who live, but it is Christ who lives in me' (Gal 2:20)? Give thanks for the effects of the resurrection on our lives, our sharing in his risen life, the gifts of the Holy Spirit. What do you need to do to use those gifts more effectively?

I do not know this man you are talking about. The words of Peter denying his Master are ironically partly true, since he does not really know him yet. Lord, help us to know you truly. We know that it is our personal relationship with you, Lord, based on prayer and listening to your word, nourished by the sacraments, that really matters. Help us to know you, help us to make you known. Remember this with trepidation and with prayer: the only knowledge that some people will have about Jesus will be what they see and hear from us.

And he broke down and wept. Life can be a continual struggle to overcome our weaknesses, but Peter teaches us not to despair. Tears may be a gift. We believe, Lord, that you will always receive the sinner back. You are the saviour who does not hold grudges; you looked forward to meeting your lost disciples in Galilee, and rejoice in your power to fill empty hearts with your new life.

4. CONTEMPLATION

The picture etched on my memory is that of Jesus, hands bound, surrounded by armed men, dignified, silent in the face of false accusations, courageously speaking the truth when challenged about his identity. So I will keep the words: 'Are you the Messiah, the Son of the Blessed One? ... I am' in my mind and repeat them often to myself. 'I am' has overtones of the divine name, his union with the Father. There it is, the humanity and divinity of Jesus before our minds. '... May we come to share in the divinity of Christ, who humbled himself to share in our humanity' (Roman Missal).

The Roman Trial (Mark 15:1-20)

1. FAMILIARISATION

1.1 Getting to know the text (Mark 15:1-20)

Jesus handed over to Pilate

15:1   As soon as it was morning,
         the chief priests held a consultation
         with the elders and the scribes and the whole council.
         They bound Jesus, led him away,
         and handed him over to Pilate.

Interrogation by Pilate

2   Pilate asked him: 'Are you the King of the Jews?'
         He answered him: 'You say so.'
3   Then the chief priests accused him of many things.
4   Pilate asked him again: 'Have you no answer?
         See how many charges they bring against you.'
5   But Jesus made no further reply,
         so that Pilate was amazed.

Jesus or Barabbas?

6   Now at the festival
         he used to release a prisoner for them,
         anyone for whom they asked.
7   Now a man called Barabbas was in prison
         with the rebels who had committed murder
         during the insurrection.
8   So the crowd came and began to ask Pilate
         to do for them according to his custom.
9   Then he answered them: 'Do you want me
         to release for you the King of the Jews?'
10   For he realised that it was out of jealousy
         that the chief priests had handed him over.
11   But the chief priests stirred up the crowd
         to have him release Barabbas for them instead.
12   Pilate spoke to them again,

'Then what do you wish me to do
with the man you call the King of the Jews?'

13   They shouted back: 'Crucify him!'

14   Pilate asked them, 'Why, what evil had he done?'
But they shouted all the more: 'Crucify him!'

15   So Pilate, wishing to satisfy the crowd,
released Barabbas for them;
and after flogging Jesus,
he handed him over to be crucified.

Roman soldiers mock his kingship

16   Then the soldiers led him into the courtyard
of the palace (that is, the governor's headquarters);
and they called together the whole cohort.

17   And they clothed him in a purple cloak;
and after twisting some thorns into a crown,
they put it on him.

18   And they began saluting him:
'Hail, King of the Jews!'

19   They struck his head with a reed,
spat upon him, and knelt down in homage to him.

20   After mocking him,
they stripped him of the purple cloak
and put his own clothes on him.
Then they led him out to crucify him.

1.2 Background

1.2.1 Bringing Jesus to Pilate: A full meeting of the Sanhedrin took place very early in the morning (v 25 says the crucifixion happened at nine o'clock in the morning). This was either to give a semblance of legality to their night proceedings or to formulate a charge that would cause the Roman prefect to take action, or possibly both. From now on the chief priests make the running, and others from the Sanhedrin are 'with' the chief priests (15:1, 31). Their charge of blasphemy will not impress the Romans, and Mark doesn't tell us what actual charge they gave to Pilate. (Luke 23:2 states the charges: 'We found this man perverting our nation, forbidding us to pay taxes to the emperor, and saying that he himself is the Messiah, a king.') From the question asked of Jesus by Pilate (v 2): 'Are you the King of the

Jews?' it is logical to suggest that they charged him with claiming to be a king, which would have to be taken seriously by Pilate. This is supported by v 12, 'the man you call the King of the Jews.' They led him bound and handed him over to Pilate.

1.2.2 *Pontius Pilate:* The 'prefect' appointed by Rome to the minor province of Judea, 26-36 AD, under the supervision of the 'legate' of the larger province of Syria. He normally lived at Caesarea Maritima (on the coast), but moved to Jerusalem during the important feasts like Passover in case of trouble among the crowds. In Jerusalem he resided at the former palace of Herod the Great to the west of the temple area (the *praetorium*, v 16, NRSV 'the governor's headquarters'). He appears in the gospels as rather a weak character, who really did not want to execute Jesus, but was out-manoeuvred by the chief priests. The truth is that he was a hard vindictive man who had little understanding of Jewish sensitivities about their religion and their temple, and frequently seriously offended them, as a result of which he had been several times reported to Rome. The chief priests saw it as their business to keep the peace between Pilate and the people, but there was little love lost between them. There was already a current of violent opposition to Rome (see v 7 for Barabbas) and one of the things that troubled the chief priests was that Jesus would stir up a popular anti-Roman movement, which would lead to repression. It was simpler to hand him over to Pilate to be dealt with as a political threat. Ironically in the handing over of Jesus they facilitated the release of a real revolutionary leader, Barabbas. The Christian reader has to realise that Mark had not a great deal of information about the details of the Roman trial, and had every reason to play down the part played by the Romans in a time when his readers were subject to Roman persecution. So we must keep clearly before our eyes that only Pilate had the power to execute Jesus, that the decision to scourge him and crucify him was made by Pilate, and he is all the more guilty if he carried out that sentence on a man he really believed was no political threat to Rome. Pilate was probably happy enough to execute Jesus as an example of what would happen to any Jew who threatened Roman rule in Judea. It was Roman soldiers who mocked the idea of a 'King of the Jews' and Pilate who had put up over his cross the charge against him: 'The King of the Jews'.

1.2.3 Pilate's Interrogation: We have only skimpy details of the process of trying this case by the Roman prefect. The only witnesses are the chief priests, there are only two questions and one non-committal answer, and no formal verdict. To the question: 'Are you the King of the Jews?' Jesus answers: 'You say so.' That probably means 'Yes, but your understanding of King of the Jews and mine are very different.' King of the Jews is gentile wording for the Jewish concept of Messiah, which does include kingship, but in a religious sense, and for Jesus included the idea of service. Jesus then refused to reply to the charges made against him by the chief priests, maintaining the silence of the Servant of God (Isaiah 53). We are only told that Pilate was amazed, and the impression we get is that Pilate was more convinced that the chief priests were playing a game of their own than that Jesus was really a political threat. Pilate did not like the idea of being used by the priests, and it would be true to his character that he would thwart them if he could. For his part Jesus seems to have decided that he was not going to respond to any more questions, to accept the inevitable and drink the cup that was prepared for him.

1.2.4 Who will he release, Jesus or Barabbas? Close attention paid to the text here, vv 6-15, will reward the reader with clearer understanding of what is going on. We attend to Mark's text as probably the earliest evidence, setting aside for the time what the other evangelists have to say about it. Firstly Mark tells us of the custom of Pilate to release on amnesty a prisoner whom the people requested at the feast of Passover. Then he names a prisoner called Barabbas 'who was in prison with the rebels who had committed murder during the insurrection.' This insurrection is not otherwise known to us, but Mark calls it 'the insurrection,' suggesting it was widely known at the time. Presumably Barabbas was a leader of this movement against Rome, and most authors presume that the two 'bandits' (*lêstai*) crucified with Jesus belonged to this group, and presumably that would have been the fate of Barabbas too if he had not been released. Then, v 8, Mark abruptly introduces 'the crowd', hitherto unmentioned and unexpected so early in the morning, for it is reasonable to presume that the chief priests, who had been unwilling to arrest Jesus in daylight because he was popular with the crowd, would have been trying to bring him to Pilate quietly at this early hour. What crowd is this and why have they come? Mark tells us: 'the crowd came and began to ask Pilate to do for them according to his custom.' This crowd has not come about Jesus, but about the amnesty for a prisoner. This is not then the Galilean pilgrim crowd that cried 'Hosanna' as he approached Jerusalem on the donkey (11:1-10), nor the Jerusalem crowd who listened with interest to Jesus in the temple (11:18, 32; 12:12, 37; 14:2). It is possible to believe that they were not interested in the release of any particular prisoner, and v.11 says that the chief priests 'stirred up the crowd to have them release Barabbas for them instead (of Jesus).' But Barabbas would never have been the first choice of the chief priests, for people like Barabbas were precisely those who made trouble for the priests by stirring up violence against the Romans, so it is more likely that they were pushing a moving wagon. This crowd were probably supporters of anti-Romans called Zealots, and they had come to ask for the release of Barabbas.

1.2.5 Pilate's strategy: Vv 9-10 explain Pilate's strategy. He had no wish to release Barabbas, who was a leader of rebellion against Rome, and he believed that Jesus was less of a threat to Rome than Barabbas, and more popular with the Jerusalem crowd than with the priests (the Romans made it their business to know what was going on during the pilgrim feasts in Jerusalem). 'For he realised that it was out of jealousy that the chief priest had handed him over,' indicates that Pilate thought that the chief priests saw Jesus as a threat to their own authority with the people. So he decided to gamble: anticipating a demand for the release of Barabbas, be decided to offer the crowd the release of Jesus instead. His fatal misjudgement was that he mistook the crowd; these were not the people who had been listening to Jesus in the temple area and who would have been outraged at an attempt to arrest him by the chief priests. This crowd wanted the release of Barabbas. When Pilate said to them: 'Do you want me to release for you the King of the Jews?' their answer was: 'We want Barabbas!' The chief priests knew their crowds, and were able to encourage the crowd to demand Barabbas, and when Pilate persisted in asking what they wanted him to do with Jesus, they persuaded the crowd to shout for

crucifixion (for Jesus instead of Barabbas). Pilate's gamble mis-
fired badly, and to prevent trouble from the crowd, he decided
reluctantly to do what they asked for, release Barabbas. The
total injustice of Pilate's gamble is that he offered on amnesty
someone he had not found guilty. Then when his offer is refused, Jesus is a condemned prisoner without ever being found
guilty. Pilate decided that the only thing he could do was to
have Jesus crucified as an example to Barabbas and all of like
mind of what would happen to those who set themselves up as
leaders of the people against Roman rule. Therefore Jesus'
crime is calling himself 'King of the Jews', and that charge will
be publicly displayed for all to see at his crucifixion. Probably
Mark sees irony in the name Barabbas, which could mean 'Son
of the Father', while the one who was addressed from heaven
as the Beloved Son is condemned unjustly as a leader of revolu-
tion and crucified with revolutionaries. Some manuscripts at
Matthew 27:16 give Barabbas the name 'Jesus Barabbas'. Mark
certainly sees the irony of Jesus the man of peace being condemned as a threat to Rome while the real revolutionary is set
free, and the double irony of the chief priests getting rid of Jesus
as a threat to their temple, while the coming rebellion against
Rome by people like Barabbas will actually be the cause of the
temple's destruction in 70 AD.

1.2.6 Crucifixion: '… and after flogging Jesus, he handed him
over to be crucified.' The sentence of crucifixion was usually reserved for slaves and provincial rebels against Rome. It involved very severe flogging, in order to weaken the victim so
that he would not live too long on the cross, for it was a slow and
painful death. We cannot be certain in individual cases, and the
evangelists do not describe the crucifixion in detail because it
was well known to their readers, but usually the upright part of
the cross was left permanently in place and the condemned man
had to carry the heavy crossbeam on his bleeding shoulders in
his weakened condition to the place of execution.

1.2.7 Mockery of Jesus' kingship: Jesus' kingship is only recognised in mockery. After the Jewish interrogation he was mocked
as a prophet, now he is mocked as 'King of the Jews' which was
the issue in the Roman trial. The Roman soldiers were not
Romans but provincial recruits from surrounding areas. They

brought Jesus into the inner courtyard and are said to gather together 'the whole cohort', which might be up to 600 men, too
many to be stationed at the palace, and means 'all of the cohort
who were there'. They clothe him as a mock king in purple and a
thorny crown, and kneel before him, hailing him as 'King of the
Jews' with blows and spittle. After their humiliation of Jesus, the
kind of thing that soldiers seem to do even today with captives
seen as representing 'the enemy', to which superiors turn a
blind eye, they clothe Jesus in his own garments again, and lead
him out to be crucified.

2. REFLECTION

2.1 Mystery

The one who is to share in power at the right hand of God, and
so become judge of all nations, is permitted to be judged by very
fallible mortals. God's judgement on them we would expect to
be terrible: it is to be the offer of forgiveness and reconciliation!
God's thinking is not our thinking. God's reign is at hand, even
when it appears to be astonishingly absent. Jesus submits to
mockery and violence believing that through his suffering good
will come. God's power is at work in the suffering, or perhaps
more in the self-sacrificing love of sinful humanity which Jesus
shows. We are invited to make our sufferings valuable by uniting them to those of Jesus, or by uniting ourselves to Jesus' love
and self-giving.

2.2 Christology

The title for Jesus in this section is king, though not in the sense
that Jesus would use it. Three times in this passage Pilate uses
'King of the Jews', once in a question, twice in a way that he
thought might appeal to the crowd, and lastly it is used by the
soldiers in mockery as they dress Jesus as a mock king and call
out: 'Hail, King of the Jews!' As 'King of the Jews' he is rejected
by the chief priests and by the crowd who choose Barabbas. Yet
Jesus' reply to Pilate is not a total rejection of the title, but more a
reluctance to accept it in the sense that Pilate understood. Given
the deliberate echo of the Servant of Isaiah 53 in Jesus' silence
before his accuser, we may have Mark's indication of the sense
in which Jesus would be able to accept the title king. He is the

Messiah of Israel, the expected Davidic king, only when that is qualified by the sense of Servant of God who has come 'to give his life as a ransom for many' (10:45); then indeed Jesus is 'the King of Israel', the title which Jewish usage prefers to 'King of the Jews'. The chief priests and scribes will mock him on Calvary, telling him to come down from the cross and then they would believe that he was 'the Messiah, the King of Israel' (15:32).

2.3 Discipleship

Jesus is alone. There is not a disciple in sight. All those who hung on his words are somewhere else, and the crowd who gathered had their own agenda, which they thought was for the good of their people. Mark shows Jesus abandoned by all his friends during the passion; Jesus has experienced the loneliness that human beings often suffer, so that he knows our sorrows. Mark is casting a glance to disciples who may have abandoned Jesus in times of persecution, hoping that they may repent and return. In the future the disciples may well be in this position, as Jesus prophesied. 'As for yourselves, beware; for they will hand you over to councils; and you will be beaten in synagogues; and you will stand before governors and kings because of me, as a testimony to them' (13:9). Mark hopes that his readers, who may have to face Roman courts and judges, will learn courage from Jesus, and know when to be silent and when to speak. We may well be brought before the bar of ridicule and mockery for our faith, and it is difficult to accept it with the silent dignity of Jesus. The antidote is prayer and closeness to Jesus.

2.4 Conversion

It behoves all Christians and all who speak and act in the name of their God to think deeply about what they do in God's name, to try to be sure that it is God's kingdom they are building and not their own. We may blame the chief priest and the Roman prefect for wrong judgements, while we continue to make wrong assumptions ourselves, and be guilty of prejudice. In particular, Christians down the centuries have blamed 'the Jews' in general, then and for ever after, for the death of Jesus, with terrible results, of which the Holocaust is the worst, but far from the only one. A little careful study of the Gospel will show us that it was a very small minority of the Jews of the time, in particular the Sadducees, who included the chief priests, who must take blame for handing over Jesus to the Romans, and if Pilate had been a different man, he would have refused their request. It was his decision to crucify Jesus, no one else had the power. It hardly needs to be stated (but it does!), that relatively few Jews, and quite a number of Gentiles, were involved in the death of Jesus at that time, and that no Jew of subsequent generations has any responsibility for the death of Jesus. But anti-semitism is hard to eradicate and keeps rearing its ugly head. Christians need to remember that Jesus was a forgiver, loved his own people and first and foremost saw himself as suffering for them. The least his followers can do is to be aware of those who are accused in the wrong, beware of false and shallow judgements and beware of shirking responsibility for things we pretend are not our business.

3. RESPONSE

Make your personal response by rereading the text, pausing to pray with any verse or phrase that strikes you.

Are you the King of the Jews? Pilate wants a black or white, yes or no answer. But it won't do, as so very often in life it won't do. Lord, I know you are King of Israel, the one who fulfils all the promises to David, but you have not claimed any royal privileges, in your birth, in your life, and certainly not in your approach to death. We thank you for being among us as one who serves, who qualifies every title with the prefix 'servant'. Help us to learn from you about power, success, titles, honours, and help us to aspire only to be servants of God and servants of God's people.

Do you want me to release for you the King of the Jews? Help us, Lord, to do what is right when we know it to be right, and not to try to worm our way out of it, as Pilate did. Help us, Lord, in making our choices. It is easy in a crowd to be carried away and follow the leaders. Very bad choices were made by the crowd and the chief priests. But am I sure that I would have done better myself? Forgive me the bad choices I have made. For going with the flow. Every time I have done what is contrary to my principles meant saying no to Jesus. Help me to understand your words, 'Whoever does the will of God is my brother and sister and mother' (3:35).

Crucify him! … Why, what evil has he done? Lord, we know that members of a pressure group, or a gang, supporters of a team, or a party, are capable of doing things when the group is in full cry that they would never do by themselves. Most members of the crowd who yelled 'Crucify him,' did not come to have Jesus crucified; they probably did not know he had been arrested. Yet they allowed themselves to do this thing to an innocent man because by that they got what they wanted, the release of Barabbas. Help us to know this about ourselves, that we are capable of passionate and irrational behaviour in support of what we care deeply about, or ideas that are deeply ingrained in us. That does not mean that we should not care deeply, just that we need to be careful about what it makes us do or say. Lord, what we do to vulnerable others we do to you. Save us from hatred, prejudice against strangeness or difference, blindness to other people's goodness, unexamined assumptions about what is acceptable. Pilate unfortunately had not the courage to stand up for an innocent man; Jews were expendable. Lord, give us respect for every person, for you have offered your life for us all.

'And they began saluting him, "Hail, King of the Jews!" Father, forgive all the mockery and cruelty towards your Beloved, and towards so many of your children. Father, we mock what we do not understand or what we fear or what is weak – it gives us a sense of power. In mocking Jesus, the soldiers mock all your chosen people, the Jews. Lord Jesus, servant of God, we offer you the praise and thanks of all believers through two thousand years, the love of all the saints, the courage of the martyrs, the goodness of the children, and we unite our own small thanks to all that homage. No one has ever been loved as you are. Forgive us for disrespect, indifference, and carelessness. We are slow to learn that 'the fear of the Lord is the beginning of wisdom.'

Then they led him out to crucify him. All you prophesied, Lord, is coming true. Servants carry things for others, and you carry the weight of the cross-beam on your lacerated shoulders. Thank you for accepting to the end your role as servant of God and servant of sinful humanity. Help us to carry the crosses we find in our lives, and help those whose crosses are very heavy, for whom the journey seems endless.

4. CONTEMPLATION

What lasts in the memory is the silent dignity of Jesus while others decide his fate on expediency. The only words of Jesus are: 'You say so,' in answer to the question: 'Are you the King of the Jews?' So for this time I will remember the silent Jesus while others play out their agendas around him, and I will ask for the grace to be silent when it would be wiser to say nothing, and the grace to be quiet in the presence of the mystery of Jesus' passion and death.

The Crucifixion of Jesus
(Mark 15:21-41)

1. Familiarisation

1.1 Getting to know the text (Mark 15:21-41)

'And they crucified him …'

15:21   They compelled a passer-by,
        who was coming in from the country, to carry his cross;
        it was Simon of Cyrene,
        the father of Alexander and Rufus.

22   Then they brought Jesus to the place called Golgotha
        (which means the place of a skull).

23   And they offered him wine mixed with myrrh;
        but he did not take it.

24   And they crucified him,
        and divided his clothes among them,
        casting lots to decide what each should take.

25   It was nine o'clock in the morning
        when they crucified him.

26   The inscription of the charge against him read:
        'The King of the Jews.'

27   And with him they crucified two bandits,
        one on his right and one on his left.
                    (V 28 omitted by all editors; cf Lk 22:37; Is 53:12)

Jesus is taunted on the cross

29   Those who passed by derided him,
        shaking their heads and saying,
        'Aha! You who would destroy the temple
        and build it in three days,

30   save yourself, and come down from the cross!'

31   In the same way the chief priests,
        along with the scribes,
        were also mocking him among themselves and saying,
        'He saved others; he cannot save himself.

32   Let the Messiah, the King of Israel,

come down from the cross now,
so that we may see and believe.'
Those who were crucified with him also taunted him.

Darkness, death and glimpses of light

33   When it was noon, darkness came over the whole land
      until three in the afternoon.

34   At three o'clock Jesus cried out with a loud voice,
      'Eloi, Eloi, lema sabachthani?' which means,
      'My God, my God, why have you forsaken me?'

35   When some of the bystanders heard it,
      they said, 'Listen, he is calling for Elijah.'

36   And someone ran, filled a sponge with sour wine,
      put it on a stick, and gave it to him to drink,
      saying, 'Wait, let us see whether Elijah will come
      to take him down.'

37   Then Jesus gave a loud cry
      and breathed his last.

38   And the curtain of the temple was torn in two,
      from top to bottom.

39   Now when the centurion, who stood facing him,
      saw that in this way he breathed his last,
      he said, 'Truly this man was God's Son!'

Faithful witnesses

40   There were also women looking on from a distance;
      among them were Mary Magdalene, and Mary
      the mother of James the younger and of Joses,
      and Salome.

41   These used to follow him
      and provided for him when he was in Galilee;
      and there were many other women
      who had come up with him to Jerusalem.

1.2 Background

1.2.1 The events in all their stark reality: Mark's description of
the crucifixion is factual, graphic and harrowing, even though
he does not give details of the suffering involved in crucifixion –
there was no need, for his readers were all too familiar with it.
His account is unrelieved by any visible nearness of Jesus to

God, conscious offering of himself into God's hands as in Luke, or by hints of glory as in John. Jesus is crucified between sinners, mocked and bad-mouthed by passers-by, priests and scribes, and even by those who were crucified with him, his personal dignity assaulted, taunts from those gloating over his helplessness. Even God seems to have deserted him. He cries out: 'My God, my God, why have you forsaken me?' and dies with a great cry on his lips. He is totally abandoned, apparently without a friend. The victory of his enemies seems complete, all his hopes vanquished.

1.2.2 Signs of hope: Thankfully, that is not the whole picture. There are signs that even in the midst of Jesus' total humiliation the hand of God is at work, but in the Markan manner they are mostly rather enigmatic, asking the reader to look carefully. We may list these as: scriptural allusions, especially to Psalm 22 which Jesus quotes in Aramaic, suggesting that even this apparent defeat is the fulfilment of scripture; a bitter irony which the Christian reader perceives, when things are said or done in mockery which will be revealed as profoundly true; the darkness that covered the land from noon to three o'clock; the curtain of the temple being torn from top to bottom; the amazing turn about, *con-versio*, of the centurion in charge of the execution party; and lastly, the presence, though at a distance, of faithful friends of Jesus, the women who will be the first witnesses to the resurrection. We will develop these below to help our re-reading of the text.

1.2.3 The way of the cross: Of the traditional way of the cross only one event is recorded, Simon of Cyrene carrying the cross. The Roman soldiers had the right to compel provincial natives to undertake work for them, and Simon seems to have been in the wrong (right?) place at the wrong time, coming into the city from the country. He was probably a retired member of the Jewish diaspora from Cyrene (modern Libya) spending his retirement in Jerusalem. His sons, Alexander and Rufus must have been known in Mark's church, presumably as Christian converts. The place of execution is Golgotha (from Aramaic *gulgulta*, Hebrew *gulgoleth* meaning skull), which would have been in a public place outside the city gates near a road as a deterrent to others. The site was perhaps a small hillock shaped like a skull. An outer city wall was added later so that the identified site, inside the church of the Holy Sepulchre, is now within the old city, where tombs cut into rock have been excavated, and a piece of rock, now venerated as the site of the crucifixion, was providentially preserved by being used as a pedestal for a pagan statue to deter Christian pilgrims. Before the crucifixion Jesus was offered 'wine mixed with myrrh', the one sign of compassion, as it was intended to dull the senses to the pain of crucifixion. There is some speculation that it would have been prepared by Jewish women, based on Proverbs 31:6: 'Give strong drink to one who is perishing, and wine to those in bitter distress.' It would be nice to think it was prepared by the women disciples mentioned in 15:40-41, but Mark gives no indication of this. Anyhow, Jesus refused to take it, commonly interpreted as his wish to accept the full pain of crucifixion, and probably also remembering his pledge at the Last Supper, 14:25: 'Truly, I tell you, I will never again drink of the fruit of the vine until that day when I drink it new in the kingdom of God.'

1.2.4 Crucifixion: Mark merely states: 'And they crucify him,' (using the historic present), and moves on to accompanying events. But he gives emphasis by repeating the verb 'crucify' three times (vv 24, 25, 27; similarly, three times before Pilate, 15:13, 14, 15). Mark's time scheme has divided the day into three hour periods, from early morning (6 am) to 9am with Pilate, from 9am to noon on the cross, subject to mockery, from noon until 3 pm darkness over everything (v 33, lit. from the sixth to the ninth hour), and soon after 3 pm Jesus died. The burial took place about 6 pm. John's Gospel conflicts with Mark's timing, for John 19:14 says Pilate handed him over to be crucified about noon (of the previous day, at the time when they began to slaughter the Passover lambs in the temple). Both want to associate Jesus' death with sacrifice, since Mark's timing of the crucifixion at 9 o'clock corresponds with the morning sacrifice in the temple, and his death about the 9th hour, 3 pm, corresponds with the evening sacrifice in the temple. Two other things need comment: the division of his garments (v.24), and the crucifiction between two 'bandits' (v 27). The soldiers were entitled to share whatever possessions the condemned man left, and their doing so brings our first reminiscence of Psalm 22, which is a lament of a man suffering unjustly and mocked by enemies, who nevertheless ends up by putting his trust in God. 'They divide my clothes among themselves, and for my clothing they cast lots' (Ps 22:18). This and later echoes of Psalm 22 serve to indicate that all Jesus' suffering is the fulfilment of prophecy, and that God will deliver him in the end. The two bandits crucified with him (v 27) are called *lêstai*, a word which was later used by the Jewish historian Josephus to describe members of the Zealots who rebelled against Rome. The likelihood is that these two were some of the people involved in the insurrection mentioned by Mark in 15:7. Since he had been persuaded to release Barabbas, Pilate used Jesus instead as an example, with the charge 'King of the Jews', and crucified between two murderers who had been involved in rebellion. Note the emphasis given by Mark, 'one on his right hand and one on his left'. Some manuscripts include a v 28, "And the scripture was fulfilled which says, 'And he was counted among the lawless." This is a reference to Isaiah 53:12 and is quoted by Luke 22:37 in a different setting. It is not found in the best manuscripts, and omitted by all editors. But the addition was probably to make explicit something that Mark intended us to remember anyhow, that Jesus' association with sinners on the cross was foretold in the Servant Song (Isaiah 53: 12 above), reminding us of his words in 10:45: 'The Son of Man came not to be served but to serve, and to give his life as a ransom for many.'

1.2.5 Mockery (vv 29-32): Jesus on the cross is subjected to triple mockery, by passers-by, priests with scribes, and the two men who were crucified with him. The passers-by are not casual passers-by, for, with shaking of heads, they taunt him about the threat to destroy the temple alleged against him during the appearance before the high priest. There may be a deliberate reference by Mark to Lamentations 2:15: 'All who pass along the way … hiss and wag their heads at daughter Jerusalem' (after its destruction by the Babylonians in 587 BC). The motif of wagging heads in mockery is also in Psalm 22:7: 'All who see me mock at me; they make mouths at me, they shake their heads.' They also call on him to save himself from the cross to show that he is God's friend. The chief priests, along with the scribes, taunted him among themselves with the same delight in his helplessness, incidentally admitting that he saved others: 'He saved others; he cannot save himself.' Then they take up the chief accusation in the trial before Pilate, the claim to be King of the Jews; but the priests use the more Jewish title: 'Let the Messiah, the King of Israel, come down from the cross now, so that we may see and believe.' The reader knows that Jesus has not come to save himself, but others, and remembers 8:35: 'For those who want to save their life will lose it, and those who lose their life ... will save it.' When they say: 'Come down ... so that we may see and believe,' we remember also how Jesus told them (14:62): 'You will see the Son of Man seated at the right hand of the Power ...' Their taunts betray a worry that indeed God might bring him down from the cross, and they rejoice in his helplessness, relieved that he isn't able to come down, and that therefore he cannot be the chosen one of God. Mark probably intends the mockery by the men crucified with him to be the depths of his humiliation; absolutely no one, not even his fellow-sufferers, have anything good to say of him.

1.2.6 The death of Jesus and accompanying events (vv 33-37): From noon to three there was 'darkness over the whole land'. The darkness, which may well have been caused by thunder storms, or some other natural cause, is intended by Mark to be a sign of God's hand at work. Amos 8:9 says: 'On that day, says the Lord God, I will make the sun go down at noon, and darken the earth in broad daylight.' 'That day' was to be the day when God punishes the leaders of the people for their exploitation of the poor of the land, but the term 'that day' tended to be cast into the future and refer to the day of the Lord when God will decisively intervene in judgement upon human affairs. So we have a powerful hint that, in the weakness and humiliation of Jesus, God is at work to accomplish his plans for his people. Then Jesus cried out in a loud voice in Aramaic, which Mark translates for his reader, the first verse of Psalm 22: 'My God, my God, why have you forsaken me?' That he was able to cry out in a loud voice, here and soon after on his death, is unexpected of one who has now been on the cross for six hours. The horror of crucifixion is partly the constriction put on the chest and respiratory system that renders the victim unable to breathe except by pushing himself up with his nailed feet, so that the lungs fill with fluid and breathing becomes more and more difficult. So crying out with a loud voice is remarkable in itself. But experts are divided about the implications of the recital of Ps 22:1. Does it mean that Jesus is experiencing the absence of God in such a way that he is totally desolate, abandoned by all human support, and feeling abandoned by God as well? Psalm 22 is one of the psalms of lament, in which innocent sufferers cry out against their sufferings and beg God to come to their help. These psalms go on to express confidence in God's help and often end with faith and praise of God, as does Psalm 22. Therefore some believe that we should look to the whole psalm, which Jesus was praying, and not concentrate solely on verse 1. So does the cry of Jesus express despair or confidence in God's help? The answer probably lies in avoiding extremes. Even if Jesus was praying the whole psalm, Mark chooses to focus on the sense of isolation in verse 1 rather than on a positive part of the psalm, so he thinks the desolation of Jesus was real. None the less, Jesus is appealing to his God in prayer, so he is by no means in despair. Dying is a lonely business, and dying on the cross in agony, struggling for each breath amid taunts and mockery, is an extremely lonely business. Mark wishes to stress that Jesus, crucified between sinners, himself experiences the isolation that human beings suffer in their separation from God and from loved ones in times of distress. The Son of Man is bringing the suffering of sinful humanity to God, and is really experiencing the terrible reality of it himself. This is the meaning of the psalms of lament, which became a rich quarry from which the early Christians drew answers to the questions raised by Jesus' suffering. It is characteristic of Jewish prayer that a sufferer has the right to bring his suffering and distress to God in total frankness, without hiding his anger and sense of injustice, and demand that God take notice, for isn't he the God of the covenant, whose qualities are strong love and fidelity? In the very action of bringing the suffering to God, the sufferer is convinced that God is with him, and will confound the forces of evil that assail him.

There follows a sort of distraction, a bystander mishears (or pretends so) Jesus' call 'Eloi, Eloi ...' and says he is calling on Elijah; so Jesus was offered a drink, sour wine on a sponge, presumably an attempt to allay his thirst until Elijah has a chance to save him. Elijah was thought of as a rescuer of those in dire straits, and Malachi 4:5 promises Elijah's presence on the 'day of the Lord' ('Lo, I will send you the prophet Elijah before the great and terrible day of the Lord comes'). Most likely this is another of the negative jibes; if Elijah does not come to save him, then he cannot be Israel's Messiah. A reference may be implied to Psalm 69:21, another psalm of lament, '… for my thirst they gave me vinegar to drink.'

Then Jesus gave a loud cry and breathed his last' (v 37) No words are given for this cry, and we remarked above on the un-expected loudness of the cry from one dying of slow suffocation on the cross. Some think of a cry of triumph, a cry of defiance, others associate it with the more hopeful parts of Psalm 22. Something in the way he died impressed the centurion, as we shall see, and that could not have been despair or terror. Perhaps the cry affirmed that God's work has been done, later developed by John in the words: 'It is ended (accomplished)' (John 19:30). The Servant of God had given his life as a ransom for many (10:45), poured out his blood for many (14:24).

1.2.7 Signs after his death (vv 38-39): The first sign is the tear-ing of the temple curtain, stated but not interpreted for us. Mark emphasises the completeness of the tearing by repeti-tion, 'torn in two,' and 'from top to bottom.' There were two curtains, one veiling the Holy Place, where the sacrifices were offered by the priests, and one veiling the Holy of Holies, where only the High Priest was allowed to enter once a year on the Day of Atonement to anoint the 'mercy seat' (the place of God's presence) with blood for the sins of the people. Neither of these could be seen from the place of execution, and the inner curtain only by the priests, so it may be for Mark the be-ginning of what Jesus foretold at the High Priest's interroga-tion: 'You will see the Son of Man seated at the right hand of the Power' (14:62). But Mark is probably more interested in its symbolic meaning, the opening up through the death of Jesus of access to the presence of God for all who believe in him. It may also point to Jesus' prayerful cry being answered immedi-ately on his death, his immediate access to the loving and mer-ciful presence of God, the affirmation of all his service for oth-ers.

Next, Mark carefully words the confession of faith by the centurion, the soldier in charge of the execution party (a Gentile, but probably a provincial rather than a Roman). 'When the centurion, who stood facing him, saw that in this way he breathed his last, he said: 'Truly this man was God's Son.' It is the gazing at Jesus as he dies, rather then the after-effects, that prompts the centurion in Mark. Compare Matthew 27:54. 'Now when the centurion and those who were with him … saw the earthquake and what had taken place (ie the effects of his death), they were terrified and said, 'Truly this man was God's Son.' Jesus' identity is revealed at his lowest moment, paradoxically by a Gentile who has just overseen his execution, who professes his identity not just as Messiah but as God's Son. The Greek words, 'this man was Son of God' do not have a definite article before 'son', so some translate it as 'a Son of God', rather than 'the Son of God,' making it something that might be more easily expected from a Gentile soldier. But that is definitely not Mark's intention: he began his gospel with the affirmation of Jesus as Christ (Messiah) and 'the Son of God' (1:1, again without the definite article), and the words from heaven at the baptism (1:11), and at the transfiguration (9:7) clearly affirm Jesus as 'my Son, the Beloved.' The Greek sentence with the verb 'to be' does not require the article (nor would the equivalent in Latin, Aramaic or Hebrew). The NRSV translation, 'Truly this man was God's Son,' allows a certain ambiguity, which Mark did not intend. For he was allowing the centurion to articulate the faith of the Christian community in Jesus' divinity, at a moment when there could be no doubt either about his humanity. What the centurion meant historically is another question. Gentiles in the service of the Roman emperor were quite used to professing the 'divinity' of human beings in the emperor's family, mostly after their death, sometimes before it. Many Christians will be asked to sacrifice to the divine emperor to prove that they are not 'guilty' of being Christians. Mark is glad to hold up the example of the Gentile centurion, showing his reverence for Jesus at his death, to his Gentile Christians. Luke 23:47 has a perhaps more 'historical' confession, 'Certainly this man was innocent.' But it is conceivable that the centurion historically referred to Jesus as divine or 'Son of God', though he would not have been able to give it the full Christian meaning, rather than something like a Roman emperor officially 'deified'. And that 'treason' could have endangered his life, never mind his job.

1.2.8 The faithful women disciples (vv 40-41): it is only now that Mark draws attention to the group of women disciples who had accompanied Jesus from Galilee, and who were witnesses to the crucifixion, although from a distance (kept at a distance by the soldiers). He mentions three by name, Mary Magdalene, Mary the mother of James the younger and of Joses, and Salome. Disconcertingly, though they are the important witnesses who saw the death of Jesus, his burial (15:47), and who went to the tomb on the Sunday morning to find it empty, Mark is not consistent about their names, apart from Mary Magdalene. With Mary Magdalene watching the burial was 'Mary the mother of Joses'. Those who came to the tomb with Mary Magdalene are, 'Mary the mother of James' and Salome. Presumably this second Mary is well enough known to his readers that they will not be confused. It is interesting to speculate whether James 'the little' (ho mikros) and Joses are the same as the James and Joses mentioned among the 'brothers' of Jesus in 6:3 during Jesus' visit to Nazareth. It would take a while to tease that out, but I rather think the case for their being the same is too lightly dismissed by commentators. The women have obviously ministered to Jesus and his group during their travels (compare Luke 8:2-3, where Mary Magdalene is the only name in common). And they remained faithful, and will not be missing at the burial or at the tomb as soon as possible after the Sabbath is over. They show more courage than the male disciples, even if they were less likely to be arrested.

2. REFLECTION

2.1 Mystery

The great and terrible day of the Lord has come, when God will judge the world in its sinfulness. 'On that day, says the Lord God, I will make the sun go down at noon, and darken the earth in broad daylight. I will turn your feasts into mourning, and all your songs into lamentation' (Amos 8: 9-10). A day to be feared, but the one to suffer for the sins of the world is Jesus, the

Beloved Son, crucified between sinners and identifying with all sinners and sufferers. 'I will turn ... all your songs into lamentation;' but Jesus is the one who cries out in lamentation, asking God to take the distress and suffering into his hands and overthrow the power of evil. Here is where we are asked to 'think the things of God and not the things of humans' (8:33), for while we think of vengeance, God thinks of forgiveness, and in the death of Jesus 'a ransom for many' (10:45) those who 'repent and believe in the good news' (1:15) will find forgiveness and life. 'The kingdom of God is at hand' (1:15). The mystery of the kingdom of God (4:11) is now revealed. It is God's saving power that is at work through the love and the willing service of the Beloved Son. Amos concludes the above (8:10f) with the words: 'I will make it like the mourning for an only son', and, for those who followed Jesus and hoped in him, it is time to mourn the scattered male disciples and the mourning but practical women who will try to do what has to be done. They all have little recollection and less understanding of his words: '... after three days he will rise again' (8:31, 9:31, 10:34), or 'But after I am raised up, I will go before you to Galilee' (14:28).

2.2 Christology

The terrible moment of Jesus' death is the paradoxical moment of the revelation of his true identity. The centurion is the first human being in the gospel to affirm the identity of Jesus as 'the Son of God.' Though later on some Christians had difficulty with the concept that the Son of God could die, and developed the notion that he only appeared to die, Mark's story affirms also the reality of his humanity, all too able to suffer and to die. It will take the theologians years and years to try to formulate the mystery, but Mark asks us to stand beneath the cross with the centurion and declare our faith in the Son of God. The psalms of lament like Psalm 22, which promise the distressed victim of suffering God's saving help and vindication, helped the early Christians to make some sense of Jesus who suffered for others and will be vindicated by God. Likewise the Songs of the Servant of God in (Second) Isaiah, especially Isaiah 53, made sense of Jesus accepting suffering for others that they might be saved.

2.3 *Discipleship*

The disciples, though they heard the prophecies of the passion and resurrection, could not face the former, and have apparently no hope of resurrection, nor any understanding of what it could mean (9:10, 'questioning what this rising from the dead could mean'). Up to the last did they believe that God would rescue him? Now they are at their lowest point. More positive is the presence of the faithful women, introduced at last by Mark, but it is hard to believe that they did not also see this as the end of the dream, though like women do, they will not run away until the body of Jesus has been attended to with love and reverence. The model of faith is the centurion, a reproach to his 'real' disciples. The centurion had no schooling in the religion of Israel with its expectations of a Messiah, had spent no time with Jesus or heard his teaching or his prophecies. Indeed he had presided over his humiliation by the soldiers in the courtyard of the praetorium, perhaps even took part in it, and had been in charge of the crucifixion. But in all the hours that he had to keep watch under the cross, observing the behaviour of the hostile bystanders and the Jewish leaders, the silence of Jesus and the way he bore his suffering, his prayers and above all the manner in which he died, led to a total change in his attitude, to his voicing an act of faith in his divinity, remembered by the Christians (legend has it he became one himself) as the first one to voice the faith of the Christian Church, 'Truly this man was the Son of God.' Mark is saying to us, stand under the cross, spend time watching Jesus as he experiences the desolation of the sufferer who feels alone and unsupported, who knows the absence of God, and learn from that who is the saviour, and how great is God's love for us.

2.4 *Conversion*

Close attention to the Markan account of the crucifixion is an incentive to conversion for everyone, as he makes clear to us by the example of Jesus how far we fall short of the new mindset we are striving to find, the 'thinking in God's way'. To see Jesus' self-giving on our behalf calls us to unselfish service of one another, to receive God's forgiveness is to learn to be forgiving. But we know that it is still a struggle to lose one's life in order to save it, to carry our crosses without complaining too much. Perhaps also we may learn from the psalms of lament to be honest in our prayers, to speak the difficult truth before God about ourselves and the people we know and love who suffer disproportionately, knowing that God has manifested his love for suffering humanity in his Beloved Son and understands the unfairness of life, and wishes to be with us in our trials. The model of conversion is the centurion, who turned his whole mindset around while spending some hours in the presence of Jesus at his weakest and most abused. Pray for courage like him to speak our faith by our words and by our lives.

3. RESPONSE

Make a personal response by rereading the text and pausing to pray with any scene, verse or phrase which moves you. Remember to get in touch with your feelings, not all of which you need to put into words. Do not try to cover the whole text at one time; there are so many things to respond to.

They compelled a passer-by ... to carry his cross; it was Simon of Cyrene. Immediately we know, Lord, that you are on the point of collapse, terribly weakened. You have to accept the help of a stranger, who models for us your own words, 'If any want to become my followers, let them deny themselves and take up their cross and follow me' (8:34). Simon takes up your cross, we have to take up our own crosses and follow you. Lord, give us strength of mind and will when our bodies fail, and help us not to be too proud to yield our independence to others when we need help.

And they crucified him. So few words for such a terrible thing to do to another human being. Just a job of work. Two more to do. Lord, you refused the only painkiller they had, the wine mixed with myrrh. We don't like to think about the hours and hours of suffering ahead of you, the pain, the heat, the thirst, the flies, the struggle for each breath as your chest is stretched taut and your arms pinned, how you have to push your body weight up with nailed feet to breathe, people around you enjoying the spectacle of your humiliation and helplessness. We commend to your compassion all who are suffering and especially those on the point of death, that they may feel your presence.

And with him they crucified two bandits, one on his right and one on his left. By their company you will know them! He always associated with low types, didn't he! They are determined to label him as revolutionary by placing him between two rebels. Only more obvious sinners than the rest of us! That is what you came to do, Lord, seek out the sinner and offer hope. 'Those who are well have no need of a physician, but those who are sick. I have come to call not the righteous but sinners' (2:17).

Save yourself, and come down from the cross. We know, Lord, that you had no wish to die, and did not hand yourself over meekly to martyrdom. You are the Lord of life, and death is the enemy of life. But some things cannot be done, even to avoid death. As Thomas More said: 'I die the king's good servant, but God's first.' So you could not change your mission to save yourself from death. The kingdom of God is not based on saving one's skin by compromise. Lord, we thank you for identifying with sinful humanity and bringing hope to all. May you bring strength to us to live without betraying the truth of the gospel we profess; pardon our many compromises with truth and justice and goodness.

When it was noon, darkness came over the whole land until three in the afternoon. We fear that goodness is being overcome on the cross by this darkness. But God is light. This darkness is a sign, not of the triumph of evil and death, but of God's judgement on evil and death. God our Father and the Father of Jesus, we thank you that you are a God of life, who will overcome death and evil through your Son's refusal to save himself, through his great desire to save others. You ask us to die to ourselves, but not to stop living; rather to be really alive. Lord of life, help us to overcome the darkness in ourselves, help us to be life-giving for others.

My God, my God, why have you forsaken me? Jesus, you prayed during the long hours on the cross. Through your prayers, you couldn't save yourself, but your prayers during that ordeal must have been immensely powerful for us. In heaven, and in our liturgical gatherings, you continue your prayer for sinful humanity as on the cross. You prayed for your frightened disciples and for all weak disciples down the ages. You prayed for suffering humanity, and placed them in the hands of your Father. You prayed for those who condemned you and drove the nails, and for those who heedlessly jeered at your sorrow. Even when you felt so alone on this cross, you clung to your conviction that God's immense and eternal love can still accomplish his plans. My comfort is, that on the cross and in the Eucharist, and at God's right hand, you pray for me and for each of us. We have no need to fear our weakness!

And the curtain of the temple was torn in two, from top to bottom. Twice, Lord, something is torn open and you are pronounced 'Son of God'; by your Father at your baptism when the heavens were torn open, and soon by the centurion when the curtain of the temple is torn from top to bottom. Lord, we rejoice that on your death you go straight to the presence of your Father. We rejoice too that you have opened up access to God for all of us, that he is ready as a loving Father to forgive us, heal us, and welcome us as his people. This you have done for us, Lord, and we thank you. By your goodness, do not allow us to remain selfish and hard of heart, after we have witnessed your selflessness and courage. Take away our hearts of stone, and give us hearts of flesh.

Truly, this man was God's Son. Lord, your power to heal and change hearts has already worked on the centurion, as he confesses in our name the faith of the church. Help us, like him, to stand beneath the cross and contemplate your death, that our hearts may be changed.

There were also women looking on from a distance. We are glad that not all your friends deserted you. We thank you for the faith, love and courage of these women who served you in life and in death, and who will be your first witnesses to the resurrection. We thank you for all the women, mothers, sisters, wives, carers, healers, life-givers, who have taught us love and fidelity down through the years, and have loved you with faithful hearts.

4. CONTEMPLATION

How unforgettable an experience for the centurion, who 'stood facing him, saw that in this way he breathed his last,' and made his declaration of Jesus' divinity. Carry in your mind and heart the experience of living with Mark's account of Jesus' death in all its rawness and its hope. Contemplate the desolation of Jesus which unites him with all suffering humanity, with each of us in our moments of doubt and suffering. Remember his prayer, 'My God, my God, why have you forsaken me?' but also the declaration of the centurion, 'Truly this man was God's Son.'

The Empty Tomb (Mark 16:1-8)

1. FAMILIARISATION

1.1 Getting to know the text (Mark 16:1-8)

The stone already rolled back

16:1   When the Sabbath was over, Mary Magdalene,
and Mary the mother of James, and Salome
bought spices,
so that they might go and anoint him.

2   And very early on the first day of the week,
when the sun had risen,
they went to the tomb.

3   They had been saying to one another,
'Who will roll away the stone for us
from the entrance to the tomb?'

4   When they looked up,
they saw that the stone, which was very large,
had already been rolled back.

The Easter proclamation

5   As they entered the tomb,
they saw a young man, dressed in a white robe,
sitting on the right side;
and they were alarmed.

6   But he said to them, 'Do not be alarmed;
you are looking for Jesus of Nazareth,
who was crucified.
He has been raised; he is not here.
Look, there is the place they laid him.

7   But go, tell his disciples and Peter
that he is going ahead of you to Galilee;
there you will see him, just as he told you.'

The women flee in fear

8   So they went out and fled from the tomb,
for terror and amazement had seized them;
and they said nothing to anyone,
for they were afraid.

1.2 Background

1.2.1 Mark chapter 16: Though normally translations of chapter 16 have 20 verses, it is unanimously agreed that only vv 1-8, the finding of the empty tomb, were written by Mark, while vv 9-20, about resurrection appearances, are an addition attached to the gospel much later, different in style and character from Mark, though accepted by the church as part of the official canon of scripture. Sometimes seen as a summary of the post-resurrection events from the other gospels, these verses are more probably an earlier summary of events that were developed by the other evangelists in their own way. Another very short ending is found in one manuscript, a couple of sentences in Greek, not usually printed in our bibles, saying simply that the women disciples brought their message about the resurrection to Peter and the others, and that Jesus commissioned them to spread the proclamation of salvation from east to west. We will deal only with vv.1-8, and return below to the question of why Mark has no resurrection appearances.

1.2.2 The women witnesses. As we saw at the end of the crucifixion narrative, Mark has carefully noted the presence of women witnesses at the crucifixion, naming Mary Magdalene, 'Mary [the mother] of James the younger and of Joses', and Salome (15:40). Then he describes how Joseph of Arimathea, a member of the Sanhedrin, asked Pilate to release the body of Jesus to him, and buried it, wrapped in a linen cloth, in a tomb cut out of the rock, and closed the tomb with a stone. Mary Magdalene and 'Mary the mother of Joses' (Mark is not consistent in how he describes this Mary) saw where the body was laid (15:47). This was on the eve of the sabbath, i.e., before sunset on Friday, and there was not time to anoint the body for the burial. On the sabbath day they rested. Then we come to 16:1, 'when the sabbath day was over', ie after sunset on the Saturday, the three women originally named, Mary Magdalene, 'Mary the mother of James' (presumably the same lady), and Salome, who was not named at the burial, bought spices to anoint the body, so as to be ready early on the Sunday morning to visit the tomb. Mark says they went 'very early', and then more precisely, 'when the sun had risen' (v 2). He probably intends the symbolism of the rising sun after the darkness of the Friday to suggest Jesus rising as the light which conquers the darkness. Then with some artistry Mark mentions the human forgetfulness of the women as they realise that in their effort to get there early with spices all ready, they have forgotten about the heavy stone rolled across the mouth of the tomb, and wonder how on earth they are going to find anyone strong enough to roll it back so early in the morning; and thus the reader's attention is focused on the tomb. Then the women lifted up their eyes and gazed at the tomb (Mark uses two verbs), and the stone was already rolled back, the huge great thing. ('For it was very large.') We are not told what they thought, but they must have been very upset, for the thought of someone interfering with the tomb of your loved one just after his burial is a severe shock.

1.2.3 The Easter Proclamation: On entering the tomb, they were 'alarmed' (NRSV) to see a young man already there, sitting opposite the place where Jesus' body had been laid, dressed in white. Pretty certainly Mark intends us to believe this was an angel. The verb Mark uses seems much stronger than 'alarmed'; they were frightened out of their wits. The angel then makes the declaration that is found, though with variations in wording, in Matthew, Mark and Luke at the finding of the empty tomb. 'Do not be frightened; you are looking for Jesus of Nazareth (lit. 'the Nazarene'), who was crucified. He has been raised; he is not here.' The passive verb, 'has been raised' means 'God has raised him', though Mark's prophecies used the wording '(he will) rise again' (8:31; 9:31; 10:34). ' Look (singular, ie 'behold'), ('there is', supplied by NRSV) the place where they laid him.' The women are quite unprepared for this; they, like the male disciples, had not understood what Jesus said about his resurrection. But, though Mark's Gospel is to end abruptly, this is the tremendous announcement of the resurrection of Jesus, the Father's answer to the jibe: 'He cannot save himself', and to the prayer of Jesus: 'My God, my God, why have you forsaken me.' The implied question for the women must be: 'Where is he then? Will we ever see him again?' And the angel tells them: 'But go, tell his disciples and Peter that he is going ahead of you to Galilee; there you will see him, just as he told you.' This is a reference back to Jesus' words on the way to Gethsemane: 'But after I am raised up, I will go before you to Galilee' (14:28). The Greek verb *proagein*, 'to go before' can also mean 'lead'. It's most likely sense here is that Jesus will be awaiting them in Galilee, but Mark intends the ambiguity. Since shepherds in Israel lead their sheep to pasture, there are also overtones of the scattered sheep being gathered together again, a reconciliation with Jesus and a renewal of their discipleship.

1.2.4 The strange reaction of the women (v 8): That the women fled from the tomb in 'terror and amazement' we understand, but that they 'said nothing to anyone, for they were afraid' has become the subject of endless debate. We would expect that Mark would go on to say that after a time they got over their fear and told the disciples about it. But he doesn't. How does Mark know about the women going to the tomb if they never told anyone about it? Either he has it from an earlier source, which would show that they did talk about it, and that it was part of the early preaching about the resurrection, or he meant that they did not tell anyone at that time (but they did later). Matthew and Luke probably knew of Mark's version, and imitated his format, though not the details. Scholars say they cannot prove that Matthew or Luke knew of any Markan material beyond 16:1-8. But if we consider that the longer ending, 16:9-20, represents an early source which was later developed by the other evangelists (see 1.2.1 above), 16:10, though it doesn't mention the tomb, says that Mary Magdalene saw the risen Lord and told the disciples, though they did not believe her. So even if they were too frightened to tell immediately, an appearance of the Lord to the women, represented by the later accounts in John 20:14-18 (to Mary Magdalene, cf. Mark 16:9), and Matthew 28:9-10 (to Mary Magdalene and 'the other Mary'), changed their minds. So we are left with the puzzle of Mark 16:8, that they told nothing to anyone.

1.2.5 Did Mark intend to stop at 16:8? Up to 1950 the fairly unanimous answer would have been no, of course not! In 1950 Professor R. H. Lightfoot published *The Gospel Message of St Mark*, (Oxford University Press), in which he carefully examined the arguments for and against, and came down on the side of saying that Mark deliberately stopped there. He then tried to show why Mark did so and what he meant by it, thereby creating a new industry, since many commentators followed his lead, though giving their own literary reconstruction of why exactly Mark acted in this way. Anyhow, the net result is that nowadays the vast majority of scholars accept that Mark intended to end his gospel at 16:8, though there is no corresponding agreement about the explanation of why he wanted to do so and what it means. If you wish to see a sober approach to the question of why Mark may have intended to end at 16:8, based on exegesis of the gospel, read M Mullins, *Commentary*, pp 444-448. For those who are able to handle biblical Greek, see R. T. France, *Commentary*, pp 670-684, for the opposite opinion, and Nineham, *Saint Mark* (Pelican), pp 439-442, for a survey of the pros and cons. I confess that in the course of working through Mark's gospel over many months, I have gone back to the old answer, no, of course not! It is now very much a minority opinion, and as far as praying with the gospel is concerned, we do not have to decide one way or the other. For those who are interested, I have outlined below only a few of the arguments for and against. It is really a sort of draw, balancing the improbability of an author who has flagged up twice a reunion of Jesus, after his resurrection, with his disciples in Galilee (14:28; 16:7), has carefully set up the women disciples as witnesses and messengers, and then fails to describe it, with the other improbability of the ending having been totally lost or the author having been prevented from finishing, perhaps by illness or arrest, with nobody else in a position to supply the intended finish.

1.2.6 Reasons to expect a longer narrative.

- The twofold promise that Jesus would see the disciples in Galilee (14:28; 16:7).
- The careful references to the women witnesses at the crucifixion, burial and empty tomb. Mark treats them as faithful, practical women, not as fearful or foolish.
- Frequent references to future seeing of the Son of Man exalted: 9:1, 'some standing here who will not taste death until they see the kingdom of God coming with power.' 13:26, 'Then they will see the Son of Man coming in clouds'. 14:62, 'You will see the Son of Man seated at the right hand of the Power'. 16:7, '... he is going ahead of you to Galilee; there you will see him, just as he told you.' These texts should not be seen as primarily referring to the Parousia, but to the risen

Lord, exalted to the right hand of the Father.

- It is very odd, even for one who is often careless of the niceties of classical Greek grammar, to end a book with the word *gar*, meaning 'for'. *Gar* always comes after the verb it qualifies, but extremely rarely at the end of a sentence, as in *ephobounto gar*, 'for they were afraid' (modern 'they were scared, like!'), not at the end of a paragraph, and never at the end of a book. There are, however, a couple of instances in the Septuagint Greek translation where it does end a sentence: Genesis 18:15 and 45:3, once with the same verb *phoboumai*, to fear.

- Mark is sometimes labelled as a 'dark night theologian' (eg Montague, *Mark, Good News for Hard Times*, pp 187-8), who stresses the absence of Jesus during persecution, so he does not encourage readers to think they will 'see' the Lord. 'He has been raised; he is not here.' The angel also says, 'He is going ahead of you to Galilee; there you will see him.' Mark begins the Gospel with the Christian faith, 'the good news of Jesus, Christ, the Son of God', and at every 'dark' time in the Gospel he gives a note of hope, transfiguration after passion-prophecy, declaration of coming glory before the High Priest, confession of faith after the crucifixion. The reader just feels the need of the good news being completed by the appearance of the risen Christ and the renewal of the disciples' call and mission. 'The good news must first be proclaimed to all nations' (13:10). How can the good news end on such an anticlimax as 'they said nothing to anyone, for they were afraid'? Are Peter's tears after his denials (14:72) not to find reconciliation in Galilee, even though he is specially mentioned, 'tell his disciples and Peter' (16:7)?

1.2.7 Reasons to think that Mark intended to end at 16:8.

- It is hard to explain how the ending got lost. If it did, it happened very early, before the manuscript was copied even once; no trace exists of a longer ending by Mark in any surviving manuscript. If the last portion of the original scroll was lost or damaged, there must have been people who had heard or seen the full text, and could have given at least an outline of it for a new copy. There seems to have been quite a time gap before a longer ending was added.

- Mark likes paradox, and likes to leave his readers to work out the meaning for themselves. So it is not impossible that he ends with paradox. 'The challenge for the reader at this point is to see that Mark's narrative is complete, but the Christian story is not' (Mullins, p.446).

- Throughout Mark's Gospel, there is continued reference to human failure and lack of understanding. Revelation is met with fear and astonishment, with an inability to understand or articulate the new insight. Mark's women disciples are just another example of this inability to understand or articulate; 'trembling and amazement had seized them.' We do not depend on them to articulate the fact of the resurrection; it has been done by an angelic messenger from God. Trouble is, only the women saw and heard the angel.

- Mark knew his readers were already familiar with at least oral narratives about the appearances of the risen Jesus. He was more concerned with their neglect of the hard reality of discipleship, taking up the cross and following a crucified Messiah. Mullins, p 446, insists that Mark did say in 1:1: 'The beginning of the good news of Jesus Christ, the Son of God.' He did not necessarily intend to complete the story to suit our expectations at a different time.

2. REFLECTION

2.1 Mystery

'To you has been given the mystery of the kingdom of God' (4:11). We now have in kernel the big picture that the disciples did not have in Galilee. God's power to rule over people with free will is made effective only in those who listen to Jesus, come to know his true identity and believe in him, and the numbers at this moment do not need a computer to tally. But the death and resurrection of Jesus are the work of God's power, and their potential to change the world and its people is infinite. The power of love, service and self-giving has been vindicated by the resurrection, the Father's yes to all that Jesus has tried to do and teach. Jesus in weakness and in service to humanity has confronted all the power of opposition, self-serving, violence, cruelty, suffering and mockery, all that belongs to the kingdom of Satan, the power of the state, the power of death, that old enemy

273

who steals human hope, and through the power of God has overcome them all. The kingdom of God is truly at hand. All things are possible to God's love. The power of the resurrection will rehabilitate the disciples, the fulfilment of the promise of John the Baptist is to come: 'He will baptise you with the Holy Spirit' (1:8). The meeting between the disciples and the risen Jesus did take place in Galilee, even though we lack Mark's account of it, and the spreading out of the good news has been wondrous, though crosses have to be carried, and opposition met by disciples in their struggle to bring the message to every nation (13:10). It is God's power that will realize all that potential, but all believers are called to be workers for the kingdom, and to pray, 'Thy kingdom come, thy will be done.'

2.2 Christology

The 'was' of the centurion's confession under the cross is for ever changed: 'Truly this man was God's Son' embodied the sadness of his death. Now 'Jesus of Nazareth who was crucified … has been raised' by the power of God and lives forever. Truly this man (his humanity glorified) is the Son of God. The theology of what resurrection means is given to us only in the tremendous sense of awe that comes to the women; they sense they are in the presence of the supernatural. For this is not like the daughter of Jairus coming back to life, wonderful though that was. This is not Jesus coming back to life as it was before, it is a new dimension of being, life with God, where his humanity is - we have no words for it – glorified, transformed, transfigured with new and eternal life. All the intimations in the gospel are now made real: Jesus is the new place of the presence of God among us, the new temple 'not made with hands', but also the shepherd who will gather together his scattered sheep, bringing them healing and new strength. 'He is going ahead of you to Galilee' means that he will be waiting for them in Galilee, but also will gather them together in Galilee as the shepherd calls his sheep, cares for their wounds, and leads them to pasture. We have to visualise that promised meeting for ourselves; we have no account of it from Mark.

2.3 Discipleship

The women disciples are the link between Jesus and the male disciples, but the link seems to fail. They are seized by 'terror and amazement' (*tromos*, trembling, *ek-stasis*, dislocation, they are 'beside themselves'), at least temporarily unable to deliver their message. Disciples are weak, but weak disciples are summoned to Galilee for healing by the living shepherd. The narrative calls for them to be given a new commission to spread the good news, which must be proclaimed to all nations (13:10). The joy of the resurrection and their reconciliation with Jesus will not mean that their task will be easy. Jesus has already in chapter 13 warned of the dangers ahead: 'Beware, for they will hand you over to councils; and you will stand before governors and kings because of me, as a testimony to them ... When they bring you to trial and hand you over (Jesus' own fate), do not worry beforehand what you are to say ... for it is not you who speak, but the Holy Spirit' (13:9-11). All of us who have travelled this journey through the Gospel, reflecting on our own discipleship, wondering how to meet the challenges of today, may take comfort from the love and care of the good shepherd, and the accompaniment of the Holy Spirit. The Father's kingdom requires that we lead lives of faith, hope and love.

2.4 Conversion

Jesus said to Peter, when Peter's half understanding of Jesus' identity leads him to be an obstacle to the kingdom: 'The way you think is not God's way, but the human way' (8:33). Two things emerge: firstly, that a shallow understanding of Jesus is not good enough, and may lead us to do harm rather than good. Shallow understanding leads to shallow relationship with Jesus, and that will not sustain us either, or help us to build the kingdom of God. Secondly, we ask ourselves what have we learned about this new mindset, thinking in God's way, that will give direction and meaning to our lives and further the kingdom of God? We can only learn to think in God's way by listening to and learning from Jesus. Aware of our human weakness, we depend upon the risen Jesus, our shepherd and guardian, for healing and strength. New thinking means that we learn to use only the 'weapons' of Jesus, truth, love and service, in our personal relationships and in our work for the kingdom. It means using the gifts that Jesus' death and resurrection gave us, his new life within us and the power of the Holy Spirit. It also means refusing to be dis-spirited in the face of the tasks that confront anyone concerned for the future of faith today. Believers in the resurrection must be people of hope.

3. RESPONSE

Make your personal response by rereading the text, pausing to pray with any verse or phrase that strikes you.

Very early on the first day of the week, when the sun was risen, they went to the tomb. Blessed day of the week, the Lord's Day, Sunday of the Son, resurrection day, weekly celebration of the resurrection of Jesus. The new dawn, dawn of hope, as the sun rose to light the world, so the Son of God rose to be the everlasting light of the world. Enlighten us.

Who will roll away the stone from the entrance to the tomb? Who has power over death? Only you, God of the living, who rolled back the stone to reveal that death could not hold your beloved Son in its weakened grip. Blessed be the Son who allowed death to do her worst so as to take away her sting. The grip of death cannot hold the children of God because of the new life of God's Son.

They saw a young man, dressed in a white robe ... and they were alarmed. Angel of the Lord, no one ever brought us a more welcome message. Blessed women, the first to hear the message of life and hope. You have shown us, wisely, that before the mystery of God's power, we should be filled with awe and wonder; something beyond our dreams is happening in the destruction of the power of death. God of life, give us the desire and the power to spread this good news around us, that all may experience the new life of the risen Jesus.

He has been raised; he is not here. This, the kernel of the Easter Proclamation, prompts us to make our deepest thanksgiving to God for raising up Jesus to his side in glory. 'He is not here' any more, and the first disciples will miss his physical presence. Risen Lord, live in us, fill us with your presence, give us the Spirit to strengthen us to be witnesses.

He is going ahead of you to Galilee; there you will see him. Lord, Mark's text does not tell us whether this momentous meeting took place, but we know it must have. You drew your disciples back to yourself, and gathered them together with your shepherd's call, for they had been scattered since the shepherd was stricken. You healed their guilt, you remembered Peter's tears more than his denials, and gave him back his identity as a disciple. Thank you for filling them with life and hope and strength to go out and spread the good news everywhere, for therein lay our salvation, the hearing of the good news. Good shepherd, raised to the throne of God, confirm us, sustain us, inspire us, make us alive to your word, that we may hear it with love, speak of it with enthusiasm, live by it, and spread the word.

They said nothing to anyone, for they were afraid. Are we to end on a note of fear? Lord, we confess to the fears within us, the prevarications and excuses we make for avoiding challenge and taking responsibility. Help us to face up to our fears, to allow your strength and your gifts to give us courage. We are followers not just of 'Jesus of Nazareth, who was crucified', but of the Son of Man raised to the throne of the Father, the conqueror of death, the life-giver. So make us courageous, fill us with enthusiasm for life and for the kingdom of God, help us to bring your compassion and service to those who are 'sheep without a shepherd.'

4. Contemplation

Through this journey through St Mark's Gospel, we have met wonder, enthusiasm, misunderstanding, betrayal, opposition and hate, the power of the establishment and of the state to rid themselves of uncomfortable challenges to their power. We have walked with Jesus in his astonishing authority over Satan, death, the forces of savage nature, in his compassion for the sick, the weak and the lost, in his bonding with his new family, brothers and sisters who wish to do the will of God. We have been with him in his weakness and distress of soul, in his suffering and isolation, in his death and humiliation. But the abiding reality is his defeat of death, his everlasting life, his glory at the right hand of God, his life-giving power to heal and make new, to inspire love, service and the spread of the good news. We carry with us the message of the angel, 'You are looking for Jesus of Nazareth, who was crucified. He has been raised, he is not here.'